# e-Learning and Social Networking Handbook

## Resources for Higher Education

### Second Edition

Digital resources—from games to blogs to social networking—are strong forces in education today, but how can those tools be effectively utilized by educators and course designers in higher education? Filled with practical advice, the *e-Learning and Social Networking Handbook, Second Edition* provides a comprehensive overview of online learning tools and offers strategies for using these resources in course design, highlighting some of the most relevant and challenging topics in e-learning today, including:

- using social networking for educational purposes
- designing for a distributed environment
- strengths and weaknesses of delivering content in various formats (text, audio, and video)
- potential constraints on course design
- implementation, evaluation, induction, and training

Illustrated by short, descriptive case studies, the *e-Learning and Social Networking Handbook, Second Edition* also directs the reader to useful resources that will enhance their course design. This helpful guide will be invaluable to all those involved in the design and delivery of online learning in higher education.

**Frank Rennie** is Professor of Sustainable Rural Development at the University of the Highlands and Islands, Scotland.

**Tara Morrison** is a Lecturer at the University of the Highlands and Islands, Scotland.

# e-Learning and Social Networking Handbook

## Resources for Higher Education

### Second Edition

## Frank Rennie
## and
## Tara Morrison

Routledge
Taylor & Francis Group

NEW YORK AND LONDON

Second edition published 2013
by Routledge
711 Third Avenue, New York, NY 10017

Simultaneously published in the UK
by Routledge
2 Park Square, Milton Park, Abingdon, Oxon OX14 4RN

*Routledge is an imprint of the Taylor & Francis Group, an informa business*

First edition published by Routledge 2008

*Library of Congress Cataloguing in Publication Data*
Rennie, Frank.
    E-learning and social networking handbook : resources for higher education / by Frank Rennie and Tara Morrison. 2nd ed.
    p. cm.
    Prev. ed. cataloged under Mason, Robin.
    Includes bibliographical references and index.
    1. Internet in higher education—Handbooks, manuals, etc. 2. Online social networks—Handbooks, manuals, etc. 3. Instructional systems—Design—Handbooks, manuals, etc. I. Morrison, Tara M. II. Mason, Robin. E-learning and social networking handbook. III. Title.
    LB1044.87.M26 2012
    371.33'44678—dc23
    2012026083

ISBN: 978-0-415-50376-1 (hbk)
ISBN: 978-0-415-50375-4 (pbk)
ISBN: 978-0-203-12027-9 (ebk)

Typeset in Minion
by EvS Communication Networx, Inc.

Printed and bound in the United States of America by Walsworth Publishing Company, Marceline, MO.

# CONTENTS

# PREFACE TO THE 2013 EDITION

In revising this book for a second edition, we are very aware of the enormous changes that have taken place in the intervening three years. Not least, one of the original authors has tragically died. The changes in the field of educational technology have also been full of surprises. At the time of writing the first edition, Facebook was an up-and-coming social networking tool, but no one could have predicted the astonishing growth the network has had over the last few years. Similarly, Twitter was something that birds did, and although neither of these applications have been fully analysed for their transformative educational potential, there is now the expectation that they both have potential strengths and drawbacks, and that these aspects should now be systematically explored. There has, of course, been an explosion of new applications, particularly in terms of social networking, but also for, broadly speaking, social learning—both formal and non-formal. Among advocates of online education, there is a recognition that online social networking could play an enormous and positive role in the overall student learning experience—for student support, peer-interaction, and educational "play-spaces." Social networks provide opportunities for a community of enquiry, almost without fixed boundaries, and can assist with social constructivist techniques. Most of these applications are still in the "discovery" phase and remain untested on a large scale for their full educational potential. Due to the nature of things, many applications may simply disappear from lack of use, but it is an exciting time to be exploring technology enhanced learning.

In this edition we have revised and updated the academic reading, and through this we have also brought up-to-date the examples of "how it works in practice" for the different technological solutions. As much as possible we have tried to anchor the reported practice to published academic sources that the reader can trust and can follow-up independently. We believe that much of what was expressed in the text of the first edition about the general approaches to the use of educational technology is still valid, in fact the experiences of the last few years has served to reinforce much of what we said. Here too we have tried to insert citations to newer works of academic reference and to refresh what these publications can tell us about the application of various online applications, or the match between pedagogy and the technology. In addition, we have added a postscript to the original book to raise awareness of some current issues in online education, although in the main these are live issues that are still evolving.

Inevitably we have been selective in our choice of applications and the priority allocated to the affordances that they display, for our aim is not to comprehensively cover every nuance of every new online application. Rather we want to showcase some of the most popular applications, highlight their strengths and potentials, and to suggest what sorts of pedagogical approaches would work well with each application. Despite the wealth of experience that provides information to the contrary, there is often a temptation to adopt a new technological application first (perhaps because it appears to be innovative and exciting) and then attempting to use this application without regard for the pedagogical situation where it is being applied. We firmly believe that the considered and efficient use of educational technology can provide at least as good an experience as "traditional" face-to-face education —and in many instances can improve upon the learning experience for students. This book attempts to document some of the significant evidence that supports this view. Not only that, but we are convinced that the educational process of re-thinking a programme of study for a fully online style of delivery makes the course designers reason more clearly and more consistently about putting the learner at the centre of the educational process, and ultimately creates greater value for the educational experience. To do this, however, we require to understand what we really want the student to learn, and to enable the student flexible opportunities for learning in their own preferred style. This is the challenge that this book seeks to explore. We look forward to the educational challenges of the immediate future.

**Frank Rennie and Tara Morrison**

# 1
## SOCIAL NETWORKING
## AS AN EDUCATIONAL TOOL
### *Yet Another Trend ...*

The popularity of a wide range of social software, particularly with young people, has led many educators to think that this practice and enthusiasm could be turned to educational use. The purpose of this book is to assist this process by providing some guidelines for integrating social networking into course design and by documenting the activities of the early pioneers who are experimenting with innovative practices in their teaching. In this first chapter we aim to show that the roots of social networking are not a paradigm shift from what went before but a growth or development from previous practice and theory. Of course, there have been other media which educators were convinced could transform teaching and learning:

- Television and then videoconferencing were going to render most ordinary lecturers redundant because every student would have easy access to outstanding lecturers, with resulting cost savings.
- Computer-based training was going to allow learners to work at their own pace, practicing as often as necessary and receiving programmed feedback from the ever-patient computer.
- Artificial intelligence was going to provide a truly responsive "tutor" who would "understand" the student's misunderstandings and respond appropriately.
- Asynchronous computer conferencing was going to support global education in which students from different time zones around the

world could take courses from prestigious universities without having to leave home or work.

The list could go on. Educational hype has a long and resilient history of jumping on the latest technology as the means of making education better, cheaper, more available or more responsive. Is social networking going to be any different? Our answer is, probably not, but this may be the wrong question. Ignoring social and technological trends is not the way forward for educators any more than is chasing after every new movement because it is new. If a university were to issue each student with a slate and chalk it would be ludicrous, but equally, to expect all students on all courses to benefit from keeping a blog or creating multimedia items in their e-portfolio, is not a sensible way forward either. What we are advocating in this book is an open mind to the possibility that using some form of social software could be beneficial in most courses, given imaginative course design. The emphasis is squarely on how to use social software creatively, not on any assumption that these tools are predisposed to improving education, reducing costs, widening participation or any future priorities of higher education. These are merely tools; however, as we know, man is a tool-using animal!

## WHAT ARE THE TOOLS?

The various tools to be considered in this book are all part of what has been called web 2.0 (O'Reilly, 2005). The underlying practice of web 2.0 tools is that of harnessing collective intelligence, and we have explored the relevance of this for education in a previous book (Rennie & Mason, 2004). As users add new content and new sites, they are connected through hyperlinking so that other users discover the content and link to it, thus the web grows organically as a reflection of the collective activity of the users. O'Reilly cites Amazon as an archetypal example:

> Amazon sells the same products as competitors such as Barnesandnoble.com, and they receive the same product descriptions, cover images, and editorial content from their vendors. But Amazon has made a science of user engagement. They have an order of magnitude, more user reviews, invitations to participate in varied ways on virtually every page—and even more importantly—they use user activity to produce better search results. While a Barnesandnoble.com search is likely to lead with the company's own products, or sponsored results, Amazon always leads with "most popular," a real-time computation based not

only on sales but other factors that Amazon insiders call the "flow" around products. With greater user participation, it's no surprise that Amazon's sales also outpace competitors. (O'Reilly, 2005)

Other examples of social software with relevance to education are:

- Wikipedia is an online encyclopedia in which the content is created and edited entirely by users.
- Folksonomy sites such as del.icio.us and Flickr in which users tag with keywords their photos or other content entries, thus developing a form of collaborative categorization of sites using the kind of associations that the brain uses, rather than rigid, preordained categories.
- Blogging, a form of online diary, adds a whole new dynamism to what was in web 1.0, the personal home page.
- Really Simple Syndication or Rich Site Summary (RSS) is a family of web feed formats used to publish frequently updated digital content, such as blogs, news feeds or podcasts.
- Podcasting is a media file that is distributed over the Internet using syndication feeds, for playback on mobile devices and personal computers.
- E-portfolios encourage students to take ownership of their learning through creating a dynamic, reflective, multimedia record of their achievements.
- Real-time audio and shared screen tools are used for multi-way discussions.

The web has always supported some forms of social interaction, such as computer conferencing, e-mail, and listservs. The level of social interaction they afford has become an established component of distance and even campus-based education. What has changed with web 2.0 is the popularity of social networking sites which Boyd (2006a) claims, have three defining characteristics:

1. **Profile**. A profile includes an identifiable handle (either the person's name or nickname) or information about that person (e.g., age, sex, location, interests, etc.). Most profiles also include a photograph and information about last login. Profiles have unique URLs that can be visited directly and updated.
2. **Traversable, publicly articulated social network**. Participants have the ability to list other profiles as "friends" or "contacts" or

some equivalent. This generates a social network graph which may be directed ("attention network" type of social network where friendship does not have to be confirmed) or undirected (where the other person must accept friendship). This articulated social network is displayed on an individual's profile for all other users to view. Each node contains a link to the profile of the other person so that individuals can traverse the network through friends of friends of friends.

3. **Semi-persistent public comments**. Participants can leave comments (or testimonials, guestbook messages, etc.) on others' profiles for everyone to see. These comments are semi-persistent in that they are not ephemeral but they may disappear over some period of time or upon removal. These comments are typically reverse-chronological in display. Because of these comments, profiles are a combination of an individual's self-expression and what others say about that individual.

These three attributes do not immediately suggest an educational use. Throughout this book, however, we will try to demonstrate ways in which they can be integrated in courses and programmes. More recently the term People Power on the web has been noted in relation to the success of blogging, user reviews, and photo sharing (Anderson, 2006); and observers speak of a "gift culture" on the web whereby users contribute as much as they take. Examples include YouTube, MySpace and Flickr. The primary focus in social networking is participation rather than publishing, which was the primary feature of web 1.0 activity. Bloch (n.d.) links web 2.0, mashups and social networking as "all intertwined in the brave new Internet, the so-called second phase of the evolution of the online world." The essence of social networking is that the users generate the content. This has potentially profound implications for education.

## USER-GENERATED CONTENT

The theoretical benefits of user generated content in education are fairly obvious:

1. Users have the tools to actively engage in the construction of their experience, rather than passively absorbing existing content.
2. Content will be continually refreshed by the users rather than require expensive expert input.
3. Many of the new tools support collaborative work, thereby allowing users to develop the skills of working in teams.

4. Shared community spaces and inter-group communications are a massive part of what excites young people and therefore should contribute to users' persistence and motivation to learn.

However, this assumes a transition between entertainment and education which has never in the past been an obvious or straightforward one. The early champions of educational television had a difficult time persuading learners that this entertaining (but passive) medium could be a tool for active and demanding education. Similarly, how will current users of computer games, blogging, podcasting, and folksonomies be convinced that they can use their favourite tools for getting a degree? O'Reilly suggests that we look at what commercial organisations are doing:

> One of the key lessons of the web 2.0 era is this: *Users add value.* But only a small percentage of users will go to the trouble of adding value to your application via explicit means. Therefore, web 2.0 companies *set inclusive defaults for aggregating user data and building value as a side-effect of ordinary use of the application.* As noted above, they build systems that get better the more people use them…. This architectural insight may also be more central to the success of open source software than the more frequently cited appeal to volunteerism. The architecture of the internet, and the World Wide Web, as well as of open source software projects like Linux, Apache, and Perl, is such that users pursuing their own "selfish" interests build collective value as an automatic by-product. Each of these projects has a small core, well-defined extension mechanism, and an approach that lets any well-behaved component be added by anyone, growing the outer layers of what Larry Wall, the creator of Perl, refers to as "the onion." In other words, these technologies demonstrate network effects, simply through the way that they have been designed. (O'Reilly, 2005)

What is the comparable onion in relation to education? We claim in this book that it is course design. Through appropriate course design, we can help learners to pursue their "selfish interests" of passing the course, while at the same time adding value to the learning of other students.

Another way of looking at user-generated content, and one that is possibly less contentious, is to see it as a network. In a report from FutureLab, Rudd, Sutch, and Facer (2006) note that:

Castells, for example, argues that the network is now the fundamental underpinning structure of social organisation—that it is in and through networks—both real and virtual—that life is lived in the 21st century. This perspective is also advocated by social commentators such as Demos, who argue that networks are the "most important organisational form of our time," and that, by harnessing what they describe as "network logic," the ways we view the world and the tools we use for navigating and understanding it, will change significantly. The ability to understand how to join and build these networks, the tools for doing so and the purpose, intention, rules and protocols that regulate use and communications, therefore, become increasingly important skills. This concept of the "network society" calls into question what it means to be "educated" today—what new skills, what new ways of working and learning, what new knowledge and skills will be required to operate in and through these networks? It requires us to ask whether our current education system, premised not upon networks but upon individualised acquisition of content and skills, is likely to support the development of the competencies needed to flourish in such environments. (p. 4)

The wise use of web 2.0 technologies in education addresses this call for students to develop 21st-century skills. Blogging, wikis, e-portfolios and social networks are all excellent tools for allowing learners to clarify concepts, establish meaningful links and relationships, and test their mental models. Furthermore, they provide a public forum in which the cumulative process of concept formation, refinement, application and revision is fully visible to student peers and teachers. By providing a comprehensive record of how concepts take form through multiple clusters of knowledge, such media can promote more complex and lasting retention of course ideas among students (Boettcher, 2007).

## WHAT ARE THE LIMITATIONS?

Critics of user-created content refer to a breakdown in the traditional place of expertise, authority and scholarly input. They express concerns about trust, reliability and believability in relation to the move away from the printed word to the more ephemeral digital word (Poster, 1990). The web contains a plethora of unauthenticated, unfiltered information and most students lack the critical skills to penetrate this mass of undifferentiated material. In short, traditional notions of quality in higher education seem to be abandoned in the move to web 2.0 learning.

Another line of criticism is that course designers who use these technologies are merely pandering to the net generation, which is not in their best interests. Carlson (2005) notes that "not everyone agrees that Millennials are so different from their predecessors, or that, even if they are different, educational techniques should change accordingly." These critics feel that new technologies encourage a short attention span and lead students to demand immediate answers, rather than thinking for themselves.

Furthermore, if content is created by users on different systems (e.g., podcasts, blogs, wikis, chat systems, and other social networking software), then it can be difficult to keep track of where everything is, and to access it with ease, both for the users and the casual visitor. This in turn calls for new tools to help users search and integrate across content that may be quite fragmented.

Other commentators question whether social networking has real learning value and point to the superficiality of this informal mode of learning. Learning from websites and online discussion groups is very different from the orientation of formal courses, where stress is laid on learning step by step, just in case one needs it later or for the exam. By contrast, informal learning is just-in-time and just the amount necessary to put to immediate use. However, Kapp (2006) argues that:

> We can contemplate whether "real" learning happens with web 2.0 technologies, we can be philosophical about the value of informal learning versus formal learning, we can tout the virtues of "collective wisdom" but in the end … none of that matters.
>
> What matters is that kids are already using web 2.0 technologies comfortably and effectively. If we old folks (over 30) don't figure out how to effectively use these tools to help the younger generation learn what they need to be successful in our baby boomer-run companies, government agencies and other large organizations then we learning and development folks will be irrelevant. Conducting traditional classroom lectures for these gamers is not going to cut it and neither is our multiple-choice question, e-learning module format. We better stop bad mouthing web 2.0 or eLearning 2.0 and start using these technologies or be passed up by the "digital natives" as Prensky calls them.

Others of the same persuasion apply the dictum, "If you can't beat them, help them." They focus on developing critical thinking skills, analysis of the content of websites, and peer commenting on student assignments. In a similar way, Cross (2007) takes a positive stance towards integrating informal learning and web 2.0, and describes an approach which has implications for the role of the teacher:

> Because the design of informal learning ecosystems is analogous to landscape design, I will call the environment of informal learning a learnscape. A landscape designer's goal is to conceptualize a harmonious, unified, pleasing garden that makes the most of the site at hand. A learnscaper strives to create a learning environment that increases the organization's longevity and health, and the individual learner's happiness and well-being. Gardeners don't control plants; managers don't control people. Gardeners and managers have influence but not absolute authority. They can't make a plant fit into the landscape or a person fit into a team. A learnscape is a learning ecology. It's learning without borders.

In the following chapters we describe a wide range of learnscapes and provide practical methods for implementing them.

## STUDIES OF STUDENT BEHAVIOUR

The predictions that students who have grown up with digital media will learn differently and demand a more engaging form of education, have led to a number of studies and surveys of student attitudes, behaviours and uses of technology. A study by Oblinger and Oblinger (2005) talks about Millennials, those born since 1982, whose learning characteristics are defined as follows:

- Ability to multitask rather than single task;
- Preference to learn from pictures, sound and video rather than text;
- Preference for interactive and networked activities rather than independent and individual study.

However these characteristics have the following disadvantages:

- Shorter attention spans or choosing not to pay attention;
- Lack of reflection;
- Relatively poor text literacy;
- A cavalier attitude to quality of sources.

Millennials could be described as having hypertext minds, craving interactivity, easily reading visual images, possessing good visual-spatial skills, and having the ability to parallel process. They will prefer learning in teams, will seek to engage with problems and enjoy experiential forms of learning. Another study of Millennials by Raines (2002) lists similar characteristics:

- Skilled at teamwork,
- Techno-savvy,
- Preference for structure,
- Desire for entertainment and excitement,
- Biased toward experiential activities.

Two European reports, one from Germany (Veen, 2004) and the other from Hungary (Karpati, 2002), both largely confirm the description of millennials outlined in the Oblingers' study (2005). The German report refers to millennials as *Homo Zappiens* because of their habit of using remote controls, and outlines four characteristics:

- Scanning skills,
- Multi-tasking,
- Processing interrupted information flows,
- Non-linear learning.

Not all of these skills, whether positive or negative, can be attributed to social networking, although a number of online gaming sites have web 2.0 characteristics.

An extensive study in the UK of largely pre-university students' use of online technologies (Livingstone & Bober, 2005) has some sobering conclusions:

- Young people lack key skills in evaluating online content and few have been taught how to judge the reliability of online information ;
- Most online communication is with local friends ;
- Nearly one quarter of the sample admitted to copying something from the Internet and passing it off as his or her own.

The researchers note, however, that the opportunities and risks of these technologies go hand in hand, and the more users experience the one, the more they experience the other. We turn now to what researchers are investigating in the web 2.0 world.

# RESEARCH ISSUES

## *Web 2.0 Research Literature*

The technologies which have come to dominate the activities of young people have also been taken up by researchers, academics and lecturers as methods of disseminating their thinking and their practice. A simple browse through the reference section of this book shows that URLs dominate the entries, rather than publisher citations. Much of the literature on the educational use of web 2.0 technologies is online—in blogs, podcasts, wikis and social networking sites. For those trying to keep abreast of developments, it is more important to have the right RSS feeds than the right journal subscriptions.

Of course, in many scientific disciplines, printed journals and books have long been an outmoded form of dissemination for research—too late, too inaccessible, and too expensive. Web 1.0 was an improvement over print as a means of transmitting and consuming research. What is different with web 2.0 technologies is that real interaction, peer commenting and collaborative research are actually happening in a distributed, global environment. Knowledge is created, shared, remixed, repurposed, and passed along. In short, web 2.0 is a research network as well as a learning network.

However, do web 2.0 networks constitute research? The 2007 *Horizon Report* notes that "academic review and faculty rewards are increasingly out of sync with new forms of scholarship." Will academics list blog entries in their CV? (See, in particular, Weller, 2011.) The *Horizon Report* goes on to say, "The trends toward digital expressions of scholarship and more interdisciplinary and collaborative work continue to move away from the standards of traditional peer-reviewed paper publication" (New Media Consortium, 2007). The essence of research has always involved notions such as ownership and copyright, objectivity and replicability. Blogging is very different: it is much less formal; it is usually written from a personal point of view, in a personal voice. Wikis do not privilege personal ownership and are ephemeral or at least are constantly changing. Some researchers counter these criticisms by underlining the fact that our relation to knowledge is changing. The shelf life of information is now so short that knowing where to find information is more valuable than knowing any particular piece of information. The capacity to form connections between sources of information, and thereby create useful information patterns, is what is needed in a knowledge economy. Knowledge used to be organised in strictly classified disciplines and subjects, but is increasingly becoming more fluid and responsive, allowing it to be organised in different ways for different purposes. Furthermore, as Stephenson (n.d.) notes:

> Experience has long been considered the best teacher of knowledge. Since we cannot experience everything, other people's experiences, and hence other people, become the surrogate for knowledge. "I store my knowledge in my friends" is an axiom for collecting knowledge through collecting people.

Experienced academic bloggers find that this forum for airing ideas and receiving comments from their colleagues helps them to hone their thinking and explore avenues they might otherwise have overlooked. The *Horizon Report* lists new scholarship and emerging forms of publication as one of its six key trends in 2007 as most likely to have a significant impact in education in the next five years.

> While significant challenges remain before the emerging forms of scholarship we are seeing are accepted, nonetheless, there are many examples of work that is expanding the boundaries of what we have traditionally thought of as scholarship. In the coming years, as more scholars and researchers make original and worthwhile contributions to their fields using these new forms, methods for evaluating and recognizing those contributions will be developed, and we expect to see them become an accepted form of academic work. (New Media Consortium, 2007, p. 21)

Knowledge is no longer acquired in a linear manner. We can no longer personally experience and acquire all the learning that we need in order to act. We must derive our competence from forming connections with other people. Blogs and wikis are ideal tools for this and what we see in these tools are examples of networks of growing knowledge and understanding. In terms of the use of web 2.0 tools in education, research on the whole is not to be found in print-based literature. Knowledge and understanding of practice are developing within a network of interactions through web 2.0 tools online.

Why then are we choosing to write a book on the use of these technologies for education? Isn't this contradicting our case that there is a change in how knowledge is being created and accessed? Yes, the book will be out-of-date before it is printed, much less read, but no, we are not trying to suggest that there is no place for printed books. What we are aiming to do in this book is draw together what is already known about how to use web 2.0 technologies and to provide direction in how and why to use them in course design.

## The Changing Learner

One of the questions which have arisen due to the phenomenal uptake of new technologies by young people is whether and to what extent learners are changing. That is, what is the effect of computer games, mobile phones, the Internet, and social networking on learners who have grown up with these as an integral part of their environment? The most widely quoted respondent to this question is, of course, Prensky whose papers on "digital natives" (the net generation for whom everything digital is natural) and "digital immigrants" (those who have had to learn the language of these technologies as mature adults) have sparked controversy, further studies, and commentators on both sides of the fence (e.g., Allen & Seaman, 2006; Conole, de Laat, Dillon, & Darby, 2006; Kvavik & Caruso, 2005). Prensky (2001a, b) holds that digital natives are different in kind from digital immigrants.

> It is now clear that as a result of this ubiquitous environment and the sheer volume of their interaction with it, today's students think and process information fundamentally differently from their predecessors. These differences go far further and deeper than most educators suspect or realize. (Prensky, 2001a)

Prensky's conclusions are based (loosely) on research into the neuroplasticity of the brain and he suggests that there may be an actual change in the brains of young people who have spent hours of their growing period as screenagers, gaming, interacting online, and creating online content. Owen (2004) counters such sloganising with a reference to Brown and Duguid (2000):

> In this study Brown and Duguid's central theme is that access to information does not equate to knowledge. Brown and Duguid note, much of what we recognise as learning comes from informal social interactions between learners and mentors. These social interactions are difficult to achieve in mediated instruction. They recognise that technology can enhance instruction in remarkable ways; however, it cannot replace the insights that students receive by struggling to make sense of information with both peers and mentors. They contend that the gung-ho tunnel vision of commentators like Prensky—seeing only one way

ahead (if all you have is a hammer, everything looks like a nail!), has led to erroneously simplified and unrealistic expectations of what our future in the information age will be like. (Owen, 2004)

Nevertheless, Owen agrees with Prensky that the tools we use inevitably change how we think, how we learn, what we may think and what we may learn, but he sees this as evolutionary rather than revolutionary. Johnson and Johnson (2004) reiterate this point of view:

> Because the nature of technology used by a society influences what the society is and becomes, individuals who do not become technologically literate will be left behind. Influences of a technology include the nature of the medium, the way the medium extends human senses, and the type of cognitive processing required by the medium. (p. 785)

Johnson and Johnson (2004) are confirming the idea already suggested above that educators need to use the tools that are common in the social context of the day, because they are determining the way people learn.

A major piece of research on student reactions to the use of information technology (IT) in education was carried out by Kvavik and Caruso in 2005. Reassuringly, students in this survey still saw faculty knowledge and expertise as the most important element in learning, but the majority wanted instructors to make moderate use of IT, whilst equal numbers wanted extensive use or limited use.

Another aspect of the changing learner is the increasing multiculturalism of most university classes. This is especially true of online, distributed courses, as students from outside the originating institution may be part of each cohort, making a more culturally diverse online environment than was the case for traditional classrooms in the past. Course design manuals used to begin with the process of identifying learners' needs and background knowledge. This may be possible with a relatively homogeneous student body, but becomes impossible in a multicultural context. Cultural backgrounds are inextricably related to how we learn, and hence learning needs of students may well vary by culture. Attitudes to particular content (political correctness, contextuality in meaning-making and views about absolute reality), variations in writing styles (formality, vocabulary, directness), and above all, concepts about the role of the learner and of the teacher (criticism, authority, politeness); these are all culturally specific, and hence highly variable in multicultural learning environments. The practices of peer evaluation, student-generated content, and teacher-as-equal-partner may make students from some non-Western cultures feel uncomfortable and leave them floundering rather than participating. Experienced practitioners of online multicultural environments usually recommend flexibility and openness on the part of course designers. For example, Palloff and Pratt (2003) suggest "recognizing the different ways in which students might respond to instructional techniques online and being sensitive to potential cultural barriers and obstacles is yet another means by which the online classroom can become more culturally sensitive."

Similarly, Henderson (1996) promotes an eclectic paradigm which does not assume that any one instructional pedagogy is immutable but provides an epistemological and pedagogic pluralism that allows students to interact with materials that reflect multiple cultural values and perspectives. Another approach to cultural pluralism is to recognise that every student is individual in his or her learning requirements regardless of cultural background. Providing diversity in types of resources, assessments, communication tools, and learning activities not only creates greater flexibility for all learners to customise their learning, but also provides a self-reinforcing learning environment for creativity and innovation (Price & Rennie, 2005). The issues raised by multicultural classrooms are not new and not restricted to online learning, though they will undoubtedly be exacerbated by web 2.0 technologies.

### Collaborative Learning

Johnson and Johnson (2004) analyse the history of cooperative and collaborative learning and the way in which these practices have been revitalised by the advent of online learning. They cite a range of studies which demonstrate that cooperative learning online results in higher achievement than individualistic learning. They conclude that "few educational innovations hold the promise that technology-supported cooperative learning does ..." (p. 806). Jenkins (2006) points out that one of the implications of online collaborative work is that educators need to rethink the individualistic foundations of assessment in higher education. Social networking encourages collective contribution, not individual ownership. Creativity is different in an open source culture. He uses the term *distributed cognition* and outlines the new skills educators need to develop in their learners:

> Applications of the distributed cognition perspective to education suggest that students must learn the affordances of different tools and information technologies, and know which functions

tools and technologies excel at and in what contexts they can be trusted. Students need to acquire patterns of thought that regularly cycle through available sources of information as they make sense of developments in the world around them. Distributed intelligence is not simply a technical skill, although it depends on knowing how to use tools effectively; it is also a cognitive skill, which involves thinking across "brain, body, and world." The term "distributed intelligence" emphasizes the role that technologies play in this process, but it is closely related to the social production of knowledge that we are calling collective intelligence. (Jenkins, 2006, p. 38)

Course design is a particularly important component of successful online collaborative learning. Wenger (1998, p. 229) clarifies the relation between course design and learning: "Learning [itself] cannot be designed: it can only be designed for—that is, facilitated or frustrated." The essence of online collaborative course design is the use of activities appropriate to the subject and level of the students. Generic models include: an online debate, joint creation of a website, group presentations, and peer comments on student work. Web 2.0 course design involves collaborative uses of blogs, wikis, e-portfolios and podcasts. These are in their infancy, although educational uses of blogging have a marginally longer history.

### Student-Centred Course Design

The issue of student versus teacher centred course design is another long-standing one which continues to evolve with the impact of social networking. Designing a course around the learner's needs is a cornerstone of open and distance learning where it usually involves passing at least some control to the learner over pacing, interaction with the course content, and timing of the assessments in order that part-time students can fit studying around work and family commitments. Garrison and Baynton (1989) argued that control is a dynamic relationship between independence, power and support, and Hall, Watkins, and Eller (2003) talk about the need to find a balance between providing the student with enough structure to keep their studying on track, and enough freedom to work creatively and flexibly on the course.

The advent of user or student generated content adds a new dimension to the debate. There are a number of ways in which students can participate in creating the content of a course. Discussions and debates have been standard practice on campuses and have been used regularly in online courses where asynchronous conferences are the established mode of communication. Similarly, the practice of resource-based and problem-based learning pre-dates social networking by some decades. Both of these design models imply that students find appropriate material in order to study the course. Student-generated content takes this a step further by students not just finding content (in the form of resources), but actually creating it (through blogs, wikis, e-portfolios, and other multimedia presentations).

The obvious implication of student-created content is a changing role for the teacher and for the educational institution. There is a need for teachers not only to master the new technologies, but also to understand and capitalise on the pedagogical implications. There is a need for institutions to monitor student access to the technologies and consider what to provide for students and what to leave to social trends to determine. Many of the web services are free and may already be familiar to students from social and informal learning activities outside of their studies. A Vice Chancellor of the UK Open University, in considering the implications of student-created content for the university, posed the following issues:

> how best we deliver customer service and student support in this new world and how we harness this gift culture to enhance student support with peer-to-peer mentoring and collaborative learning models; how we deal with the shifting boundaries between formal and informal learning. What we see on the Web are people from all over the world creating communities of interest (some of them very sophisticated indeed) on a whole range of subject matter—and what we need to do is ask ourselves how we harness this energy and recognise the learning—if that is indeed useful to people as they negotiate their careers and lives. (Gourley, 2006)

Mason and Lefrere (2003) define the essence of this move to a sharing environment as involving processes for developing trustworthiness. Jameson, Ferrell, Kelly, Walker, and Ryan (2006) also conducted research on the importance of trust in collaborative online learning networks. Course designers need to set up learning systems that recognise the need for building trust and exploit the learners' social networks.

The changing role of the student obviously has implications for the role of the teacher. Beldarrain (2006) notes the transition from teacher as deliverer of knowledge, to facilitator of online interaction. With the advent of student-generated content, she predicts that "the future instructor may have to be more of a partner in learning than a facilitator. The instructor must view the students as contributors of knowledge, and thus allow them to participate in the creation of content" (p. 149). The instructor, therefore, needs to provide feedback and build rapport. Papert noted in 1998 that there was a clash between the dominant ideology of curriculum design and the empowerment learners get from games and other technologies which enable the user to take charge of his or her learning. Rudd et al. (2006) have reiterated this point:

> Currently most discussions about increasing learner "choice" and "voice" are focused around giving learners a greater variety of routes through predetermined and predefined subjects and curriculum content. However, a truly personalised system requires that learners will not only have greater choice and influence over the pace, style and content of learning but that they are also supported to become active partners in developing their own educational pathways and experiences. (p. 7)

Student-centred learning and the technologies which enable them to generate content will continue to have profound effects on the inter-relationships of students, teachers, and course content. We develop this theme at greater length in chapter 6.

## BEYOND CONSTRUCTIVIST THEORY

Many researchers consider that course design based on constructivist theories of learning is highly compatible with the use of web 2.0 tools. Constructivist curricula favour an open-ended, negotiable approach which structures activities so that students have opportunities to collaboratively negotiate knowledge and to contextualise learning within an emergent situation. This reflects the two tenets of constructivism: that (1) learning is an active process of constructing knowledge rather than acquiring it, and (2) instruction is a process that involves supporting that construction rather than of communicating knowledge (Duffy & Cunningham, 1996, p. 171).

Through the provision of activities for students to direct their own learning, the designer acknowledges the students' need for autonomy in the learning process in order to construct their own understanding. The provision of realistic or authentic contexts for learning is the basis for many constructivist learning environments, as the purpose is to stimulate learners to relate their thinking to actual practice.

Communication through the learning environment is a key feature of constructivist design, especially where the students are geographically isolated. It is through dialogue in chat rooms, commenting on blogs, collaborating through wikis and self-expression through e-portfolios that students are able to develop as members of their learning community, to create shared understandings, to challenge and to question the key issues of their area of study.

Learners are considered to be distributed, multidimensional participants in a socio-cultural process. This concept moves away from the idea that learning is effective internalising of knowledge, toward one that involves a connection with communities and a pattern of participation in community. It should not be a lonely act of a single person but a matter of being "initiated into the practices of a community, of moving from legitimate peripheral participation to centripetal participation in the actions of a learning community" (Duffy & Cunningham, 1996, p. 181).

Learners in a constructivist environment need to be active and interactive, and web 2.0 software is inherently participative.

> Web 2.0 is where anyone can not only *take* information down *from* it but also create content and upload *to* it. In this respect the Web is not simply a one-way means of *obtaining* knowledge, but also a place where you *interact* with the materials and *annotate* and *contribute* to the content. Such sites frequently display other Web 2.0 characteristics such as automated access through RSS feeds and ability to find related materials through tagging and other social networking devices. (Stevens, 2006)

Nevertheless, other educators are beginning to look beyond constructivism and to associate it with web 1.0 thinking. For example, Siemens (2004) claims that web 2.0 technologies have changed the learning landscape such that the three pillars of learning theory (behaviourism, cognivitism and constructivism) are no longer adequate for describing the world in which we now are learning:

> Constructivism suggests that learners create knowledge as they attempt to understand their experiences (Driscoll, 2000, p. 376). Behaviourism and cognivitism view knowledge as external to the learner and the learning process as the act of internalizing knowledge. Constructivism assumes that learners are not empty vessels to be filled with knowledge. Instead, learners are actively attempting to create meaning. Learners often select and pursue their own learning. Constructivist principles acknowledge that

real-life learning is messy and complex. Classrooms which emulate the "fuzziness" of this learning will be more effective in preparing learners for life-long learning.

Learning theories are concerned with the actual process of learning, not with the value of what is being learned. In a networked world, the very manner of information that we acquire is worth exploring. The need to evaluate the worthiness of learning something is a meta-skill that is applied before learning itself begins. When knowledge is subject to paucity, the process of assessing worthiness is assumed to be intrinsic to learning. When knowledge is abundant, the rapid evaluation of knowledge is important. Additional concerns arise from the rapid increase in information. In today's environment, action is often needed without personal learning—that is, we need to act by drawing information outside of our primary knowledge. The ability to synthesize and recognize connections and patterns is a valuable skill. (Siemens, 2004)

Siemens (2004) posits instead, a theory he calls connectivism, whose principles he defines as:

- Learning and knowledge rest in diversity of opinions.
- Learning is a process of connecting specialized nodes or information sources.
- Learning may reside in non-human appliances.
- Capacity to know more is more critical than what is currently known.
- Nurturing and maintaining connections is needed to facilitate continual learning.
- Ability to see connections between fields, ideas, and concepts is a core skill.
- Currency (accurate, up-to-date knowledge) is the intent of all connectivist learning activities.
- Decision making is itself a learning process. Choosing what to learn and the meaning of incoming information is seen through the lens of a shifting reality. While there is a right answer now, it may be wrong tomorrow due to alterations in the information climate affecting the decision.

Connectivism as a theory presents a model of learning that reflects a society in which learning is no longer a personal, individualistic activity. It acknowledges the fact that the ways people learn and function are altered when new tools are used. Siemens is critical of educators for being slow to recognize both the impact of new learning tools and the environmental changes in what it means to learn. Connectivism is his theoretical foundation for the learning skills and tasks needed for learners to flourish in a digital era.

## Learning Design

A new area of research has emerged recently called Learning Design. It reflects a shift of focus in course design from an emphasis on providing content to an emphasis on designing activities that help students learn through interaction with sources, people and ideas. Learning designs provide a way of representing learning activities so that course designers can easily identify the essence of a design or learning sequence and apply it to their own curriculum area. Through a process of breaking down activities into constituent parts, it guides individuals through the process of creating activities and incidentally, highlights policy and technology implications. It also provides a common vocabulary for course designers to understand how students learn through activities. In short, learning design offers a method for reusing good practice across many disciplines. An example of research in this area comes from Australia.

In a climate where individual institutions are experiencing increased costs at the same time as they face increased demand for more flexible approaches to learning, the Australian Universities Teaching Committee (AUTC) considers there is benefit to be gained in developing shared resources and disseminating successful, generalisable templates between institutions. One product of this assessment is a project, now completed, which is captured here as "Learning Designs."

The project was commissioned in 2000 by the AUTC to explore the use of Information and Communication Technologies (ICTs) to facilitate flexible learning opportunities for students by identifying learning designs that have been demonstrated to contribute to high quality learning experiences and determining which learning designs may be redeveloped in a more generic form (http://www.learningdesigns.uow. edu.au/project/index.htm).

There are a number of learning design tools which have been developed to support the process of course design from creation, through technical implementation, to actual presentation to students. One of these, developed by researchers at Oxford University, is called Phoebe (http://phoebe-project.conted.ox.ac.uk). Another is the Joint Information Systems Committee (JISC) Pedagogic Planner (http://www.wle.org. uk/d4l/), and a third is called Compendium and was developed at The

Open University (http://compendium.open.ac.uk/). The value of these tools is currently untested on any significant scale. They are essentially decision support tools and some (e.g., the JISC Pedagogic Planner) are highly structured, while others (e.g., Phoebe) are open-ended. Early indications are that some users welcome them and others with different working and thinking practices find it preferable to design on paper or from instinct about what works with students.

## OUTCOME-BASED DESIGN

What should drive the process of course design: pedagogical principles, specific problems to be addressed, or tools to be used? It is generally acknowledged that there is no best approach to begin the process of course design. However, there are fashions or trends and currently outcome-based design is in vogue (and definitely out of fashion are technology-driven rationales and teacher-centred approaches).

Learning outcomes are statements of what students will know or be able to do, if they have learned everything in the course. Outcomes are subtly but distinctly different from learning objectives, which are statements of what is going to be taught, although they may be expressed as if the students were going to learn it. Objectives are normally written using behavioural verbs: list, define, calculate, state. Unfortunately, behavioural objectives are not so easily adaptable to the higher forms of learning such as understanding and being creative or to critical reflection or transformative learning. With learning outcomes, there is a slight shift from content to process as the outcome is more explicit about how evidence is to be provided, rather than the evidence itself.

Apart from this shift to a focus on process, learning outcomes have also become the driver for the assessment strategy of a course. Coats and Stevenson (2006) claim that it is important to "ensure that assessment strategies and assessment methods support the development of the stated outcomes and enable them to be appropriately assessed." Furthermore, the learning outcomes and their assessment should make a positive contribution to the learning process.

> Good assessment now is that which most closely reflects desired learning outcomes and in which the process of assessment has a directly beneficial influence on the learning process. (Boud, 1995)

Knowing the expected outcomes and being clear about the criteria that will be used to assess whether or not they have been achieved gives more control to the learner and thus enables him or her to use that assessment as a learning experience. Assessment can be, indeed always is, a learning experience, with or without an outcomes-based approach and clear assessment criteria. The point is that appropriate outcomes and shared criteria can enhance that learning.

How can an educational assessment methodology (or paradigm) that places emphasis on the learners and supposedly encourages them to take more responsibility for their own learning—stressing autonomy and empowerment at the same time—subject that learner to a pre-scribed curriculum and defined outcomes to learning? One approach to this seeming contradiction is to see assessment as an integrated part of teaching and learning, in which both teacher and student play an inter-active role, and in which teaching and learning are seen as complex and socially mediated (Coates & Stevenson, 2006).

Another approach to this contradiction is proposed by Irlbeck, Kays, Jones, and Sims (2006) who suggest using emergent models of instruc-tional design, rather than the top-down models in which the "experts" decide the objectives, assessment criteria, learning outcomes, and activities. Emergent theory suggests a radical alternative—that design should proceed from the ground up using a process of natural selection that will weed out less useful information. Boettcher (2007) sees the unpredictability of a course which is allowed to evolve with the stu-dents, as highly engaging:

> Other valuable features of games and simulations are their unpredictability, their interactive qualities, and their infinite variety. Canned, predictable, and static learning resources such as books, pre-programmed tutorials, and linear video experi-ences are less interesting and less engaging. The more dynamic and interactive the learning experience, the more likely it is that students will invest greater amounts of time in the learning process.

The subject of emergent design is further developed in chapter 6.

## ANOTHER BOOK ON COURSE DESIGN?

There is a substantial literature on course design in higher education and particularly so for distributed and distance education (e.g., Gagnon & Collay, 2006; Jochems, van Merrienboer, & Koper, 2003; Rabinowitz, Blumberg, & Everson, 2004). Why is another book needed? Evidence from the literature on the use of new technologies in education shows that many educators appropriate the new technology—be it computer-based learning, videoconferencing, or computer conferencing—but use them to mirror existing practice rather than to exploit their real affordances. Conole, Oliver, Falconer, Littlejohn, and Harvey (2007) argue that this gap between the potential of technologies and the reality of actual use is due to a number of interconnected issues:

- Lack of understanding of how they could be used,
- Lack of appropriate guidance at the course design stage,
- Immaturity of the tools,
- Organizational barriers.

Waller (2007) predicts a similar misuse of web 2.0 tools:

> You find nowadays that PowerPoint is inevitable and used with the slightest of excuses. In the main it no longer supports the speaker as it should but instead acts as a crutch…. Now we all just stare at the PowerPoint, looking but not seeing, thereby relieving our brain of the tiresome task of seeing what the speaker is saying. Very soon we will have death by podcast as people with uninspiring voices dump what they have to say onto enormous mp3 files. We will have death by short learning programme, rapidly produced by someone who is convinced that this will always produce the required results. We will have death by blogs and wikis and we will be inundated with demands to share what we know in online communities…. If these interventions are not designed by people who know about these things, these events will fail in their purpose.

The role of the course designer is arguably *more* relevant with web 2.0 tools than with traditional forms of teaching and learning. It is the intention of this book to address this need by providing a framework and above all, examples of how web 2.0 tools can be used appropriately in distributed and distance education settings.

## CONCLUSIONS

This synopsis of some of the issues affecting web 2.0 course design has emphasised a number of critical issues. We summarise these in several aphorisms:

1. The medium is only as good as the design of the instructional strategy the educators have used.
2. Cooperation is the watchword, not control. Web 2.0 applications work on the basis of participation not coercion.
3. Course design is no longer about transmission and consumption; it is about co-creating, sharing, repurposing, and above all, interacting.

But as with many areas of web 2.0, the new tools and approaches are only a development or fuller realization of the true potential of the web platform. This gives us a key insight into how to design educational uses for these applications and services.

This overview of the issues related to using web 2.0 tools in education has tried to convey an important concept: that web 2.0 is actually more than a set of tools and services. It is the powerful ideas behind the tools and services that have so much potential for education: the reality of user-generated content, the network effects of mass participation, and the openness and low threshold for easy access. These factors are inherent in the original concept of the web, just as their application to education builds on long established principles of best practice: student engagement and interaction in learning, and student ownership and management of learning.

# 2
## DESIGNING FOR A DISTRIBUTED ENVIRONMENT

## DEFINITION OF TERMS

Before we go much further, it is useful to clarify what we mean by the terms *distributed*, *blended* and *flexible* learning. In recent years a strong interest has developed in the support of distributed learning systems that are flexible enough to permit easy access to multi-mode educational resources, over a wide geographical area. Amongst the plethora of definitions of distributed learning, however, there is little common ground. The term *distributed* in relation to education, particularly higher education, encompasses a number of different practices. For some the term is synonymous with distance education and e-learning (Oblinger, Barone, & Hawkins, 2001); for others it is identical to the term *blended learning* (e.g., Bonk & Graham, 2006); others prefer to distinguish between these terms. For example, according to Tarleton State University (2004):

> Although the phrases "distributed education" and "distance education" are often used interchangeably, distributed education has a broader meaning. The primary characteristic of distance education is that learning takes place independently of place and time, allowing students to absorb the content from a distance. On the other hand, the principal goal of distributed learning is to customize learning environments to better-fit different learning styles, whether students are on or off campus. In this new pedagogical model, students are encouraged to learn in an interactive and collaborative environment.

Distance education is a subset of distributed learning, focusing on students who may be separated in time and space from their peers and the instructor. Distributed learning can occur either on or off campus, providing students with greater flexibility and eliminating time as a barrier to learning. A common feature of both distance and distributed learning is technology. Regardless of whether students are on campus or online, there are many implications of integrating technology into education, i.e., in making learning distributed.

*Blended learning* is also a term that encompasses a range of different practices, though usually it refers to learning that combines face-to-face teaching with online resources. The learners may be full-time campus students or they may be located partially on campus and partially at a distance. Although these terms are always changing in their application, it might be fairly safe to say that distributed learning is commonly used for the teaching model of an institution or university, whereas blended learning tends to be used at a course level to describe particular design components. A few researchers (Oliver & Trigwell, 2005) have argued against the term *blended learning* altogether, from both philosophical and pedagogical perspectives, but even allowing for (or perhaps because of) the vagueness and imprecision in terminology, both *blended* and *distributed* learning activities are frequently described in the literature and seem likely to continue in use for the foreseeable future.

As these descriptions make clear, technologies of varying sorts are a central component in the practice of distributed learning. In this chapter we will consider successful ways of conveying different kinds of content, and how this content can be made available in different formats, both synchronous and asynchronous.

As noted, while *blended learning* is a contentious term, it generally refers to a combination of face-to-face and online learning (such as using e-learning to complement classroom activity or vice versa). A study into the undergraduate experience of blended e-learning in the UK (Sharpe, Benfield, Roberts, & Francis, 2006) comprehensively explored recent literature and practice, and came up with some key "recommendations to guide future policy, practice, and research." This report forms important background reading to the present chapter, but a slightly wider interpretation is taken here to accommodate the fact that (1) blended learning may take place on one campus (i.e., without necessarily any geographical distribution) and (2) distributed learning, although combining distance and e-learning, may not necessarily include any face-to-face activity (as is normally implicit in the term *blended learning*).

For the purposes of this chapter, we will assume the following properties define distributed learning:

- The components of the course are distributed across multiple media and this tends to imply a certain amount of choice of media as well as a tendency towards a student-centred learning approach.
- Distributed learning can be used to augment traditional classroom-based courses, to deliver distance education courses or to create wholly online courses, and therefore the "distributed" nature may contain a component of geographical distribution of learning resources.
- Providing flexibility for students in terms of time or location of study is one key aim of the pedagogy of distributed learning.

Schematically, the relationship between blended learning, e-learning, and distributed learning can be illustrated in Figure 2.1.

The apparent lack of consistency amongst the various definitions can be partially explained by the fact that distance education and campus-based teaching are converging due to the growth of ICT and the web, as well as the growing student demand for flexible learning options (Tait & Mills, 1999). A number of universities that introduced online courses as a way of attracting new learners, have found to their dismay that their campus students also opt for these courses, often creating

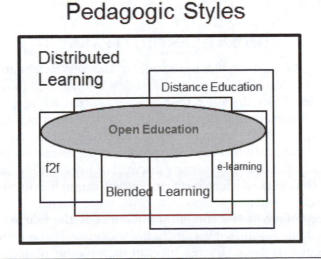
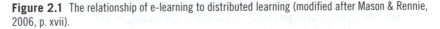

**Figure 2.1** The relationship of e-learning to distributed learning (modified after Mason & Rennie, 2006, p. xvii).

their blend by taking one online course plus several face-to-face courses (Young, 2002). Across the sector, provision is moving towards a pattern characterised by brief, intensive face-to-face interventions punctuating longer periods of independent or group study facilitated by learning technologies (Middlehurst, 2002). Distributed learning has arisen as a term which bridges educational practice from face-to-face to distance learning (Lea & Nicoll, 2002). The availability of new learning technologies, both synchronous and asynchronous, has added depth and richness to the potential of distributed education.

A growing number of institutions also make use of videoconferencing for higher education, often in combination with their own online virtual learning environment (VLE) in a manner that combines asynchronous access (discussion boards, e-mail, tutorial resources, online libraries) with synchronous access (instant messaging, Skype audio and video) to facilitate the interaction between tutors and students. New communication tools such as instant messaging, Skype, shared whiteboard technologies, and reflective tools such as blogging, wikis, and e-portfolios have been added to long-established means of asynchronous communications (print, e-mail, discussion boards, etc.) to become part of the distributed learning designer's palette of options in creating dynamic and varied educational environments. To be effective in combining these new media, it is important to analyse what choices are being made by practitioners, and for what reasons. How do course designers decide what technologies to use? What considerations underpin their design solutions?

## STUDENT-CENTRED LEARNING

According to existing literature, one of the key factors in designing courses with a high level of flexibility must be the development of a student-centred, rather than teacher-centred learning environment (Gudmundsson & Matthiasdottir, 2004; Meyers & Jones, 1993; Motschnig-Pitrik & Holzinger, 2002). Based on constructivist theories of learning, student-centred approaches to course design create an environment in which learners discover or work out for themselves an understanding of the subject or concept through critical analysis and reflection, often in conjunction with other learners. By combining a range of media and communication modes, the course no longer consists of one authorised version of knowledge such as is conveyed by a lecture or a textbook. The resources of the web, the interactions with other learners, the guidance of the teacher, and the experiences resulting from collaborative activities all combine to effectively distribute the inputs of the course so that the onus shift s to the individual students to construct their own understanding of the topic. Relan and Gillani (1997) confirm this analysis of the impact of distributed education: "The predominant source of content shifts from the textbook and the teacher to a more varied source of information. Further, the nature of the content becomes dynamic, versus the static texts published on a certain date" (p. 44).

The role of the teacher or tutor is to generate an infrastructure for constructive interaction and to help students individually and collectively to negotiate their own meaning. The course designer, who may or may not be the same as the teacher or tutor, needs to understand the strengths and weaknesses of available technologies and to know something about the background of the potential students. Even with this understanding, it is still problematic for course designers to decide what components to use and where to start. Anecdotal evidence suggests that many courses are technology-led; that is, a new piece of software appears to be gaining followers, so the course designers decide to "have a go with it." This can result in technologies being peripheral to the core content of the course. Students immediately detect this and avoid engaging at all or only superficially with this component. In some cases communication technologies are used on a course where only a proportion of students have access.

In a practical guide for the UK Quality Assurance Agency, Casey and Wilson (2006) provided a theoretical and practical framework to consider flexible learning in the context of further and higher education, and this is also a good conceptual starting point for distributed learning. In particular, the "five dimensions of flexibility" proposed by Collis and Moonen (2004) formed a useful framework for staff interviews and could be further developed as an empirical tool for quantifying the level of flexibility of distributed learning courses. The five elements of flexibility they defined are: time, content, entry requirements, delivery and logistics, and institutional approaches and resources.

In this context also, it is worth considering the proposed model for analysis and implementation of flexible programme delivery offered by Normand and Littlejohn (2006) although they acknowledge the fact that that their selected case studies reflect an "instructor-offered flexibility" rather than a more comprehensive institutional approach. They base their model on previous work that identified a framework of five components for successful design of flexible programme delivery. These are strategy, structure, roles and skills, management processes, and technology, but their new model refined this to just three components by combining the central role of technology with the grouping of strategy and structure as "contextual factors," grouping roles and skills and "management processes as process factors" (both of these factors being embedded within the strategic thinking of the institutional structure), to provide a "set of tailorable tools to manage learning."

## SOCIAL NETWORKING AND LEARNING

The development of online community structures to facilitate learning is as old as the Internet itself. A considerable, one might almost say exhaustive, amount of academic literature has been produced on the subject of constructing, maintaining, supporting, and evaluating online communities for educational (and other) purposes (e.g., A. J. Kim, 2000; Preece, 2000; Smith & Kollock, 1999). We have written previously about the powerful significance of networked communities for creating intimacy and support for self-directed learning (Rennie & Mason, 2004, chap. 2) and we do not propose to elaborate further on this topic, except to try to relate it to the increasingly flexible online environment of web 2.0 applications. Weller (2007a, 2011) has argued that the design features of the Internet—particularly its capacity for robust, decentralized, open communication—have been transformed into recognisably social features of the system, and that these have a particular importance for the way online learning communities function. Using the examples of a number of successful online communities, Weller asserts that the openness inherent in the Internet encourages the sharing, group editing, and self-policing of information in online learning communities which, he argues, are a logical conclusion of e-learning.

The decentralised nature of the communication systems allows users access from a variety of locations using a variety of devices, and this placing of greater responsibility on learners to manage and direct their own learning will have profound implications for educators and the education establishment. In effect, "teachers" and "tutors" will need to change roles from being the sole repository of knowledge, to roles in which their experience is utilised to help facilitate and focus learners to contextualise knowledge within the wider framework of their experience. This multi-level hyper-interactivity is critically encouraged by the technical and social construction of web 2.0, and can be considered an emergent property from what is effectively a complex adaptive system. Thinking about web 2.0 in terms of the systems analysis of a complex adaptive system is crucially important, and helps to understand how the system functions in three key aspects:

1. **Feedback**: The interchange of ideas peer-to-peer and teacher-to-student can help to modulate the flow of information through and between communities. A positive feedback can help to accelerate change; for example, good user experiences with new applications such as text messaging, YouTube, or blogging results in a rapid spread of new users seeking to share in the experience. Negative feedback helps to resist change and promote stability; for example, the dampening down of rapid adoption of new applications after a few bad experiences; or the modification of over-enthusiastic claims on a Wikipedia entry to achieve a general consensus or compromise position.

2. **System ecology**: The intricate structure of collaboration and complementarily between applications and users can be considered analogous to the functioning of a natural ecosystem, in that each part is, even indirectly, connected to every other part, and changes in one component will have a knock-on impact to other components. This is of supreme significance for course design, and illustrates simply the reason why adding new technology to "solve" a course problem without considering the knock-on effects may simply create other problems elsewhere on the course.

3. **Self-organisation**: An important feature of complex adaptive systems is their self-organizing properties, known as community assembly. Web-based learning generally requires a high level of self-regulatory skills (Niemi, Launonen, & Raehalme, 2002). In part this is determined by technical features—whether one device can communicate with another—but with the growing convergence between devices, and between different software applications, this may be less of a problem in future. In part, also, self-organisation is user-defined, with learners selecting subject areas, levels, and modes of flexible access that suit their lifestyle or personal requirements—in effect, a specific ecological niche for each learner.

## LEARNING OUTCOMES

It is well established in academic literature that a considered approach to designing distributed learning courses is to begin with learning outcomes. As we become more learner-centred, instructors move from covering content to helping students master learning outcomes. This transition can have profound impact on how faculty structure their courses and curricula, and generally leads to increased interest in depth of processing rather than breadth of coverage (Allen, 2004).

Learning outcomes are specific understandings or skill sets that a student is expected to achieve at the end of a learning experience. They can be applied to a course, a program, or a complete degree. The use of learning outcomes as the focus of course design provides a rationale for the selection of resources and media.

Outcome-based education is a method of teaching that focuses on what students can actually do after they are taught. All curriculum and teaching decisions are made based on how best to facilitate the desired outcome. This leads to a planning process in reverse of traditional educational planning. The desired outcome is selected first and the curriculum is created to support the intended outcome (Lorenzen, 1999).

The use of learning outcomes as a starting point for course design generally has become standard practice in UK higher education in recent years. At least four factors are implied in this approach:

- What the student is to learn must be clearly identified.
- This must be achievable and demonstrable.
- The course should provide multiple instructional and assessment strategies in order that each student can demonstrate what he or she has learned.
- The course design must allow adequate time and provide adequate assistance so that each student can reach the maximum potential (Towers, 1996).

A significant problem with this approach is that if the outcome-based approach is too rigid, it flies in the face of demands for more student autonomy in learning choices. How can it be a truly self-directed learning experience if the outcomes and the paths to these outcomes are preselected before the student even signs up for the course? We will come back to this in more detail in chapter 6.

## ON LEARNING STYLES AND PERSONALIZATION

It might be useful at this stage to deal with the issue of individual learning styles. A considerable amount has been written on this subject but there appears to be little general agreement over definitions, or on how to measure the variation claimed to be predicted in the models of analysis that attempt to predict an individual's learning style. Put simply, the theory of learning styles, or "multiple intelligence" attempts to use a series of tests to predict the main way that a learner actually learns (e.g., the self-administered test at http://www.ldpride.net/learningstyles. MI.htm). It is generally accepted that people favour different ways of getting to know a subject: perhaps you like to find a quiet corner with a good book (text) or you prefer to see a practical demonstration on TV (visual). There is a difference between the person who prefers to learn by doing (experiential) to the person who likes to talk things over then think about it for a while (reflective). The controversy, however, begins when we attempt to reach agreement on how we measure these preferences and how robustly we can rely upon any measurements that suggest that a certain person *always* learns in a particular way.

The arguments for and against the concept of definitive learning styles have swung to and fro over recent years, but there is a broad, if reluctant, agreement that there *are* several different generic styles of learning, even if most educators baulk at the idea of designing course materials to fit rigid stereotypes. Against this background we have seen the evolution of increasingly sophisticated web-based software that enables complex user profiles to be built up to personalise the user interface for a variety of purposes. Personalised profiles are built up either by the user deliberately creating a record of likes and dislikes, or by the automatic recording of preferences as a result of the user's behaviour online. Common examples of user-selected personalised profiles might include the social networking spaces such as Bebo (http://www.bebo.com) and MySpace (http://www.myspace.com) or Facebook (http://www.facebook.com) through which users seek to communicate with other like-minded individuals online. An example of an automated profile might be the Amazon shop (http://www.amazon.co.uk) where the choices of the users as they browse or buy online are recorded in a database and combined with similar results from millions of other users to create a complex cross-matching of personal preferences that can sometimes be stunningly accurate. The more people use it, the better the service becomes. In educational terms, the incorporation of personalisation into course design is intended to facilitate opening up choice for the learner, although compared to the commercial applications the educational use is in its infancy.

A critical application of personalisation in relation to educational social networking stems from the desire to recreate the connectedness of the face-to-face environment in an online setting. In the desire to create effective online communities that can enhance the educational experience, a number of institutions are seeking to enhance the value of peer-to-peer connections between remote students by enabling them to create personalised spaces online, usually behind well-developed institutional firewalls to deter unwanted intruders. Woods and Ebersole (2003) describe this as a form of "communal scaffolding" that helps to bridge the gap between the cognitive and intellectual tasks of e-learning and the other (social and interpersonal) requirements of online education. A major role provided by the hyperactive web 2.0 technology applications is to engender and support the heightened sense of intimacy, group identity, and safe environment in which to participate in the learning experience. LaRose and Whitten (2000) identified three main sources of intimacy in online educational settings: (1) between teachers and students; (2) between students; (3) between students and the computing system (VLE) used to support courses. Significantly, although Woods and Ebersole detail numerous ways of enhancing intimacy online in the educational setting, they emphasise:

> How do we transform a dialogue of texts into a community of learners characterized by intimacy and interconnectedness? Perhaps the starting place is to recognize that a positive social dynamic requires intentionality—that is, community online just doesn't happen but is created through the intentional use of a variety of verbal and nonverbal communication cues. Or perhaps we begin by recognizing that there are no shortcuts to developing community. In other words, it takes time, and there is no substitute for time spent in communication with others. (Woods & Ebersole, 2003)

Two further elements come into play here, even though they might initially appear to be occasionally contradictory. The flourishing of online communities requires the establishment of interpersonal trust, often between people who have rarely, if ever, met face-to-face. This trustworthiness is a common feature of online communities, educational, recreational, or business, but it is hard to define. In educational terms, there is considerable experience to indicate that the level of trust required to stimulate a high level of sharing and open-ended thinking is most quickly achieved when the participants either know each other prior to joining the online community or when they come together face-to-face in an initial meeting. After participants have met in person, there seems to be a greater willingness to share and a higher bond of familiarity is achieved. In part this may reflect upon the second important element, which is the accuracy of the information contributed by the participants. Internet lore abounds with stories of people adopting other personalities online than they have in real life, i.e., males pretend to be female, older people to be younger, and so on. This may indeed be a common feature of chat-room communication, or it may be apocryphal and exaggerated, but either way the level of occurrence is difficult to determine accurately. In the commercial world, the accuracy of the participants is often judged by their peers, as in the credit rating applied to sellers on eBay, or the comments and star awards given to books, music and film on Amazon. In the educational world peer review is more generally based on the usefulness of the contributions made by participants, and it would be interesting to investigate whether the confidence of learners in the usefulness of the contributions of their colleagues is enhanced by being able to triangulate the usefulness between different social networking applications. For instance, if a learner has his or her interest raised by a useful-sounding contribution on a discussion board, follows it up by an exchange of exploratory messages with the contributor, then has a longer telephone or Skype conversation to discuss the issue in depth before submitting an assessment, does the contributor have a higher status "credit rating" than a remote contributor with whom the learner has had no in-depth, multi-media communication? All of this is, of course, to a large degree dependent upon the learner's willingness to engage both with the learning resources and with the diverse media resources used for communication and sharing. It is a fundamental supposition of the design of distributed learning that learners will selectively choose the particular media (telephone, e-mail etc.) and the level of engagement (regular, enthusiastic participant, or lurker) that is most appropriate for their own particular situation. Their level and type of engagement may of course change several times in the duration of a particular block of study.

Cho, Gay, Davidson, and Ingraffea (2007) drew attention to the fact that some academics are attracted to "the idea that individuals exhibit personality-like differences in their basic communication styles." They claim evidence in their studies for both individual and structural factors (i.e., communication styles and a pre-existing friendship network) significantly influencing the manner in which learners developed collaborative learning social networks: "More specifically, learners who possessed high willingness to communicate or occupied initially peripheral network positions were more likely to explore new network linkages" (p. 309).

## INDIVIDUALISATION VERSUS GROUP INTERACTION

This raises the issue of the value of social learning. In designing a course or module, how much should the educator allow the learner to customise, personalise, or opt out of course elements and how much should the learner be "forced" to complete certain activities, share with peers, or submit fixed assessments? There is a tension between allowing the individual to select his or her own educational path—at the risk of the student drifting aimlessly between a random selection of superficial items of knowledge—and compelling the learner to learn in a very narrow, inflexible manner decided by the tutor or teacher. From the point of view of providing equity of access to learning resources as well as that of making best use of the resources available, it does not seem logical to avoid using one of the most diverse and flexible resources available on any course—the body of student participants themselves. Particularly when trying to encourage transferable skills such as teamwork, problem-solving, and articulate presentations to others, the design of learning activities that compels students to "practice what they preach" and undertake these tasks together as a form of course assessment seems a natural example of good practice. Social networking tools, although not primarily designed for formal educational activities, are specifically designed to ensure an open flow of information, easy networking, and ease of use of technology in diverse contexts.

As we have said elsewhere, the generic term of *virtual learning environment* (VLE) has become devalued, partly due to advocates stressing that the use of the word *virtual* is a derogatory term that does not acknowledge the real and intimate relationships that a good online learning environment can support; partly, also, the rapid evolution of the VLE now encompasses such a very diverse range of software applications, from very basic to extremely sophisticated, including the incorporation of independent social networking applications, that there is no longer a simple, clear definition of what a VLE should contain. For this reason, some educators have moved toward the term *course management system* (CMS) to encompass the "conventional" VLE and also include a growing array of web-based software tools, activities, and course management procedures that can be described and specified in detail. In a paper addressing "the need for the development of an e-learning environment within a CMS that addresses learner's diversity in terms of metacognitive skills, learning styles, prior knowledge, and cultures," Vovides, Sanchez-Alonson, Mitropoulou and Nickmans (2007, p. 5) made the case for course management design that emphasised the ability to allow students to personalise and customise their learning experience, rather than try to provide individualised paths to instruction. With an acknowledgement to dual coding theory, which proposes that multiple content representations enhance memory recall, the authors draw upon the evidence of several previous studies to suggest why and how CMS design must support the development of self-regulated learners.

... the e-learning environment in a CMS should provide opportunities for students to learn how to: select, combine, coordinate their cognitive strategies in connection to the new knowledge, and [be] prompted to reflect on their strategy use, extending their metacognitive knowledge with strategy and capacity beliefs. Despite this strong recommendation, the CMS is often used as a "one size fits all" service to learners, irrespective of their knowledge level, goals, and interests. All students have access to the same instructional material and the same web-based tools without personalised support. All students receive the same exercises irrespective of their pre-existing knowledge and experience. It is not taken into consideration that the educational material is presented to a large number of learners who have varied knowledge levels, skills, and learning strategies. (Vovides et al., 2007, p. 68)

For this reason, they stress that the student learning support within the CMS needs to be adaptive in order to foster and motivate student self-regulation in these highly flexible learning environments. In other words, leaving aside the danger that highly flexible learning environments may appear difficult and unstructured to some types of learner, we need to acknowledge that even many well-organised and powerful CMS are under-utilised in their potential by students and by teachers, and both groups need to explicitly recognise that the development of self-organised, self-directed learners, playing an active role in their own learning, is the ambition of all educational courses. The design of the CMS needs to be structured well enough to scaffold learners who are hesitant in online education, yet responsive enough to adapt to the individual learning needs of students and allow them to open out individualised learning paths that are more contextually suited to the range of diverse learning needs, interests, and requirements.

Drawing from several previous studies, they attempt to synthesise the key features that a CMS should incorporate in order to deliver successful online courses, including:

• Availability of technology
• Reliability of technology
• Standards of course design
• Instructor (teacher) training
• Learning effectiveness,
• Student satisfaction
• Faculty satisfaction

- Cost effectiveness
- Access

A fundamental distinction here, however, is the need to view these key features from the student-centred perspective, rather than from the tutor or the institutional view. The course management system needs to function as an interlinked system for the benefit of the learner, not a cluster of individually useful but stand-alone technology applications that are bolted together according to some personal philosophy, preference, or whim of the course tutor.

## THE RESEARCH ISSUE

This review of some of the literature on blended learning and distributed learning suggests that course design should be student-centred, provide a flexible, interactive and dynamic learning environment, yet have a rationale for the choice of media and methods used in the course. Sharpe et al. (2006, p. 3) in a comprehensive review, found that "student response is overwhelmingly positive to the provision of online course information to supplement traditional teaching." Individual case studies and evaluations of distributed learning courses abound in the literature (e.g., Langenbach & Bodendorf, 1997; Matheos & Archer, 2004; McConnell, Lally, & Banks, 2004), but remarkably few of these articles have a central focus on the design process, most preferring to report on student or faculty satisfaction with the results of the "delivery" of a course or module. The research described here aimed to discover how course design for distributed learning takes place in practice. What rationale determines media choice? What assumptions do course designers make about students' readiness to engage with particular media? What implications are there in terms of student support?

There are two key points to recognise before we embark upon a consideration of the actual practice of distributed learning, and these relate to an appreciation of the context of education. Firstly, flexible learning is not a new phenomenon. Ever since the first person sat by the fire with a course textbook to revise a topic that she or he had discussed or listened to in a lecture earlier that day, or the first person retired to a quiet corner of the library to re-read the hand-written notes that had been given out in an earlier tutorial, learners have been making use of different forms of learning material that are flexibly suited to their needs. This means, almost by default, that learning regularly takes place out of the formal course settings. The phenomenon of recent years is that digital technology allows us a vastly more diverse range of high-fidelity forms of information that are able to be replicated and shared easily. It is the challenge of systematising the use and development of these new resources in a meaningful manner that is currently exercising (some of) the educational establishment today. In particular, there is an urgent need to mainstream the incorporation of digital learning resources as an embedded part of the curriculum, rather than simply regard them as resources to turn to in order to pep-up a course that has problems or is failing to interact with students in a satisfactory manner. The acknowledgement that much (most?) of our learning takes place outside the context of a formal course requires us also to acknowledge that the sorts of tools that children of all ages, and young techno-savvy professionals are using extensively in their leisure time may (some would say must) have a valuable contribution to make in the parts of their lives given over to more structured educational activities.

In their discussions on flexible learning, Collis and Moonen (2001) identified four key components of flexible learning:

- Technology
- Pedagogy
- Implementation strategies
- Institutional framework

They then quote from previous work, identifying 19 "dimensions of learning flexibility," and note that this is not intended to be an exhaustive list. Significantly, only one of the 19 dimensions is specifically concerned with the distance between the tutor and the location of the learner.

A summation of flexible learning by Collis and Moonen (2001) focussed upon the benefits to the learner:

> Flexible learning is a movement away from a situation in which key decisions about learning dimensions are made in advance by the instructor or institution, towards a situation where the learner has a range of options from which to choose with respect to these key dimensions. (p. 10)

## CHALLENGES FROM THE INSTITUTIONAL PERSPECTIVE

So far we have largely addressed distributed learning and social networking from the perspectives of the students and staff, but in reality, of course, the enthusiasm and motivation (or lack of it) that the staff have for new educational technology is fundamentally influenced by the corporate attitude(s) of the educational institution as a whole. This is particularly the case with the highly interactive, peer-to-peer, and cross-institutional applications of web 2.0.

> Web 2.0 is a potentially disruptive technology because of its potential to change the model of higher education from the traditional classroom framework to an asynchronous 24/7 mode. Institutes of Higher Education historically do not cope well with disruption, especially in the short term; however, coping with this disruptive force could mean engaging students in extended collaborative learning opportunities. From this perspective, the perceived disruption could entail many positive implications for higher education. (Thompson, 2007, p. 5)

This optimism is not always fully shared. Concerns among the educators generally centre on a combination of four key areas of potential conflict:

- Administrators may regard online learning solutions as a way to cut the costs of "traditional" education.
- A move toward online tuition is a way of cutting jobs and diluting subject expertise.
- IT service staff may be antagonistic toward more open or flexible Internet applications that they might perceive as being a threat toward institutional security or simplicity.
- Academic staff may feel that they are not well trained or prepared for the adoption of new educational technology in their subject area.

The first two areas of concern can largely be answered by a mature appreciation of the development of online learning. As more and more of the curriculum in an increasing number of higher education institutions has moved online, a truer assessment of the actual costs of online learning systems has evolved. While the subject is still hotly contested in some quarters, it is now generally agreed that the true costs of online development are certainly no less than the true costs of traditional development, and while the investment in both is largely upfront (in software and content or bricks and mortar) it has historically proved easier to gain funding for brick and mortar, though the near ubiquitous access to the Internet may change this. Certainly, a willingness to experiment with new business models for higher education delivery, even for traditionally face-to-face students, would seem to be a prerequisite for success in the Internet age. Even here, however, a form of social networking is emerging, with numerous consortia of educational institutions coming together, even temporarily, to share the development, and frequently give various levels of public access to, newer generations of online resources, templates and tools. This has been encouraged by the growing scale and complexity of web-based applications, which have spread the cost, and risk, of development over several institutions; the increasing popularity of open source solutions; and the recent trend among educational funding organisations to place a premium on the added-value of inter-institutional collaboration rather than fostering competition over smaller and smaller areas of educational turf. Examples of this collaboration can be seen in numerous developmental projects through organisations such as JISC (http://www.jisc.ac.uk) including initiatives such as their "pedagogic planner" for higher education at http://www.wle.org.uk/d4l/. Given the nature of the evolving scale of online learning activities, it seems likely that multi-institutional collaboration in the development of online learning and social networking applications will be *de rigueur* in the foreseeable future, with an emphasis upon designing the technology to suit the pedagogical requirements, rather than vice versa. Lamb (2007) concluded that:

> Educators and higher education decision-makers have an obligation to carefully and critically assess new technologies before making radical changes. Taking a more freewheeling approach to content reuse and making campus technologies more accessible to data mashups require significant changes in existing practices and attitudes. These changes won't happen quickly or easily. (p. 22)

Critical to our vision in this book, however, he also speculated about "What might happen if we allow our campus innovators to integrate their practices in these areas in the same way that social networking application developers are already integrating theirs?" and suggested that there may be different levels of collaboration to safeguard "mission-critical data" ranging from selected development consortia to full public disclosure.

## CONCLUSIONS

We began with a review of various definitions relating to the increasing flexibility in the design of learning resources and suggested that the term *distributed learning* should be used to describe learning resources that seek to optimise the flexibility to a diversity of learner types, in location, time, and type of media access to educational support.

The distributed learning opportunities within a course management system need to address the diversity of learners' requirements in terms of prior knowledge, learning styles, metacognitive skills, and cultural context. The new requirements of flexible course management systems and online social networking opportunities for learning have shifted the focus of the tutor from a teacher to a facilitator of learning.

Although some of the responsibilities of this new role remain similar—guidance, knowledge of the subject area, supervision, and advice on sources of knowledge—two areas in particular are new and potentially challenging for staff: (1) the power shift in favour of student-directed learning, and (2) the requirements to understand and master the full capabilities of the new technological applications.

In order to support both staff and students, educational institutions need to develop a support strategy for the use of their course management systems, and a realistic mechanism to adequately support this strategy.

# 3

## SELECTING THE MEDIA PALETTE

So, where do we start when we want to actively plan for the incorporation of educational technology in a course in order to facilitate learning, not impede it? The Electronic Training Needs Analysis (ETNA) in Scotland (Dailly & Price, 2007) surveyed the situation in the Further Education network and compared this with previous surveys in 2001 and 2003. Among the many conclusions and recommendations noted, three stand out as generalities that could be applied to the entire formal education sector:

1. The enormous development of the technical capacities of IT systems, even over the previous six years since the first survey;
2. The hugely improved access (individual and institutional) to online resources and networks; and
3. That "the rapid pace of change presents a challenge to staff in simply being aware of the possibilities presented by new technologies" (Dailly & Price, 2007, p. 7).

Two further points, explicit in this study—and reinforced time after time in interviews for this book—have a major importance for this chapter. Firstly, though most institutions now have a virtual learning environment (VLE) (some operate routinely with two or three platforms) staff are often confused over the function of the VLE and do not consider it essential to carrying out their role. Secondly, staff and students frequently have better (less restricted) access to online resources at home than from their institution, a cause for concern if we seek to relate learning to the real world and exploit the best of technology to improve education. We will come back to both of these points later.

The fact is that "the environment of higher education is changing rapidly. Costs are rising, budgets are shrinking, and the demand for new services is growing" (New Media Consortium, 2007). In a rare case of rhetoric living up to reality, increasing globalisation is changing the way that we work and communicate, and this means that research, scholarship, and learning are not exempt from the significant shifts that are being unleashed by web 2.0 and beyond. Philip (2007) tried to summarise these changes by what he calls the "knowledge building paradigm" and related this to his perception of the changes that are happening among "the Net generation" in business, society, and education. In particular, he noted earlier work by Tapscott (1998) that identified interactivity in the learning process as the key characteristic common to these changes, and listed eight areas for attention:

- From linear to hypermedia learning,
- From instruction to construction and discovery,
- From teacher-centred to learner-centred education,
- From absorbing material to learning how to navigate and how to learn,
- From schooling to lifelong learning,
- From one-size-fits-all to customised learning,
- From learning as torture to learning as fun, and
- From the teacher as transmitter to the teacher as facilitator.

Other researchers (Lohnes & Kinzer, 2007) emphasise the fundamental importance of the learning context, and caution us against making overly generalised assumptions about the learning preferences of even the digitally literate students—variously described as "the net generation" (Obliger & Obliger, 2005), "millennials" (Howe & Strauss, 2000), and "homo zappiens" (Veen & Vrakking, 2006). The latter authors also stress that learning is not simply a one-way process. In an attempt to tease this out, we propose the following matrix as an early working plan to identify various ways in which educational technology can be adopted to enhance the process of interactive learning (see Figure 3.1).

## HOW CAN MEDIA BE BEST USED IN DIFFERENT CONTEXTS?

Not all learners want to engage with all of the learning technology resources, so it is important in course design to be clear about what is "need to know" (i.e.. watching a chemistry experiment—face-to-face or on a video-clip—and what is "nice to know" (adding depth, offering , or simply providing additional resources to allow specialisation). A good

**Interactive Learning A Matrix of Educational Technology Options**

| Media | Basic | Intermediate | Advanced |
|---|---|---|---|
| Text | One-way **Print** Interactive **e-mail** | One-way **Webpages** Interactive **Computer conferencing** | One-way **Blogs** Interactive **Wikis Blogs** |
| Audio | One-way **Audio clips** Interactive **Telephone support** | One-way **Podcasts** Interactive **Telephone conferencing** | One-way **Ipod downloads** Interactive **Audiographics** |
| Images | One-way **Photographs** Interactive **Image banks, e.g., SCRAN, Creative Commons** | One-way **CD/ DVD** Interactive **Share and edit, e.g., Flickr, SplashCast** | One-way **Animations** Interactive **Simulations/games** |
| Video | One-way **Video clips** Interactive **Webcasts /TV** | One-way **Annotations?** Interactive **Skype** | One-way **Vods** Interactive **Videoconferencing** |

**Figure 3.1** Some examples of using educational technology for one-way and two-way learning

starting point for what can be considered effective practice in the utilisation of new media in an educational context is in the introduction of a report on this subject (Joint Information Systems Committee [JISC], 2004, pp. 10–11) that states:

[effective practice] should;
Engage learners in the learning process
Encourage independent learning skills
Develop learners' skills and knowledge
Motivate further learning

Nothing new, you might say, that is not already covered by good "traditional" education that makes little or no use of educational technology. The authors go on to add context by noting that:

… in the broadest sense, effective learning is likely to occur when

opportunities to learn involve:
• The right resources
• The right mode [or blend of modes] of delivery
• The right context

- The right learners
- With the right level of support

Again, this could be considered a truism, but the crucial point to appreciate is that, in the Westernised countries at least, the changing nature of society means that what were "the right resources, the right mode…" for learners 20 or 30 years ago are not necessarily the same for learners today. The reasons for this have been well rehearsed (e.g., Castells, 2001; Rheingold, 2000; 2002), so there is no need to go into the issues in depth here, but a few self-evident examples might refresh the memory.

- Even elementary school pupils are utilizing digital media resources in their learning activities and are approaching higher education with different aspirations than did their parents regarding course learning materials.
- Job mobility and skills transferability have created greater expectations of lifelong learning opportunities.
- Greater numbers of part-time and mature students are returning to learning in subjects or institutions previously dominated by residential, full-time students straight from high school.
- Financial considerations frequently mean that learners need to work full- or part-time, cannot/will not travel to study locations distant from their home/work, and want to pay for studying only what they consider useful for their personal or career ambitions.
- At the risk of using hyperbole, the Internet was in its infancy 20 years ago, and the web did not exist. Regardless of whether you think it is good or bad, it has changed the way that we think about and access information, not simply for education, but for entertainment and work as well.

There is a continuum between enthusiastic early-adopters of new technology who will immediately experiment with every new application and those who stridently (and unreasonably?) resist all forms of new-fangled ideas and technology. We think that it is important not to fall into either of the two extremes: the teacher who appears to be infatuated with each new technology and experimentally tests it on learners without adequately weighing up the strengths and weaknesses; or the neo-Luddite who disadvantages the learners by eschewing *any* new technology and claiming his or her subject is "different" and that therefore it is not easy to incorporate new ways of utilising digital learning resources.

## EDUCATIONAL ACTIVITIES TO ENGAGE LEARNERS

As we noted in chapter 1, the essence of online collaborative course design is the use of activities appropriate to the subject and level of the learner. For a course designer, it is critical to think of pedagogic models in terms of, first, "What do I want the learner to be able to do?" (transferable skill, contextual understanding, etc.) and only then "What tools (technology?) do I have at my disposal that will help the learner complete these learning activities?" It is one thing to be aware of the strengths and limitations of a particular technology and another to be able to translate these elements into learning opportunities for a student.

In attempting to define a learning activity as "an interaction between a learner and an environment, leading to a planned outcome" the authors of the JISC report (2004) acknowledge that practitioners have always planned activities for learning but also that the new technology-rich environments offer a greater diversity of available options. Different approaches to learning concentrate upon different assumptions about how people learn, and different pedagogies that might support this learning process. This may lead to the adoption of different learning activities being prescribed (e.g., to include mobile or wireless technologies; see JISC, 2005), but there is a great deal of generic overlap that can be applied in varied educational situations, and they have listed the associated pedagogy with four approaches to learning:

1. **The associative perspective**—based on the assumption of learning as acquiring competence.
2. **The constructive perspective**—assuming that learning is based upon achieving individual understanding.
3. **The constructive perspective**—assuming that learning is based upon social collaboration to achieve understanding.
4. **The situative perspective**—assuming learning as a social practice developed through participation in specific communities and practices.

It is important, however, not to be too simplistic in this and to ensure that course designers do not select media simply in an attempt to replicate a digital version of the face to face environment with which they are more familiar. We have chosen the term *distributed media* for this type of resource, meaning that the type of medium itself can support learner access across a wide spectrum of geographical locations and time constraints, thus effectively distributing the medium among many users. This distinguishes the resource from a non-distributed medium, such as a face-to-face lecture or conversation that *only* occurs at a particular locality, at a particular time, and, if it is not recorded or repeated, is not able to be distributed spatially and/or temporally. Each distributed media resource comes with its own set of strengths and weaknesses, advantages and disadvantages that, when combined in a structured ecology of learning resources, can produce quite a different effect from the original intention. In Table 3.1 we attempt to illustrate some ways by which generic learning needs can be matched to student learning activities, and how these activities might be facilitated using different levels of engagement with the media of distributed learning.

Three points should be stressed here: Table 3.1 is *strictly* to illustrate the possibilities. It is not a prescriptive document or a blueprint for course design. There is no presumption that the move from fundamental to emerging is either a more advanced trajectory or an inevitable progression for all courses. In reality, it is the learning activity that should dictate the outcomes, there may well be an intimate mixture of fundamental, extended, and emerging media used to provide a rich matrix of possible learning resources on any course or module.

## HOW CAN DISTRIBUTED MEDIA BE BEST USED?

This is a difficult question because there is no single "correct" answer. There *are* lots and lots of ways to combine distributed media, new technology (software and hardware) and educational applications, but there are so many variable factors that it is almost impossible to say "do this, and it will be successful." There are, however, some guidelines that can increase the chances of creating successful combinations of learning resources, while at the same time permitting modification or adjustment and encouraging innovation. The rest of this chapter will concentrate on how course designers can best utilise different media to present learning opportunities in different contexts.

To begin with, it is important for course designers to appreciate four fundamental "rules" when considering the use of social networking technology to facilitate distributed learning.

1. **No panacea**—The adoption of new technology or social networking applications should not just be in response to perceived problems with an existing (face-to-face) course. It has become apparent to us in the research for this book that a substantial number of educators, upon realising that they have problems with an existing course that they teach (e.g., poor student retention, lack of student participation in assignments, poor attendance at lectures), decide to graft on

Table 3.1 Examples of the Application of Distributed Media to Learning Activities

| Student learning need | Example of student activity | Level of distributed media resource | | |
| --- | --- | --- | --- | --- |
| | | Fundamental | Extended | Emerging |
| Information handling skills | Web searching Using electronic libraries | Print | Webpages | e-books Digital repositories |
| Developing understanding | Linking information from different sources | Connected document (with hot links) | e-portfolios | Mashups |
| Linking theory to practice | Learning by doing | Online quizzes | Instant messaging tutorials | Screencasting |
| Practicing discussion and argument Sharing essays online | Presentation | CD/DVD | Photos/images Online debate using threaded discussion (Flickr?) | Vlog |
| Practicing articulation of ideas | Reflective journal | Computer conferencing | Blogs Video-conferencing | Podcasts |
| Rehearsing skills and procedures | Audiovisual essay | Audio clips (Powerpoint) | Video clips | Webcasts YouTube |
| Practicing teamwork | Group projects | Online games | Social book-marking | Wikis |
| Learning professional practice | Problem solving exercises | Role playing | Animations or audiographics | Simulations |
| Feedback | Interactive Tutorial | Telephone support e-mail | Telephone conferencing | Skype |

a piece of new technology that they feel will solve the problem. As a result, hand-outs from lectures or tutorials are pasted onto a website without modification from the face-to-face class; discussion boards are established to force students to talk to each other; papers and articles are posted online (on the VLE?) to encourage students to read more. This is the equivalent of throwing a lifebelt to a drowning man—it may work, but it is better to have prevented him from falling overboard in the first place. The introduction of distributed media resources needs to be a way of creating new opportunities for sharing and extending learning, rather than constraining learners into different forms of learning participation.

2. **Pedagogy first**—Before selecting your new technology for interacting and/or communicating with the learners, be sure that you fully understand your educational goal. The applications that we will describe in chapter 4 can be used in a variety of ways in different situations—what works in one context will not necessarily work equally effectively in another context. This does not mean that there is anything wrong with the application that you have selected, nor necessarily with your learners, but due to other factors, the combination may be inappropriate for the task that you would like the learners to perform.

3. **Initial induction**—Whatever combination you select, even if it is apparently a very user-friendly technology, such as contributing to a wiki, or using SMS text-messaging, which many people use in the non-academic parts of their life, you need to provide some initial induction training for students. The key point is that learners should be completely comfortable with the new technology so that they can concentrate on the learning experience rather than being distracted by their discomfort with the technology interface. The induction to the ecology of learning resources needs not be face-to-face, though some teachers argue that initial face-to-face contact makes subsequent online interaction less intimidating for some learners. Variations of online induction could include detailed written instructions by e-mail; a screencasting of the mouse movements to select menus, download software etc.; a little video clip or podcast talking the learner through an activity; or simply a telephone conversation (one-to-one or teleconference) with the learner to guide him or her through the initial process of gaining access to and navigating through a series of online resources.

4. **Need to be serious**—The applications of new technology and the learning activities that require the use of distributed media need to have a clear learning purpose that is transparently related to the course of study—they need to be real examples that are worthwhile doing. Students, particularly mature students and students that are paying their own way through university, are increasingly strategic in the use of their time. If there is a point to the learning activity, and they can clearly see a link between the task that they have been set and the final assessment or grade that they are likely to get, then

they will respond enthusiastically. Otherwise they will spend their scarce time and attention elsewhere. As Goldhaber (1997, 1998) has argued in his work on "the attention economy," information is a commodity, and in the digital age we are often swamped by this commodity, so the more scarce resource (the ability to grab our attention) becomes the more valuable commodity. This is simply saying that the course assessments need to clearly relate to the intended learning outcomes of the course, but in the hurly-burly adoption of new technology this important aspect of course design often gets overlooked.

Let's look at how these guidelines might relate to practice by reference to a specific example. In Table 3.1, as an example of an emergent technology being utilised to support group project work, we proposed the use of a wiki. Although wikis have been around for a decade, their adoption for academic use has been comparatively slow—surprising considering their power and flexibility (Mader, 2006b; Notari, 2006). A wiki is simply a website that can be quickly and easily edited by many people so, as a piece of social networking software, it is ideal for encouraging group collaboration on a document or project (Mader, 2006a). But we are getting ahead of ourselves.

As noted earlier, the social constructivist approach or situated perspective of learning claims that, in general, learning is based upon social collaboration to achieve understanding. If this is our belief then we may want to construct a learning activity in which our students are required to work together, sharing tasks, to produce both a group product (say, a project report, or a group presentation) that will both demonstrate their team-working skills, but also provide evidence of their own individual contributions towards the product (perhaps a reflective essay, or a project diary). In the 1980s, the effective solution would probably have been limited to a process that brought the group physically together in the same room a few times, got them to discuss their ideas, partition the workload, probably go away somewhere else to prepare their individual contributions, then meet again several times to produce more refined iterations of their collective work. Today, this is still a viable option, but the application of this solution is more constrained, and other options are also available. It is constrained because it depends upon the students being able to physically get together at the same place and time—and for many students who are not co-located, and who have pressing work or family commitments, this is not a real option. Fortunately, the collaborative features of wikis make them especially suitable for use in co-operative learning environments (Schaffert et al., 2006).

In a review of the wiki as a teaching tool, Parker and Chao (2007) examined the current literature and gave numerous links to examples of how wikis are being used in practice, and suggested some additional uses. Significantly, the situation has changed slightly since their paper was accepted for publication, and some of the attributes that they list as problems in the use of wikis (such as not being able to lock certain pages against change; keeping a wiki private to a known group of contributors; and "freezing" a wiki when it has evolved to suit its end purpose) have since been overcome and are freely available as management options on the newer versions of wiki software. Duffy and Bruns (2006) summarise the uses of a wiki as follows:

- To develop research projects—using the wiki for ongoing documentation of the work.
- Building an annotated, collaborative bibliography—using links to prescribed reading and also to summarised notes on the reading.
- For publishing course resources—teachers can post hand-outs and students can post comments on these to be shared by all.
- To map concepts—ideas can be posted and edited to produce a linked network of resources.
- As a presentation tool—photographs, diagrams, and commentary can be presented on the wiki, and then subsequently edited to produce a revised version.
- For group authoring—creating and editing a single document by many authors that represents the views of each individual, but achieves a consensus.

In each of these examples the educational process and the required output(s) come first, the wiki is just an alternative solution to face-to-face meetings, with the advantages that the wiki is asynchronous and builds a written record of the interactions.

In the first example above, on the use of wikis in groupwork, the individual students might be required to provide evidence of their own contribution to the group project. In the past this might have been done solely by producing a written justification, and while this is still an option, the use of a blog might be more appropriate. Unlike a wiki (which is normally multi-authored), a blog (from weblog) is usually the product of a single author, frequently presented like a diary, but a blogger has the ability to make links to other online resources and invite other bloggers to comment on their initial postings. As wikis and blogs converge, the barriers between them blur a bit, and now it is common for many blogs to provide an opportunity for other readers to make their own comments on the blog owner's comments, to link with their own blog spots, and to suggest links for like-minded readers to investigate. Real examples of pupils and teachers talking about the use of blogging in their academic lives can be viewed by going to http://www.youtube.com and typing in search-terms such as "use of blogging" and "educational blogging" to obtain a variety of presentations. The spread of blogging has resulted in two main types of blog, the one-to-many diary type conveying the owner's comments and opinions (with or without comments from other readers), and the many-to-many message-board type in which many readers respond to an original comment or article by posting their own comment, creating a rich dialogue of experience. The latter has been extensively utilised by news agencies to gather news from the grassroots, share it as it is happening, and seek comment from other readers (see the *Guardian* blogspot at http://blogs.guardian.co.uk/index.html). Some recent blog sites allow the author to decide whether each blog posting should be shared publicly, shared with listed contacts, or remain private (only to the author). This allows a flexibility of the blog from private diary (or lab note-book) entries, through records to be shared by a team, to fully public news sites that can attract user comments.

To return to stages of course design, if we want to encourage our students to practice the articulation of their ideas, and to learn to share and comment on the work of their peers, then we start with this objective and consider what learning activities could help to achieve this. There are several ways to facilitate this of course. In a classroom we might stage a whole-class discussion, encouraging learners to offer different perspectives, answer questions, provide some answers, and generally share their experiences. In an online environment this might better be accomplished by using a computer conferencing system or a discussion board on a VLE, where learners and teachers can post their comments, responses, and questions on particular topics over a set period of time. If our preferred objective is to encourage the learners to produce a reflective journal as their learning activity, then a blog might be considered, with the added advantages that it can be shared with peers, and that both peers and teacher(s) can add helpful comments and/or questions, almost like footnotes to the main text. Similarly, if the main object of the learning activity is to encourage the student to practice the clear verbal articulation of their thoughts, then a podcast, a simple audio recording available over the Internet, might be an alternative to a conventional face-to-face presentation.

Each of the design solutions above, in addition to the previously stated advantages of enabling learner participation "as and when" (i.e., asynchronous and not location specific), have the additional benefit for the whole group of learners that they can provide a detailed record of the learning activity. Unlike a face-to-face discussion in class, which is spontaneous and generally unrecorded, the online version generates a written (or audio) record and allows time for the learners to consider previous comments and offer thoughtful additions (unless, of course, a spontaneous live response is required as part of the learning activity, in which case a distributed live session such as a chat room, an instant message session, or a Skype exchange could be selected). The written and audio records allow learners to reflect upon the learning session or topic, provide materials for slower learners or for revision, and can be archived for a period of time. With the addition of teacher notes to the learners' work, additional resources such as further reading, specific examples, and breaking news of relevant events can be made available for faster learners or those who would like to specialise in a particular aspect that is not fully covered in their present course.

To continue with our staged process of matching learning objectives and activities to more flexible uses of distributed media, the use of images is apparently particularly problematic. We say this because, although fully aware of the vibrant added-value that images (still and moving) can bring to a learning resource, we have also been struck by the apparent compulsion to use images in inappropriate circumstances. A classic example of this is the use of videoconference facilities. With the spread of the ability to link videoconference equipment over the Internet (IP connections) rather than by landlines, there has been a growth in the adoption of videoconferencing as a tool for teaching and the dissemination of research (and also for institutional meetings). While there are many fine examples of teachers playing to the strengths of this new medium—the ability to bring intimacy to a discussion among distributed participants; the ability to support multiway interaction among the group, to bring in guest presenters from geographically distant localities, to record and archive the session for future re-use—there are also many examples of bad practice. One such example sticks out as being particularly common: the delivery of a video lecture, where the teacher simply talks at the students for an hour (or more!) in an attempt to replicate the experience of the lecture theatre. This completely ignores a key strength of videoconferencing, the ability to have quality time for visual interaction. Quite frankly, in many such cases there is no need to see the teacher at all, and the lecture could better be delivered as an audio file. If visual images are essential to such a presentation, then the session can be delivered once, recorded, and made available as a webcast on the course website (or on a DVD) for asynchronous, geographically distributed access. Alternatively, if the teacher really wants interaction with the learners and visual contact is not essential, then perhaps a scheduled teleconference is more appropriate, the telephone being more ubiquitous and more mobile than videoconferencing hardware.

A second example involves trying to run a videoconference session with the same meeting etiquette as a face-to-face meeting. The strengths of the medium, being able to participate live with peers and observe body-language/facial expressions without being co-located, need to be balanced by an awareness of the disadvantages. Foremost among these, paradoxically, is the need to be inclusive in the group interaction process. The immediacy and collegial familiarity of the videoconference medium can sometimes lure participants into behaving as if they were in a face-to-face meeting, leading to several traps for bad practice, e.g., bringing a hand-out to the meeting and passing it around to the participants in the same room with you, but neglecting to circulate this in advance so that your distributed learners/colleagues could print it and bring it along to the videoconference.

Other errors include failing to clarify the identity of everybody who is participating in the meeting and checking if they can all receive the signal clearly (we tend to assume that everyone in the same room can hear us when we speak).

With videoconference, asking undirected questions such as "Any questions on that?" should be avoided. When we ask that in front of a videoconference camera, who are we asking? Students, based at different locations, either tend to hesitate and say nothing, waiting for someone else to speak, or else everyone speaks at the same time. Better to ask, "Any questions on that from....?" to each remote site.

Conversely, teachers and other confident speakers often seem to need to fill the quiet gaps by talking, making it difficult or awkward for other participants to interject. Normally, on a videoconference, the remote camera is open on the person who is talking, so we cannot usually see the body language of the other participants who are waiting their turn to speak (latecomers may be hidden from the meeting until they first speak). Tutors need to be sensitive and directive on this.

Unfocussed or rambling agendas are bad enough in face-to-face meetings, but their uselessness is magnified online. Videoconference sessions need to be more organised than face-to-face equivalents, not least because institutions that make heavy use of videoconferencing will have strict time slots and, if you over-run your allocated videoconference session because you have allowed people to ramble on, you may be cut off at the end of your pre-booked slot. You will be cut off regardless of whether you have come to the end of your agenda, whether you are a professor or a first year student, or whether a participant is in mid-sentence or not.

Tutors need to be aware of these limitations and plan for them, and, in the best of cases, the good videoconference session can be transformational, but a bad session can be truly pointless. A key point to note here is that the introduction of web 2.0 technology (in this case the ease of introducing hyper-interactivity through Internet-based videoconference connections) is not enough in itself to bring about a pedagogic change. The application of the new technology requires a corresponding shift in other components of learning and teaching (e.g., in this case, a shift from the tutors "broadcasting" their own opinions as a video monologue, to a learning session where students are encouraged/facilitated to interact with the tutor and with each other to maximise the educational advantages of interactive "live-time" sound and video).

The use of videoconferencing is a starkly obvious example of the need to combine changes in the manner of teaching and learning when changes in the media of communication and learning are introduced; but, though they may be more difficult to distinguish, similar lessons apply to using other forms of web 2.0 applications for education. We have previously described this as an ecology of learning with similarities to the functioning of natural ecosystems in that everything is connected to everything else and changes to one element will often have profound (even unpredictable) effects on another part of the system (Rennie & Mason, 2004).

Another familiar example in course design might be the use of still images and photographs as learning resources. Anyone who has used the web a lot will be familiar with the frustration of clicking on a web page and having to wait for ages while an embedded photograph is downloaded, only to discover that, apart from looking attractive, the photograph does not really add anything to the text. Broader bandwidth might allow us to download these images faster, and web 2.0 technologies might allow us to share and manipulate the images with online colleagues, but frequently we are still trying to graft new technologies onto old ways of thinking about learning resources. (A photograph looks good in a book—to break up a long piece of text—so I will stick a photograph onto the website at this point.) As with our example of videoconferencing, course designers need to fundamentally re-think the incorporation of web 2.0 learning resources into the ecology of the overall learning experience. Consider the following real life example that was shared with us during the preparation of this book:

I'm a Programme Manager on the **** e-learning team. I have responsibility for the **** e-learning transformational projects and some new projects in the innovations strand on gaming and mobile technologies. I am interested in the use of social software in a learning and teaching context and have worked with wikis and blogs in an HE institution. I am an addict of Flickr.com, my del.icio.us and have just started a combined photo/text blog.

I have done most of my recent and most effective learning in a very informal space—on Flickr. I could have taken a formal photography course and did consider doing so. However for me, in this instance, a qualification is not the important outcome—it is the learning. Flickr can be used in so many ways—as a store for images, as a social space, and as a place to share content. But it's the incredible power of the social aspects in self-organised groups that can be very powerful. There are groups that provide information (e.g., what kinds of films work in which contexts, or technical aspects of cameras), discussions (e.g., around the work of a particular photographer or genre), workshops where assignments/activities are set (sometimes with deadlines) and where we can comment or critique each other's work, games, competitions, combining creative writing with images, how to use Photoshop, etc. etc....

What I love to see is where people work collaboratively to produce images, where people tag each other's images, where people link up with other people with similar styles.

Not only that, I have made friends who I meet virtually and some who I now meet physically.

Flickr is my own university where I have choice and control. You could argue that Yahoo (who have taken over Flickr) could take that away from me and my fellow Flickr learners. Yes, they could, but we would just find another way to do it with some other software. It's not the software, or even the service (which I do pay for) but the community of people that support my learning.

Lou

p.s. After posting it I was reflecting further, and what I wanted to add, but never did, was that—in that environment/learning space I am both a learner and a teacher, because I think that whole issue of blurry, moving roles is so very significant with web 2 stuff. The other thing I nearly added was that I'm 46—just to highlight the fact that it's really not only young people using social software in that way. (Lou McGill, personal communication)

There are many significant issues that emerge from this e-mail—the exploitation of informal learning; the interest in the learning rather than the qualification; the learning aspect offered by online communities of enthusiasts; the blending of online and offline relationships; the blurring of distinctions between learner and teacher; the significance of age and gender in the digital divide. A key point for us, however, is the recognition of the almost serendipitous learning experience that is enabled by the flexibility of the media resources. A person can embark upon a simple task, not necessarily related to learning—such as taking photographs and sharing them online. This may lead to the establishment of online links to similar enthusiasts, and to the development of communities of interest or communities of practice. As the person pursues a particular personal agenda (e.g., how to improve the quality of their photographs), the online interactions become more specific, perhaps seeking help, or being referred to useful sources of information, or "dipping into" more structured photographic information such as an online course or manual. The learning activities, and to some extent the learning experience as a whole, are shaped by the learner, rather than a tutor dictating what they feel that the learner should know.

There are limitations to this. The appropriate resources may not always be available, or the community may not know of the existence of relevant resources. The danger of just-in-time learning as opposed to just-in-case learning is that the experience for the learner may be partial, incomplete, or at worst misleading. A pick-and-mix education requires that the learner is facilitated/encouraged to have an analytical approach to his or her own learning, and to view each learning activity in an appropriate context—quite a difficult task to perform on your own. For the course designer the trick is to maintain the flexibility of the pick-and-mix counter to allow optimum opportunities for self-directed learning, while at the same time providing signposts to appropriate learning resources, giving feedback on learning activities and tasks, creating opportunities for the learner to contextualise new information, and providing support by enabling knowledge to be articulated, shared, and redefined.

Returning to the earlier mention of Goldhaber's (1997, 1998) "attention economy," the prime advantage of being able to use diverse types of distributed media learning resources is that they can grab the attention of students and provide alternative ways to promote concepts or share knowledge in ways that learners find easy to assimilate. Notwithstanding our earlier scepticism about the value of being over-focussed on identifying an individual's particular learning style, it is clear that we all assimilate knowledge slightly differently at different times, in different subjects, and in different contexts. The drive to provide learners with a more flexible and more diverse range of alternative learning resources is largely a drive to contextualise learning and to shift the responsibility away from being solely teacher-led or institution-led learning to a relationship in which the learner has a far greater responsibility and shared control of the learning process.

So, how do we know that distributed learning and social networking using web 2.0 is not just inundation by another new technology? Anyone who has come back from a few days holiday to discover 450 e-mail messages has a right to feel circumspect about being swamped by the addition of new technologies. For anyone who experienced the early days of the Internet and can remember the delight in receiving a new e-mail from a distant colleague, or remember the awe of discovering the almost sci-fi technology of computer conferencing, the choice of technologies available today might seem to be a gimmick-driven overkill. But we are sure that this has been said of every new technology, as the car replaced the horse-and-cart, or the telephone replaced the telegraph cable, so the lesson is to look closely at the advantages and disadvantages of new forms of digital learning resources—not simply as stand-alone applications, but in combination with the other learning resources being proposed for the ecology of learning. We also need to be aware of the gap between the potential of technologies and their actual use, and we will try to address this in chapter 5.

Several authors have drawn attention to the fact that when the learner is given a greater diversity of choices, there is a correspondingly greater emphasis placed upon the teacher to be responsive to individual learning needs and to some extent personalise the learning experience, rather than just planning and delivering a set body of knowledge. Significantly, Collis and Moonen (2001) noted that:

> Thus more-flexible learning for the learner brings more options to the instructor as well, although not always reflecting the instructor's choice but rather in reaction to the learner's choices. (p 14)

Certainly there are significant challenges in offering a diversity of learning resources to students while still keeping the course manageable for the teacher and the institution. Equally, although there are concerns regarding the inappropriate grafting-on of new technology to courses without careful consideration of how this might alter other elements of the course, the response is not simply to do nothing, ignoring the potential benefits of new applications to help learners understand through the contextualisation of different resources. It follows that the process of matching new technology applications to satisfy particular learning outcomes and carefully selected learning activities means that we need to be aware of the strengths and weaknesses, the advantages and disadvantages of each of the new forms of distributed media resources. We will try to summarise these in the following chapter.

One final point; resist the temptation to go for technology overkill in course design simply because you can. As we have tried to emphasise, the introduction of new technology and distributed media to course design can provide some very effective ways to communicate with students or colleagues and share powerful resources, but there is no compulsion to use all of these media on the one unit or module.

Although the incorporation of distributed media can provide alternative ways of learning, and can even improve learners' access to learning resources that have previously been restricted to specific places (e.g., by the digitisation of print resources commonly held only in a specialist library), these should not be regarded simply as a replacement for the main face-to-face delivery of resources. Rather, they should be a well-designed improvement that extends the range of learning opportunities to all students, regardless of their geographical location or their ability to attend classes in physical terms. This means that the introduction of wikis, blogs, podcasts, discussion boards, and so on needs to be carefully balanced as part of a symbiotic learning system that brings benefit to the learners, rather than confusing, intimidating, or undermining their confidence. Consider the important learning activities, match them with the strengths of a particular distributed medium, perhaps provide some alternative ways to interact with key resources (e.g., an optional blog to reflect on the whole course, or a formative assessment that enables room for an individual specialisation) then consider carefully how all of your selected media function collectively. Be realistic; do not be afraid to go back to the drawing board if the cumulative results are not what you would wish for as a course designer.

## CONCLUSIONS

The design of the course as a whole is more important than the choice of specific tools or media. The choice of media needs to reflect the learning objectives of the course/module, not dictate the objectives. After the learning outcomes have been established, start with the learning activities and tailor the choice of distributed media to your course team's agreed purposes. The modes of interaction between the learners, and between the teacher and the learners, should influence but not dictate the selection of distributed media.

Although a range of distributed media encourages the adoption of a range of learning strategies, more diversified and personalised learning models are more time-consuming for the tutor to construct and maintain. They do, however, firmly shift the emphasis towards student-centred learning, and should encourage learner interactivity and higher levels of active participation in the learning processes.

Good course design needs to "open out" learning opportunities with the incorporation of new technology, not create additional constraints for learners and tutors, so the symbiotic relationship between the different components in the learning ecology needs to be carefully consider.

# 4

## THE TOOLS IN PRACTICE

In this chapter we look in detail at a wide range of web 2.0 tools, considering their advantages and disadvantages and describing an actual education application. The following is a list of the tools discussed:

- Audiographics
- Blogs/Weblogs
- e-books
- e-portfolios
- Games and Simulations
- Instant Messaging
- Mashups
- Mobile Learning
- Online Forums
- Photo Sharing
- Podcasts
- RSS Feeds
- Second Life
- Social Bookmarking
- Social Networking
- Twitter
- Video Messaging
- Wikis
- Video Clips and YouTube
- Video Chat

# RESOURCE: AUDIOGRAPHICS (OR INTERACTIVE/ ELECTRONIC WHITEBOARDS)

The combined use of voice transmission and computer networking has been used in education for at least 15 years. Nevertheless, no one term has emerged to refer to this activity, partly because the technology keeps evolving. An early term was *audiographics*, but this is not widely used; *interactive whiteboard* is a more descriptive term but tends to be used for a large physical display panel that can function as an electronic copy board. Typically, interactive whiteboards are used in lecture or classroom environments and the technology allows the lecturer to write or draw on the surface, print off the image, save it to computer and then distribute it over a network. By contrast, the term *electronic whiteboard* usually refers to a system which involves networked audio as well as screen sharing, and is more appropriate for distance or distributed learning.

Typical definitions are: real-time data conferencing combined with audio capability, or, audio conferencing on a personal computer. Whatever the name, this form of social software enables two-way communication as well as a shared screen for drawing, viewing photos or graphics, and in some cases, for sharing computer applications.

Audiographics facilitates a high degree of interactivity between students or between students and the instructor at the time the learning is taking place. The exchange of information is two-way. When students have questions about the material, they are able to ask the instructor for clarification and the instructor is able to respond in real time. In short, electronic whiteboards are a synchronous learning environment. Some products may have a feature to record and archive the tuition session for consultation/revision outside of class time. There are currently two distinct kinds of applications in distance and distributed education:

1. The students are all together in a study centre sharing one screen and the instructor is remote.
2. All of the users are accessing through a personal computer and each has a screen and audio connection. This has only become possible with recent technology developments whereby both voice and computer can be connected through one phone line.

## *The Educational Challenge*

Like all good teaching practice, the effective use of audiographics is directly proportional to the amount of effort that precedes the event. Therefore, when used as a tutorial, the instructor needs to prepare material in advance and load it onto the system so that it is easily accessible during the live tutorial.

Now that this technology can be integrated with a virtual learning environment and used with one phone line, it can also function as a communication medium amongst a small group of students for self-help or for working on joint projects. This frees its application from formal, planned tutorials to informal, spur-of-the-moment communications.

In large group settings, the main issue is turn-taking: how it is managed and controlled. Teachers can call on individual students to respond, but this can be daunting for some learners by requiring an immediate comment. Most systems also have a chat box which allows text messages to appear on the shared screen. Some systems have a method of indicating that someone wants a turn to talk.

### Strengths of the Resource

The main strength of audiographics is its application to visual and graphical subjects, such as mathematics and technology, and to auditory subjects like language learning. Text-based virtual learning environments are very limiting for these subjects, and audiographics offers a unique medium for students of these subjects studying at a distance.

The combination of audio and shared screen is beneficial in any subject for motivating and engaging remote students. The personal computer "whiteboard" can help to enhance a student's retention capability as well as attention span by giving the student something to look at while listening. This is a tremendously important advantage of audiographics. It is also a very inexpensive way to reach out to a large group of remote sites. This cost-saving becomes especially apparent when it is necessary to update and modify course materials. Audiographics then is one of the more cost-effective instructional delivery methods.

Studies have found electronic whiteboard activities to be highly motivating and learner-centred when integrated innovatively. They offer a powerful facility for enhancing content and supporting collaborative learning.

One major advantage of audiographics over other distance education techniques is that the tutorial can be modified during delivery (e.g., elaborating on a point or skipping some sections). As a real-time technology, one of its most powerful features is the capacity to enable students to interact with the lecturer and each other. There are many combinations of tutorial design: for example, a session could begin with audiographics, then move to offline group work and finish with another connection, either by audio-only or by audiographics in which students can present their offline work.

Audiographics makes it easy for teachers to enhance presentation content by easily integrating a wide range of material into a lesson, such as a picture from the Internet, a graph from a spreadsheet, or text from a Microsoft Word file, in addition to student and teacher annotations on these objects.

Many systems have a voting facility which can be used for rapid learner feedback to the presenter. Notes and resources from the session can be stored and made available to students who missed the session.

### Potential Disadvantages

Multipoint conferencing becomes increasingly complex with the number of sites involved and participant interaction tends to decrease. It requires some skill on the part of the teacher to remember to include everyone. People new to audiographic conferencing often tend to teach or speak to one location (usually to those students on site).

Higher levels of audiographic interactivity require students to have the confidence as well as skills to use a computer at their "end." Students unfamiliar with audiographics need to be eased into increased involvement by gradually increasing their level of input.

There is considerable variation in functionality across available software packages. Useful features to look for include:

- Facility to print out or save the results to the computer;
- Support for remote voting or feedback;
- Facility to store sequences of screens for playback;
- Facility to control computer applications via the screen interface.

### Key Points for Effective Practice

1. As with all slides, use large type and few words. Pictures add interest but must be relevant.
2. Combining media. Not all delivery has to be entirely by audiographic conferencing. Very effective presentations can be made by combining printed materials (distributed in advance), audio-only conferencing (for discussion), videotapes, computer-based education, audiotapes, and e-mail.
3. Promoting interaction between students at all sites is as important as good graphics.
4. Have a back-up strategy in case of telecommunications failure (e.g., revert to audio-only).

## Selected References

Jegede, O. J., Gooley, A., & Towers, S. (1996). An evaluation of the Queensland Open Learning Network Audiographic Conferencing Professional Development Programs. *Journal of Instructional Science and Technology, 1*(4) Article 2. Available at http://www.ascilite.org.au/ajet/e-jist/docs/vol1no4/article2.htm

Pullen, J. M. (2006). Scaling up a distance education program in computer science. In *Proceedings of the ACM Special Interest Group on Computer Science Education conference on Information Technology in Computer Science Education.* Retrieved from http://portal.acm.org/citation.cfm?id=1140136&dl=ACM&coll=ACM&CFID=15151515&CFTOKEN=6184618

Rowe, S., Ellis, A., & Quoc Bao, T. (2006). The evolution of audiographics: A case study of audiographics teaching in a business faculty. In *Proceedings of the 23rd annual ASCILITE conference.* Tugun, Queensland: Australian Society for Computers in Learning in Tertiary Education.

### Institution: University of Strathclyde: Postgraduate Diploma in Computer Aided Building Design

*How It Works in Practice.*    An electronic whiteboard on this programme is used to investigate the strengths and weaknesses of the Internet as a design communication medium and also to promote group working, peer learning and the development of students' ICT and organisational skills, while also encouraging cooperative and collaborative study.

The whiteboard was used for real-time sessions both amongst the design team and between the client and the design team, usually by importing and then annotating drawings (Jpegs) created on other CAD software. This ability proved very successful in the exchange of information. The drawing tools supplied with the whiteboard were rather primitive and best used only for marking up drawings created in more sophisticated packages. The students often used the text directly onto the whiteboard to add comments to the drawings rather than opening up additional text boxes which often reduced the size of the available viewable window on the screen.

Having text and drawings visible at the same time seemed essential for the development of the proposals. One criticism of working on the whiteboard was the difficulty in knowing who was in control and the students quickly had to establish a set of procedures for writing, drawing, and taking turns. Most students found it more effective to use chat messages and reserve the whiteboard for drawing.

When using the whiteboard, some groups agreed upon a colour coding system for different team members. Codes were established for ending messages in chat sessions in order not to waste too much time anticipating a longer response. Students were often misunderstood

when engaging in their virtual communications. Difficulties were overcome in the strategic wording of communications by using humour
and adopting a more informal approach to communication.

*Lessons Learned.* Establish all technologies well in advance to ensure
reliability. The latest systems are not necessarily the best—"tried and
true" is more reliable.

Allow for technical hitches and have alternative methods of continuing project workand allow students time to familiarise themselves with
the software being used. Do not overestimate what can be achieved.
Prepare students for what to expect with team work and working in
virtual environments (for additional information see http://cebe.cf.ac.
uk/transactions/pdf/HilaryGrierson.pdf).

# RESOURCE: BLOGS/WEBLOGS

A blog is a type of web page that is simple to create and disseminate and
is used as a form of online journal by millions of users. Blogs bridge the
divide between what is termed *web 1.0* and *web 2.0*, as they are one of
the older forms of communication on the Internet, but have adapted
to provide a crucial social networking function. Some blogs take the
form of regular diary entries that are posted in reverse chronological
order (newest at the top) and deal with the enthusiasms of the user
(the blogger) who will combine personal opinions with links to other
related websites, blogs, and online articles. Blood (2002) identified four
main purposes in maintaining a blog: self-expression, keeping in touch,
information sharing, and reputation building. The ability for other
users to leave comments on blog messages means that themed discussions can be built up very quickly and supporting information (other
web articles, images, etc.) can be shared with people who have similar
interests. There are a variety of different services available on the web
that enable one to set up a blog, and some use hosted software (located
at another location on the Internet) while others require you to install
the software on your own computer, however they are all basically very
similar. Due to their simplicity of use and their flexibility, blogs have
become a fast-growing feature of educational establishments, corporate
businesses, and the public sector (e.g., news media sources such as the
online *Guardian* or *New York Times*).

## *The Educational Challenge*

Blogging offers opportunities to extend discussion beyond the classroom, or can add value to the online community in blended and

distance learning courses. The immediacy of blogging encourages a very fresh approach to sharing information. While some blog spots can simply be a rant on a personal soap-box issue, most are genuinely interactive sites where like-minded users can share information and ideas. The many-to-many mode provides a learning framework that allows bloggers to acquire information very quickly, and to report on what they have learned. This can be easily used by tutors to both extend the subject matter and reinforce key learning points. As with other digital media available over the Internet, the challenge is to somehow separate the useful information in the background noise of tens of thousands of self-publicising blog sites. In order to try to minimise unhelpful blog messages (or just plain vandalism), some institutions have established blog sites that are open only to registered members (students and staff) of that institution, but this may be argued as being counterproductive in seeking to engage with the global learning community while still not being able to ensure the quality of the posted messages.

### Strengths of the Resource

As personal, even reflective online journals, blogs can encourage the skills of writing and self-expression. New resources and ideas can be easily added to the discussion for sharing and further feedback, so blogs make it easy to access new resources very quickly. A general strength is the ability to make connections with experts and opinions outside the classroom/institutional circle, and though this requires a level of trust and openness, supporting evidence can be included to contribute to the construction of a themed archive of information. This leads to the ability to categorise learning and relate it to the experience of the individual, encouraging the learner to contextualise and personalise the learning activities in ways that strengthen learning and build confidence. The ability to request automatic feedback information when a user links to their blog (trackback) allows blog authors to keep a record of who is accessing or referring to their blogs, and to receive some acknowledgement of the value of their blog site. Potential benefits are that blogs can be used to promote critical and analytical thinking on chosen topics, and that the combination of individual working and social interaction can induce critical self-reflection in a rich learning environment.

In terms of traditional assessment, blogging can be used to provide instant feedback and peer review, without having to wait. This also makes content current and contemporary as it can be commented on immediately and recent events can be applied. Blogs also provide collaborative knowledge production as students are sharing their thoughts and ideas in a learning community rather than just in a student-teacher exchange, which is the normal format for the submission of assignments. This means that the teacher becomes part of the community of enquiry and is seen as equal in the relationship between peers, the learning, and the individual students.

### Potential Disadvantages

Although extensively used in education, there are mixed views about the added-value effectiveness of the medium to enhance learning over other forms of electronic communication. Most blog spaces are public, even when contained within the firewall of a single institution, and this may discourage less confident students from contributing to the blog, much less using it to "think aloud" and expose their thoughts to scrutiny. While a strength of the blog is its immediacy, this also means that any lack of attention in maintaining a regular flow of messages may lead to the abandonment of the blog by readers, and therefore by contributors. Detractors of blogs and other online forums maintain that being unseen makes it easier for students to become lurkers who are not engaging with the learning community; but careful attention to the teacher moderation of the discussion can alleviate this to a large extent. Similarly, although the lack of technical confidence in using new software can be addressed through careful induction training for new students, as can concerns about the development of writing skills, there needs to be a strong motivation on the part of users to want to communicate and exchange ideas. This requires thoughtful course design.

Some tutors have used blogging as a private reflective tool, which means that it is a closed forum and only the student and the teacher have access. While this can alleviate the issues of confidence that some students may face, it is merely a paperless version of a reflective diary. This is not wrong in itself, but is not what blogs are designed for. The whole point of the blog is make it available for comment and feedback, and therefore an instructor wishing to use it purely for individual purposes may want to consider another technology.

### Key Points for Effective Practice

1. Start your own blog related to your own course or subject area. Start small, but without regular entries, your readers will quickly tire and move somewhere else if you allow too much time to elapse before the next entry.

2. Give your students a list of some active blog sites and get them to look at other blogs before they start to post their own comments so that they get a feel for the medium.
3. Ask students to start a blog about a subject of particular interest to the individual student, and relevant to the course. It may be more efficient to provide students with their own blog site and ask them to maintain it.
4. Setting formative or graded assessments that require students to read (and comment upon) each other's blog sites and summarise the issues can be a good way to focus the learners' attention on the essentials.

### Selected References

Blood, R. (2002). *The weblog handbook: Practical advice on creating and maintaining your blog.* Cambridge, MA: Perseus Books Group.

Conole, G., & Alevizou, P., (2010). A literature review of the use of Web 2.0 tools in higher education. *Methodology,* 17(August), 111. Retrieved from http://www. heacademy.ac.uk/assets/EvidenceNet/Conole_Alevizou_2010.pdf

Hemmi, A., Bayne, S., & Land, R. (2009). The appropriation and repurposing of social technologies in higher education. *Journal of Computer Assisted Learning, 25,* 19–30. Retrieved from http://www.malts.ed.ac.uk/staff/sian/pdfs/jcal_paper.pdf

*Guardian.* (n.d.) Retrieved from http://www.guardian.co.uk/commentisfree/uk-edition

### Institution: Hong Kong Baptist University, Hong Kong

*How It Works in Practice.* Two classes from the fourth year of a Bachelor of Education programme, majoring in English language, were originally questioned on their technical proficiency and use of blogs. Most students were familiar with instant messaging and social networking, as well as having their own personal blogs. The plan was to provide voluntary opportunities for students to engage in academic blogging as part of their study on the module Professional Studies III.

Academic blogging is different from personal blogging in that it resembles learning or research journals that record learning processes. This can be used as part of the summative assessment process as it requires students to demonstrate critical awareness and application of knowledge in a way that personal blogging does not do.

Students were required to carry out an academic blog once a week which reflected upon their teaching practice. They were encouraged to move beyond personal outbursts and think critically about their experiences and ideas. They were also prompted to read and comment on each other's blogs.

The key themes which emerged were that students used academic blogging for:

- Documentation of experience
- Keeping others updated
- Sharing teaching ideas
- Expressions of feelings
- Expressions of thoughts or reflection
- Seeking help or advice

*Lessons Learned.* Prior experience and habit of individual students affected their readiness to participate in academic blogging. If they had already been used to sharing personal thoughts and blogs, then the move to academic blogging was less daunting.

The social and environmental factors also played a part. The two groups were well acquainted with each other and therefore were less reticent to communicate using this medium as they felt they were already in a supportive environment. Therefore, if introducing academic blogging, then it is important to create a sense of community and encourage social relationships prior to the introduction of blogging.

Interestingly, where students did not have a physical environment where they were able to tap into social support networks, there was a greater likelihood they would engage with blogging as a means to share and gain the virtual support they did not have. This is particularly useful in terms of looking at using blogging with distance learning students who will be far more likely to engage as a means of creating a sense of learning community.

Although blogging was voluntary, the fact that blogs could be viewed by tutors and peers was an impetus for some students to engage. Whilst teacher encouragement was not seen as a huge motivator, teacher presence was seen as important. The more active and responsive a teacher is in terms of responding to blogs and putting up posts, the greater the participation of students.

Deng and Yuen (2012) identify the perceived values of academic blogging in Table 4.1. The overall success of academic blogging will depend on the characteristics of the student, the conditions available for interaction, and the design of the pedagogy. Whilst the first is a difficult one to predict, the latter can be considered carefully.

### Selected Reference

Deng, L., & Yuen, A. H. K. (2012). Understanding student perceptions and motivation towards academic blogs: An exploratory study. *Australasian Journal of Educational Technology, 28*(1), 48–66. Retrieved from http://www.ascilite.org.au/ajet/ajet28/deng.html

**Table 4.1**

| Individual | Social | Academic |
|---|---|---|
| **Perceived individual values** | **Perceived social values** | **Perceived academic values** |
| • Express feelings <br> • Document experiences | • Keep others updated <br> • Seek help | • Express thoughts/ reflection <br> • Share teaching ideas |
| Individual characteristics | Social and environmental conditions | Pedagogical design |

Source: Deng & Yuen (2012, p. 59).

## RESOURCE: E-BOOKS

At its simplest, an e-book is an electronic version of a conventional book that can be read on screen using a desktop computer, any portable device (e.g., laptop, PDA, mobile phone) or in a dedicated e-book hardware device such as Amazon's Kindle, or the Aldiko book-reader. There are many different kinds of e-books, varying in file formats, the diversity of functions, and their ease of use. The changing and often experimental nature of the e-book can be considered to be challenging the conventional idea of a book, as some e-books may contain audio and movie clips, as well as hyperlinks to other sources of information (which may themselves be regularly changed). Almost by definition, e-books are portable, but beyond that they vary widely in the variety of functions that they support. Some e-books simply allow the reader to browse through page after page of electronic text, most are searchable, and some allow users to annotate the text (and in some cases even to change it) or provide links to allow users to exchange electronic messages with each other. The e-book may be an electronic version of a text that is also available on paper, or may be published only in the electronic version (especially for very specialised subjects). Initiatives such as Project Gutenberg (n.d.) have popularised e-books by extending a repository of digitised books and have placed, currently, over 36,000 e-books in the public domain.

### *The Educational Challenge*

This resource allows the rapid circulation (and rapid updating) of texts at comparatively low cost, particularly of highly specialised texts and subjects that have an obsolescence factor. The incorporation of links to participative tools, such as a discussion forum or an external wiki, permit author-reader interaction, sometimes leading to user-generated content that supplements the original e-book. This shared construction of knowledge is an ideal resource in constructivist pedagogy, but some critics fear that it may undermine the authority and reliability of an e-book as a textbook or primary resource. Proponents of e-books claim that this resource can provide highly focused content for distributed learners, and that the egalitarian characteristics of e-books allow less established authors rapid access to a wider readership. This is especially true when considering that many traditional books now have very short print runs and so can go out of print very quickly—the e-book is seen by some as a promising source for materials that are no longer in print or to which access is impeded by the location of the student.

### Strengths of the Resource

The resource enables the reader to search the text and to jump quickly between subject sections, for example to check references (which may also be linked by hypertext to online journals). Some e-books allow users to annotate and/or highlight the text, and a few may even allow users to add, or even change, text. The basic text can be supplemented with other digital resources to create a rich learning resource, including images (moving and still), sound files, and detailed links to other online sources of information that can supplement and add value to the original text. The ease of online publishing allows relatively inexpensive production, marketing, and subsequent updating enabling the text to be kept accurate and up-current. For some large paper books (e.g., medical reference books) the versatility of the e-book is an attractive alternative that can be searched and cross-referenced more easily and quickly than the conventional book. The ability to enlarge the electronic font, change the colour contrast, and even to utilise text-to-speech software enables the e-book to be more flexible than the conventional book for users with reading difficulties. The ability to carry large numbers of books at any one time on a specialised e-book reader or tablet means reading materials are always to hand.

### Potential Disadvantages

The ability to copy and paste from digital sources has raised concerns about possible opportunities for plagiarism, although this is increasingly being mitigated against through software such as Turnitin. Although the basic text e-books are straightforward to use, the versions that embed some of the more complex resources may be awkward or clumsy to use, and the overuse of sound or images for their own sake is likely to annoy regular users. As with wikis, the collective or collaborative authorship of e-books challenges many established notions of copyright and ownership of the text. The main limitations, however, are that even with the tens of thousands of e-books available, there is a strong likelihood that the book you are seeking is not available as an e-book, or perhaps not available in a format that the user can easily access due to file format differences. A second major limitation is the requirement, by definition, that the user needs a computer (or similar device) or Internet access to read the material. Despite the availability of text resources onscreen, many users still prefer to print out paper copies for reading and archiving, though this may change if and when the culture of reading directly from the computer screen becomes more firmly embedded in education. However, the study by Woody, Daniel, and Baker (2010) still suggests that even the current "digital natives" still prefer a paper book. Also, many e-books are still screen captures of paper textbooks. This can be very difficult to read (small print on e-readers) and means that it is often obsolete, as it is an older edition perhaps. However, increasingly digital texts are being designed as digital versions first and books, second, and this makes the educational opportunities far more promising.

### *Key Points for Effective Practice*

1. There are various ways to utilise software in order to read e-books—students need instruction on effective use of the appropriate software.
2. Using linked documents within a course VLE, or links from a blog to specific e-books (or even relevant chapters) will help to direct students to particularly relevant information in the appropriate course context.
3. Remind students of appropriate keywords and phrases that can be used to search within e-books in order to make reading activities more strategic.
4. When permissible, downloading an e-book to a memory stick helps to make access less location dependant (e.g., the book may be read in a variety of different locations during the day, using different devices).
5. Encourage students to use linked documents to create their own notes and commentary on pieces of reading with hot-links to the relevant sections of the e-book to support their notes.
6. Simply providing an e-book section in the institution library is not enough to promote the widespread, regular use of e-book resources—it must be actively promoted.

7. It is never too early to begin discussions between the course team and the library staff about the purchase of centrally held e-books.
8. Basing the e-book resource firmly within the library service, rather than within the course team or department, gives added benefits for institutional buy-in and adoption by staff across the institution, but close collaboration with the academics is necessary to identify specifically relevant resources and links.

### Selected References

NovaNews. (2012). The new wave in education–Interactive textbooks! Retrieved from http://novanews19.wordpress.com/2012/01/23/the-new-wave-in-education-inter active-textbooks/

Project Gutenberg. (n.d.). Retrieved from http://www.gutenberg.org/

An example of Higher Education changing over to e-books: Lintner, J. (2011) E-read-ers used as textbooks at UE. Evansville Courier & Press. Retrieved from http://www.courierpress.com/news/2011/jul/16/no-headline---ev_ereading/

Spiwak, R. (2011). eText: Is It Ready? Are We Ready? Campus Technology. Retrieved from http://campustechnology.com/articles/2011/06/22/get-ready-for-etext.aspx

Woody, W. D., Daniel, D. B., & Baker, C. A. (2010). E-books or textbooks: Students prefer textbooks. *Computers & Education, 55*(3), 945–948.

Yen-Yu Kang, Mao-Jiun J. Wang,& Rungtai Lin. (2009). Usability evaluation of E-books, *Displays, 30*(2), 49–52.

### Institution: Wake Forest University, North Carolina

*How It Works in Practice.* There are a number of approaches to utilising the e-book in formal education, these can range from:

- Adopting an e-book as a course reader and giving registered students access;
- Adding an e-book to the institutional library and using this in conjunction with a paper version (e.g. to allow access to the resource for off-campus students);
- Hyperlinking other electronic information, such as a tutorial on a VLE, to specific reference sections of an e-book.

While e-books offer a digital, but so far, linear version of a book, two science Professors from Wake Forest University, North Carolina, have designed the bio-book, which they see as the pre-cursor to a new generation of digital textbooks.

The principle of the bio-book is that it allows students to organise the material in the digital resource in such a way as to make it more meaningful to them. Available online and in mobile format, the bio-book has the information on the left hand side of the screen, and readers can track their progress on the right. Students will be able to type or write notes in the book itself and also track their learning. The initial non-linear text has been an interactive iPad biology college text book, effectively creating a customisable experience for both students and educators. Learning "nodes" or connection points are linked to one or two well-defined learning outcomes. There are then supplemental materials and formative assessments. Students can complete the learning nodes in any order. They can then link the nodes to a Connection Node, and instructors can use Organisational Nodes to collate larger concepts and principles.

*Lessons Learned.* E-books are often merely printed textbooks on the screen and do not take advantage of the interactive nature of contemporary digital technologies. A 2010 survey of college stores found that over two thirds of students still preferred to have a written text book than an e-book—just not seeing the point of an e-book when it is just an electronic copy of the same. Bio-books are dynamic and re-engage the learner in the process.

There is an issue that students may get lost; with a linear text there is a clearly defined path. Students must be developed in how to interact with their texts in a meaningful way. This is a new way of learning for many and should be done slowly and sympathetically to learner needs.

Educators also need to think in less linear ways about how they construct their students' learning environment, and create a community of enquiry where the instructor, the student, and the learning material have equal billing.

Apple now, with the launch of iBooks 2—a new version of their digital books format, offers interactive text books. New features nclude videos, 3D modelling, and multi-touch functionality. So, the move towards interactive e-books is now gathering momentum.

## RESOURCE: E-PORTFOLIOS

E-portfolios are electronic collections of documents and other objects that support individual claims for what has been learned or achieved. In higher education, e-portfolios can be used at course, programme or institutional level. There is still lack of clarity about whether the term *e-portfolio* refers to the software, a particular presentation of the contents, or all of the contents. Recent work seems to confirm that while the e-portfolio concept is a simple idea, the diversity of possible permutations means in practice that the effective implementation is complex.

## The Educational Challenge

The primary challenge is in engaging students to maintain their e-portfolios. This is partly because of the tension between institutional control and student ownership of the e-portfolio. When the institution hosts the software and insists on its use either for assessment or accreditation, the student does not take ownership of the process. The challenge here is for course designers to find a way of integrating the use of the e-portfolio into the course and to motivate learners in maintaining them and to support them in understanding the value of reflection. The e-portfolio software is still immature: there are a few proprietary systems but many institutions are developing their own software, sometimes using open source approaches. Joyes, Gray, and Young (2010) summarise the history and evolution of the main features of e-portfolio design and operation.

## Strengths of the Resource

At an individual level, e-portfolios could become a portable, lifelong record of achievements, and hence there would be many advantages for individuals in maintaining them. Not only would they contain a certified record of educational qualifications, but they would be a comprehensive resource on which to draw for job interviews and promotions.

At a course level, e-portfolios can provide a strong impetus for students to take ownership of their learning. Given appropriate course design, e-portfolios encourage reflection on learning and hence a deeper approach to learning in which learners relate new material to concepts with which they are already familiar.

At an institutional or programme level, e-portfolios are ideal for encouraging students to set their own goals. The role of the teacher is to monitor students' progress toward the goals and to advise on strategies and resources that would help students meet their goals. The e-portfolio provides the focus for reviewing and discussing student work as well as the record of progress toward the goals.

Through peer and self-assessment, e-portfolios can also be used to help students develop generic skills, such as reflective and critical thinking, the ability to evaluate and provide thoughtful responses to different points of view, and the capacity to assess their own work as well as that of their peers.

As a presentation tool, e-portfolios provide the opportunity for students to make a selection of their work available for specific purposes, such as a class presentation or job interview. The e-portfolio software allows different levels of access, so for example, users can make some parts available only to themselves, other parts accessible by their teacher and still others can be open to their classmates or the Internet generally.

E-portfolios can also be used for group work, and there is no impediment technically to a group e-portfolio. The reflective element of e-portfolios bears some resemblance to blogging (and indeed some e-portfolio software contains the facility to generate public and private blogs), and e-portfolios can contain images, video clips, and podcasts as evidence of learning. In short, there is convergence amongst many types of social networking.

### Potential Disadvantages

The communication element of e-portfolios begins to blur the boundary with a virtual learning environment and hence cause confusion or overlap in trying to establish a central discussion area.

If an institution uses e-portfolios primarily for assessment and accountability, students soon cease to engage with e-portfolios as a lifelong learning tool and view it purely as a course or degree requirement.

Even so, teachers often need to be persistent, skilled and dedicated to develop reflective practices in their students. E-portfolios can all too easily be used as a "dumping ground" for odd bits of multimedia and other course work without the student engaging with the issue of what constitutes evidence of learning.

Because e-portfolio development on a technical level is still immature, there is a major problem with compatibility, as students change institutions, graduate and move to employment. Will e-portfolios be held by the individual or the institution? What happens as systems develop over time? It is hard to imagine that e-portfolios can really be a lifelong learning tool either at a technical or a personal level, given the speed of technical advance. Yet this is how their full potential will eventually be reached.

### Key Points for Effective Practice

1. Use formative or iterative assignments with comments from the teacher and peers.
2. Relate reflective activities to the learning outcomes of the course and prompt students to think further about issues and consider other perspectives.
3. Provide examples of reflective writing so that students understand what reflection means in an academic context and build activities around them.

4. Make it fun by giving students the tools to control the look and feel of their e-portfolio (and templates for those without the relevant skills).
5. Integrate the e-portfolio with the users' online workspace in order to encourage regular updating and seamless moving from course to portfolio.
6. Provide scaffolding, structure, advice and resources on what constitutes evidence of learning.

### Selected References

Chau, J., & Cheng, G. (2010). Towards understanding the potential of e-portfolios for independent learning: A qualitative study. *Australasian Journal of Educational Technology, 26*(7), 932–950. Retrieved from http://www.ascilite.org.au/ajet/ajet26/chau.pdf

Himpsl, K., & Baumgartner, P. (2009). Evaluation of e-portfolio software. *International Journal of Emerging Technologies in Learning, 4*(1), 16–22 [Special Issue on e-portfolios]. Retrieved from at http://online-journals.org/i-jet/issue/view/51

Joint Information Systems Committee (JISC). (2008) Effective practice with e-portfolios. Retrieved from http://www.jisc.ac.uk/eportfolio

Joyes, G., Gray, L., & Hartnell-Young, E. (2010). Effective practice with e-portfolios: How can the UK experience inform implementation? *Australasian Journal of Educational Technology, 26*(1), 15-27. Retrieved from htpp://www.ascilite.org.au/ajet/ajet26/joyes.pdf

Prasad, D. (200, December) Launching towards a university-wide implementation of an ePortfolio system. *International Journal of Instructional Technology and Distance Learning.* Retrieved from http://www.itdl.org/Journal/Dec_10/article04.htm

Stefani, L., Mason, R., & Pegler, C. (2007). *The educational potential of e-portfolios.* Abingdon, UK: Routledge.

### Institution: University of Cumbria, UK

The University of Cumbria is a relatively new university networking pre-existing college campuses.

*How It Works In Practice.*   In an attempt to ease the administrative burden on staff at the newly created University of Cumbria, the institution investigated the implementation of an e-portfolio system that would be integrated within a flexible learning system. Records of learning and achievement were recorded and stored for re-use as evidence of academic achievement and qualification. A wide range of digital items were able to be stored within the chosen environment and later used and/or shared by individuals to demonstrate development activities for their annual appraisal or for professional accreditation.

Used in combination with other aspects of the virtual learning system the e-portfolio application was shown to be a powerful asset for the management of personal learning plans.

*Lessons Learned.* E-portfolios have helped the institution increase consistency in assessing learning activities by students and staff through collecting and sharing records of individual achievement.

The link between the e-portfolio and other aspects of the digital ecology of the institution is an important factor in embedding the value of the e-portfolio in the learning system.

The attitude of senior staff is crucial in the success of introduction to the e-portfolio and top-down commitment from the institution is vital for embedding the use of e-portfolios for both students and staff.

The institution needs to provide a sharp focus for the use of e-portfolios; otherwise they are simply an electronic filing cabinet (for additional information, see https://portfolio.pebblepad.co.uk/cumbria/viewasset.aspx?oid=12116&type=webfolio&pageoid=12117).

## RESOURCE: GAMES AND SIMULATIONS

Games and simulations are not new to education. However, information and communication technology have been added to them, giving them a different character. Computer games, for example, can be delivered to desktop computers, TVs, consoles or mobile devices via CD-Rom, DVD, cartridge or they can be online.

Simulation games allow players to control factors from populations to pollutants, transport systems to stock trading, theme park attractions to family relationships and football teams. Games tend to be less real but more fun; simulations usually have greater realism.

Most games have goals, rules and challenges; web 2.0 games have interactivity. For many popular games, the ultimate key to success lies in deciphering the rules, and not manipulating joysticks. Some games offer an immersive environment in which students become involved both intellectually and emotionally.

Computer simulations tend to be more open-ended and allow the players to do whatever they like within the confines of the virtual world. Simulations allow the user to dynamically explore the modelled domain, and within education, the interactive, dynamic and open nature of simulations puts the user in charge and creates a valuable learning experience. The value of "sim" games is the extent to which games technology permits users to experience a simulated version of actual reality or practice.

## The Educational Challenge

Interactive games allow students to compete not only against each other, but also against students distant from themselves. This results in opportunities to develop teams competing at a distance.

Good simulation games can exemplify effective learning principles that enable students to manipulate and evaluate rather than reproduce concepts. The game should be more than an exercise for students; it should allow them to share a common experience and use this as a basis for more detailed discussions.

Simulations are appropriate when there are underlying mathematical models, when a system can be simplified to investigate the effects of a few important criteria, and when our understanding of system properties benefits from their being examined dynamically. In management education, for instance, simulations are often built around role playing activities. The people of the organisation may be simulated with artificial agents whose actions are not determined and changes in the organisation result in a variety of consequences.

## Strengths of the Resource

*Problem-solving*: One characteristic of games that supports learning is that they challenge and support players to approach, explore and overcome increasingly complex problems and thereby learn better how to tackle those problems in similar contexts in future. Good games should allow the learner to operate at the outer limits of their capability and to increase their limits with growing competence.

*Alternative solutions*: A second characteristic is that games offer the capacity for players to try out alternative courses of action in specific contexts and then experience consequences—in other words to understand how manipulating systems causes particular effects. In all simulations there are multiple paths students can take; students often play the simulation several times taking different paths to see how the results differ because there is not one right answer or one winner. The multiple decision paths allow them to enhance and expand their decision constructs.

*Practice*: Learning by playing games is a process of constant practice and interaction in progressively more challenging tasks through which players gradually come to understand underlying sets and systems of rules. Unlike reading a book, playing a game demands interpretive competence with images, sounds. and actions as well as written words. Successfully playing a game depends on the player's ability to recognise the game's multimodal features and therefore to learn its underlying grammar and how it communicates meaning. Players probe the virtual world of the game, form hypotheses about it, re-probe it with those hypotheses in mind, and then, based on feedback from that virtual world, accept or re-think those hypotheses. This process is similar to the basic procedure of the scientific method.

*Different identities*: Games may offer the experience of exploring and developing different identities and the tools and practices that support these. Games are more than simply problems or puzzles; they are microworlds, and, in such environments, students develop a much firmer sense of how specific social processes and practices are interwoven and how different bodies of knowledge relate to each other.

*Motivation*: Students who use games find that difficult tasks can be engaging, intriguing and amusing when incorporated into a story and a meaningful context. Motivation and a sense of meaningfulness are aspects they appreciate about the games, and these in turn make learning more efficient. Collaborative learning can enhance the learning process as games encourage students to work together and suggest different strategies and solutions as they interact with the games' learning environment.

*Multiple modalities*: Students who are visual learners tend to like learning through games, and generally games reinforce learning through print, sound, and image.

### Potential Disadvantages

Achieving a balance between fun, game play and learning is a goal that is very hard to achieve. Many games are simply banal and others are overly complicated. Designing an effective game is a major challenge. Educational institutions usually do not have the resources of commercial game producers, but students will be accustomed to the quality and dynamism of commercial games. All too often educational games are used as a fun diversion, a supplement to the curriculum, not a deeply-embedded, core learning element.

Commercial games tend to present stereotyped characters, genders and races. Educational games can correct this. However, the game play, interaction and story must support and be subordinate to the learning processes and knowledge objectives. The overall purpose is not to play a game but to learn in an engaging and effective way. Characters, story, and interactions must be relevant to the learning context of the specific subject or it will cause frustration.

Game playing can be addictive, and many commercial games are full of violence and aggressive behaviour. Educational games can counteract this by being action-oriented—but not action as in violence or speed but as a constant encouragement to do things—to take action. The overall idea of gaming is to engage, to be active, to be someone, to perform some kind of mission, to reach goals, and be rewarded.

### Key Points for Effective Practice

1. Games should stretch students' abilities.
2. Games should be rooted in some firm reality or present strong internal consistency and logic.
3. It is of vital importance that the user does not get stuck anywhere in the game—he or she must be able to quit the game, change strategy, use and "cross-use" different resources without becoming trapped in long sequences that are difficult or impossible to interrupt.
4. Structure and navigation must be crystal clear—no hidden features, buttons, or too many surprises! Avoid gadget and gizmo overload. The guiding principle of navigation design is simplicity and relevance—less is more. The learner should not concentrate his or her efforts on "cracking the code" of the game. And relevance and simplicity do not mean that navigation and structure cannot be elegant.

### Selected References

Clark, A. (2005). Learning by doing: A comprehensive guide to simulation, computer games, and pedagogy in e-learning and other educational experiences. Hoboken, NJ: Pfeiffer Wiley.

Creative Learning with Serious Games. (2010). International Journal of Emerging Technologies in Learning, 5 [Special issue].Retrieved from http://online-journals.org/i-jet/issue/view/97

Pan, C-C. (2011) Guidelines, challenges, and recommendations for digital game-based learning. International Journal of Instructional Technology and Distance Learning, 8(4) Retrieved from http://www.itdl.org/Journal/Jul_11/index.htm

Prensky, M. (2001). Digital game-based learning. New York: McGraw-Hill.

Whitton, N. (2010). Learning with digital games: A practical guide to engaging students in higher education. New York: Routledge.

Whitton, N., & Hollins, P. (2008) Collaborative virtual gaming worlds in higher education. Research in Learning Technology, 16 (3). Retrieved from http://www.researchinlearningtechnology.net/index.php/rlt/article/view/10900

*Institution: Manchester Metropolitan University, Manchester, UK*

*How It Works in Practice.* This initiative used an Alternative Reality Game to engage with students in order to assist their introduction to the city and the university, to encourage them to meet new friends and to improve their information literacy skills. Against a background storyline, a series of collaborative challenges were set. The game was piloted as a tool to enhance the student induction experience, and specific tasks were set to improve the student's library and information handling skills, as well as facilitating social networks. This initiative was essentially a prototype to explore the validity of using alternative reality gaming as a method of improving student induction and retention, as well as investigating the related design, support, and infrastructure issues (e.g., is it cost-effective? How would such a system link to existing campus-based procedures?). The initiative produced a very useful evaluation.

*Lessons Learned.* Although the project was successful in designing and implementing a pilot platform, it cannot be assumed that students will immediately become users, and close attention needs to be given to proper timing (not during new student orientation) as well as other induction training. Good communications is essential for sharing ideas and stimulating both activity and support in the use of the games. Continual monitoring and prototyping is of crucial importance in the ongoing development and improvement of the operation of the game. The structure of the game (rules and challenges) must be sufficiently flexible to allow the game to be used by different student groups and in different situations.

### Selected Reference

Whitton, N. (2009) Alternate reality games for orientation, socialisation and induction. Retrieved from http://www.jisc.ac.uk/publications/reports/2009/argosifinalreport.aspx#downloads

## RESOURCE: INSTANT MESSAGING

Instant Messaging (IM) is a simple form of synchronous online communication, allowing computer users to communicate across a network connection. The primary medium is text, although as with other web 2.0 tools, progressive convergence has led to many IM networks providing facilities for audio and video. Most instant messaging applications include the ability to set a status message, roughly analogous to the message on a telephone answering machine, which indicates whether the user is available, busy or away from the computer. For these reasons, IM is more akin to telephoning than it is to e-mailing. On the other hand, people are not forced to reply immediately to incoming messages, and in this sense IM is less intrusive than phoning, and also growing in popularity as a prime communication tool for young people, who prefer to use written rather than verbal messaging systems (Schwarz, 2011).

There are six main types of IM software services available. Single-protocol IMs allow you to be connected to a single network of users—whereby you can "chat" to anyone who is on the same network as you. The most popular IMs providers are AOL Instant Messenger (AIM), Facebook chat, Google Talk (Gtalk), Windows Live Messenger (formerly MSN), and Yahoo Messenger. Multiple-protocol IMs allow you to have a number of IM accounts and to access them all through one application download. This means you can chat to any of your friends regardless of what network you or they are using. The most popular ones currently are Digsby, Miranda I, Pidgin, and Trillian. Web messengers (also known as web-based IM accounts) are great for public access computer users, as this allows them to login into an application as long as they have an Internet connection and a web browser; no download is required. Web messengers tend to offer clients multiple-protocol IMs. Some examples include AIM Express, ebuddy Web Messenger, Windows Live Web Messenger, and Yahoo Messenger for the Web. Mobile IM clients are great for people who want to chat on the move, and with the proliferation of smart phones and Internet-enabled mobile phones, there are now many IM client apps available for the mobile user. Most require a free download, although there are some that can be purchased. Examples include iPhone IM Client Apps, Google Talk for mobile, ebuddy for mobile, and Facebook chat for iPhone. Enterprise IM clients are secure messaging services which can be used for business communication. Finally, portable IM clients allow users to access their favourite client IM software on a USB flashdrive, which can then be plugged into any computer and allow one to chat with one's friends and colleagues by merely executing the portable IM app; examples include pidgin portable, miniAIM, and YahELite.

As thousands of people can be signed into a service at the same time, there are tools provided to organise IM contacts. These systems allow you to add user names to a "Buddy List" or "Friends List," which can be sorted into several sub-lists. When a user on a list logs on to the IM service, a notification message or sound is played; these notifications can be customised to the subgroup in order to give the user an idea of the importance of the new visitor. In addition, a user has the ability to block or ignore other users; this is an essential tool in dealing with spammers.

## The Educational Challenge

The primary use in higher education is as a tool to encourage contact between students and faculty, usually as virtual office hours (although there is mixed evidence as to whether students do or do not prefer IM contact over face-to-face contact with their teacher). In addition, it is valuable for developing reciprocity and cooperation among students at a distance and is often used for collaboration amongst groups—usually to coordinate more sustained online work, to exchange URLs and other snippets of information. As a synchronous tool, it offers the benefit of prompt feedback and the convenience of being available from different locations. There are also administrative uses in recruiting and admissions, and as a mentoring tool or buddy system. Nevertheless, actual practice shows that the primary value is social—especially for remote students and both for student-student and student-teacher contact.

## Strengths of the Resource

Given access to a computer, the Internet, and a relative decent broadband service, this form of communication is free, easy to use, immediate and widely accepted by users of all ages. Although originally seen as a useful communications medium by shy people and by those with a hearing impairment, increasingly research suggests that young people prefer to communicate using text rather than oral methods (Schwarz, 2011). For lecturers "isolated" in their offices, it can be a positive communication tool, being more informal and intimate than the lecture hall. It is possible to save a conversation, so as to refer to it later. Also, the fact that instant messages typically are logged in a local message history provides some of the advantages of e-mails. Multiple conversations can take place between students or between students and the teacher without any of them being interrupted or disturbed. This can be particularly useful for group work. IM is relatively safe as you can control who is a buddy and who is not.

## Potential Disadvantages

The major disadvantage of IM is the security risks: message interception and infiltration of viruses. Hackers' use of instant messaging networks to deliver malicious code has grown consistently and viruses can be sent through instant messaging servers.

Also, communication cues are not so easily read and can be misinterpreted. Although the use of emoticons can help with this, it only works if people have a shared understanding of what each emoticon means, and cultural differences can make this difficult to predict, particularly on international programmes.

Students could be at risk as it is not always possible to know that the person you are chatting with is who they say they are.

For instructors, having an instant-messaging programme running in the background on the computer means that work can be interrupted at any moment. Instant messaging can disrupt a train of thought, and it is very difficult to delay responding in order to compose a well-conceived answer to a student's question. IM is seen as fuelling the expectation of ubiquitous instructor access. The time commitment, as with other web 2.0 tools, is a significant consideration.

In short, IM is viewed by many as a time-waster which encourages gossip, poor use of English and other negative behaviour, such as bullying and dangerous contacts with strangers.

## Key Points for Effective Practice

1. Use IM to develop a stronger sense of community, especially in online courses where students are remote. IM chats can be considered the virtual equivalent of the kind of communication that typically takes place in the common spaces of a campus environment.
2. Set up IM to allow communication between members of different classes, allowing a much stronger sense of community to grow between students in the same programme who are not taking the same course.
3. Encourage students to use IM to coordinate their collaborative work.

## Selected References

Dillenbourg, P., & Traum, D. (1996). Grounding in multi-modal task-oriented collaboration. In P. Brna, A. Paiva, & J. Self (Eds.), *Proceedings of the European conference on artificial intelligence in education* (pp. 401–407). Lisbon, Portugal

Habuchi, I. (2005). Accelerating reflexivity. In M. Ito, D. Okabe, & M. Matsuda (Eds.), *Personal, portable, pedestrian: Mobile phones in Japanese life* (pp. 165–182). Cambridge, MA: MIT Press

Jeong, W. (2007). Instant messaging in on-site and online classes in higher education. *Educause Quarterly, 1*. Retrieved from http://www.educause. edu/ir/library/pdf/eqm0714.pdf

Luor, T., Wu, L., Lu, H. &, Tao, Y. (2010). The effect of emoticons in simplex and complex task-oriented communication: An empirical study of instant messaging. *Computers in Human Behavior, 26*(5), 889–895.

Reynol Junco, R., & Cotten, S. R. (2011) Perceived academic effects of instant messaging use. *Computers & Education, 56*(2), 370–378.

Schwarz, O. (2011). Who moved my conversation? Instant messaging, intertextuality and new regimes of intimacy and truth. *Media Culture Society, 33*(1), 71–187.

### Institution: Graduate School of Education, University of Bristol, UK

*How It Works in Practice.* The Timmis (2012) study involved two groups of final year undergraduate students studying one of two 10-credit modules, where both required students to complete a collaborative group research project conducted in online special interest groups known as SIGs. Each SIG had up to six students, who were required to decide on a project, researching the topic and constructing a website to build upon the collective research. The various digital communication methods used by students were identified and these included the online virtual learning environment (VLE), institutional and personal email, mobile phone and text messaging, social networking sites, and instant messaging conversations using Windows Live messenger and Skype.

Results showed that all of the students involved in the study preferred to use text-based conversation rather than oral to communicate. The study also found that students were poor at communicating with each other on the task they were set. They continued to use those communication channels that had become endemic based upon their home circumstances, habitual practices, social rules and relationships, and made their existing communication channels meet the needs of the task rather than the other way around. Students also did not like to blur the boundary between work and play and preferred social media communication to be used purely for social interaction and the VLE for their studies. However, in one area of communication, students did increase their usage over the course of the task—instant messaging. The study found that the conversations were very long and that students would drop in and out at various points. Students appeared to be using IM to provide social support and affirmation as well as help and advice. Students knew how to converse successfully using this medium and could maintain their relationships through "back channelling" (using affirmative cues to imitate conversation) (Dillenberg & Traum, 1996) and "telecocooning" (maintaining a relationship without geographic or time constraints; Habuchi, 2005). The students created a private space of intimacy and playfulness which helped maintain their interaction at a social level.

*Lessons Learned.* Overall, the study found that the use of instant messaging provided a social support network and also one in which work ideas were exchanged. Students were reticent to see their interaction as one of peer "support"; they merely thought they were having conversations. However, it was obvious from their interactions that they were providing each other with mutual support but they do not recognise it as such. To be used effectively, students must be taught the value of their interactions within this medium particularly when there is now a greater emphasis on the creation of a community of enquiry whereby the instructor and students are seen as equal in the learning relationship. Timmis (2012) suggests that IM is a hybrid activity which incorporates interaction which is neither completely social, or one devoted to work. This "boundary-crossing" is a very useful tool for students and one that higher education could use to good advantage.

### *Selected Reference*

Timmis, S. (2012). Constant companions: Instant messaging conversations as sustainable supportive study structures amongst undergraduate peers. *Computers & Education*, 59(1), 3–18. Retrieved from http://www.sciencedirect.com/science/article/pii/S0360131511002430

## RESOURCE: MASHUPS

A mashup is essentially the creation of something new from parts of several separate sources in order to produce a single integrated whole. The name derives from the practice of mixing two or more songs. Typically, a mashup combines bits from existing websites or applications, but the term is beginning to be used more widely for combinations of information generally. The first mashups tended to involve the integration of information with maps and this remains a useful educational application. However, many people are now experimenting with mashups using Google, eBay, Amazon, Flickr, and Yahoo's APIs, and volunteer programmers are taking it upon themselves to combine and remix the data and services of unrelated, even competing sites. A typical example is where images and/or digital information is mashed together with Google Maps to create a unique online service. A further development is that services have appeared which allow users to create mashups without needing programming skills, so that, for example, photos from Flickr can be laid onto maps showing exactly where the photo was taken.

The phenomenon of mashups reflects the prevailing environment of web 2.0: it is no longer just a collection of pages, as people are seizing far more control of what they do online. Creativity is the key watchword of mashups as users take bits and pieces from a number of websites and stitch them together in clever ways. In this sense, mashups merely reuse information, but in the process, produce customised, personalised or novel functionality.

## The Educational Challenge

As with the other tools discussed in this chapter, the educational use of mashups can be teacher-centric or student-centric. In other words, the teacher can retain control by designing applications that put students in the position of passive receivers, or can empower students to make the tool their own. Designed with care, mashups can be a powerful learning tool, and can further advance education towards massive personalization. Students can use existing mashups to create presentations based on small chunks of learning content composed of Wiki text, multiple choice tests, movies from YouTube, GoogleVideo, Grouper, and Slideshare presentations. The challenge for the teacher is to design subject-specific problems, issues or questions which motivate learners to create unique responses. As the features and functionality of existing sites grow, so too do the opportunities for new combinations of data.

## Strengths of the Resource

Many mashups are visual, and this is valuable for visual learners. Mapping mashups provide sophisticated yet easy-to-use tools for visualization—tools that clearly show spatial relationships. In many cases, rendering data or concepts in a visual form—as opposed to simple text and numbers—helps users see and understand more thoroughly the material being represented.

As with other web 2.0 tools, mashups can be useful both as tools other people have created and as something for students to create themselves. An example of useful existing mashups are the online mapping services which allow users to navigate most of the globe through a web interface, viewing varying levels of resolution through maps, satellite imagery, or a combination of them. Mapping mashups overlay data on those maps with clickable markers showing specific points of interest. As for student generated mashups, anyone with a browser can access vast stores of information, mash it up, and serve it in new ways—a sort of endless mix and match opportunity.

There are many administrative applications of mashups used by universities: campus orientation maps for students, locations of job opportunities and graduate programmes and maps for administrators showing the location of new student recruits.

### Potential Disadvantages

As the concept of mashups becomes common, one of the dangers is that the mix and match aspect takes precedence over the value of the final product. In other words, it becomes a silly game without learning potential. The use of mashups by students, therefore, needs guidance and scaffolding by the teacher.

There are also institutional issues: as these web-based services become the medium for learning, there is a need to provide a level of service and reliability over and above that required for a more passive, resource presentation approach to the web. Similarly, whilst such technology is essentially an empowering one for all learners, there are circumstances in which some students may not have access to the web from home, and some strategy for bridging this "digital divide" should be in place.

These bottom-up efforts present tough challenges for the sites on which the new services are built. Mashups often use the data without asking first, then present it in unintended ways. Not surprisingly, some website operators have objected. Yahoo initially blocked one mashup site from using its traffic data with Google Maps (before relenting!), and Amazon asked a mashup designer to change how it made links to potential rival sites.

### Key Points for Effective Practice

1. The use of mashups by students requires the teacher to adopt a "fluid" attitude to information: that it is always changing, something that can be mixed in different ways to produce a new learning experience. For this reason, mashups represent a very different experience of learning from the traditional textbook, which presents information as static and unchanging.
2. Mashups should be viewed as a new way of presenting and analysing data, a multimedia experience to enhance understanding. For some students, the multimedia aspect of a mashup makes an otherwise abstract concept concrete, helping them see patterns and movements that explain ideas and their significance. In manipulating data and thinking critically about patterns and relationships, students can get a taste of research as well as experience authentic learning.

### Selected References

Brown, M. (2007, March/April). Mashing up the once and future CMS. *Educause Review, 42*(2), 8–9. Retrieved from http://www.educause.edu/apps/er/erm07/erm0725.asp

MashUps for Learning. (2010). *International Journal of Emerging Technologies in Learning, 5* [Special issue]. Retrieved from http://online-journals.org/i-jet/issue/view/78

Lee, K., Kaufmann, N., & Buss, G. (2011). Trust issues in web service mash-ups. *First Monday, 16*(8). Retrieved from http://firstmonday.org/htbin/cgiwrap/bin/ojs/index.php/fm/article/view/2911/3025

## Institution: Galson Estate Trust, the Isle of Lewis, Scotland

*How It Works in Practice.* The Galson Estate in NW Lewis has recently been returned to community ownership, and one of the key objectives in its business plan is the promotion of tourism based upon the unique cultural, environmental, and historical assets of the area. A mashup of web 2.0 tools is at the core of the concept of bringing together the heritage assets of the community in order to increase informal learning about the area.

The long-term sustainability of the project is based upon the motivation of local businesses and enthusiastic individuals, under the co-ordination of Galson Estate Trust, to provide ongoing content management and development with minimal further external expertise or funding.

The community's acquisition of ownership of the Galson Estate coincides with the popularisation of a number of social networking tools which are ideal for developing a sense of community, e.g., You-Tube, podcasting, Flickr, and Internet broadcasting. In this project, the aim was to "mashup" these applications for the purpose of presenting the geographical community to visitors and tourists. The project builds on the fact that broadband is now available throughout the area.

The essence of the project is that, with training, the community can generate all of the content on the site and thereby experience informal learning in the process. Some funding has been secured for:

1. The initial setup, customisation, and inter-linking of the new technology applications that provide the platform (the network ecology) to enable the local community to interact with visitors and tourists both past and future.
2. Training of members of the local community (e.g., tourism micro-businesses, local societies involved in heritage and music, school children, and local volunteers) to manipulate and input data rel-

evant to their own subject areas. A number of learning-by-doing workshops have been run.

*Lessons Learned.*   The main lesson from this project is that public participation needs time to gestate, and once it becomes established, it has its own momentum. The training opportunities were well attended, and it was evident that the most effective training revolves around the most appropriate and not the most flashy applications.

Partly because of the speed with which mashups are appearing, and partly because of the developing community involvement, it is important to balance a vision of the project's aims with a flexibility to respond to new initiatives, new tools and new participants. If a consultant had been hired to develop the website in a few weeks, it would have been a very different experience. Like many web 2.0 initiatives, the combined power of crowd participation creates a powerful and unpredictable dynamic. Community involvement and generation of content have made this an exciting and educational project (for additional information see http://www.galsontrust.com/).

## RESOURCE: MOBILE LEARNING (M-LEARNING)

Mobile learning devices currently consist of cell phones, personal digital assistants (PDAs), MP3 players, portable game devices, handhelds, tablets, and laptops. However, what used to be separate devices are now converging onto one device. For example, Smart-phones are integrated communications devices that combine telephony, computing, messaging and multimedia.

Wireless technology on campuses is becoming the norm, so that students are connected in the library, lecture theatre, cafeteria, halls of residence, and even outside on the lawn. For students off campus, Bluetooth technology makes it possible to create personal area networks (PANs) among physically proximate devices, connecting headset device to phones, which can in turn connect to a computer, a PDA, and any other nearby Bluetooth-enabled device.

According to research carried out by the National Union of Students (NUS) and Endsleigh insurance company in 2011, over 4 out of 5 students were taking a laptop to university, 14% had a desk top computer, and 4% had a tablet PC. All students had a mobile phone, with 59% having a smart-phone. In short, there are more wireless networks, services, and devices than ever before.

## The Educational Challenge

While initially innovative uses of PDAs, mobile phones, and handhelds in education tended to be organisational, administrative, and supportive, in other words, learning-related, rather than strictly learning applications per se, now there are an enormous number of educational apps available for almost every conceivable subject. From apps which allow students to ask anonymous questions in a lecture, if they are unclear on a topic, through GoSoapbox, to Poll Everywhere, whereby educators can poll their students who give them quizzes, to interactive digital books, and collaborative instant messaging, the range of educational uses of mobile devices is huge. There are so many advantages to mobility that render these devices useful for education in almost every discipline. Mobile learning is considered by many to be the next step in a long tradition of technology-mediated learning which is heading towards ubiquitous, pervasive, personal, and connected learning.

Learning is a deeply personal act that is facilitated when learning experiences are relevant, reliable, and engaging. The promise of mobile devices is that they help the innovative course designer deliver appropriate strategies, tools, and resources for different kinds of learning.

## Strengths of the Resource

The primary strength of mobile devices for learning is that so many learners own and regularly use them already. This reduces the need for training and access and adds to the rationale for integrating them into education.

Mobile learning is a response to pressures for on-demand access of learners in an information-centric world. It also connects formal educational experience (e.g., taking a class, attending a workshop, or participating in a training session) with informal, situated learning experience (e.g., field work, museums, and galleries). It also allows learners to study while travelling, commuting and at a distance from a wired computer. As campus-based students become more mobile in their learning, the divide that used to exist between distance and campus students ceases to exist. Distance learning is no longer second best. Wireless technology is improving in speed and security at the same time that it is dropping in price.

Getting students engaged in mobile learning projects might not only better facilitate learning, it might also have them learning about various 21st-century literacies like group work, composing in multiple environments, and information literacy (Rodrigo, 2011).

### *Potential Disadvantages*

Mobile devices have limited storage capacities and batteries have to be charged regularly. Data can be lost if this is not done correctly. Laptops tend to be much less robust than desktops. Bandwidth may degrade with a larger number of users when using wireless networks.

The main disadvantages for teachers is the notion of being "always on," and hence always available.

Questions have arisen about wireless devices enabling cheating on examinations, which has led to many institutions banning them in examination halls.

More challenging is the issue of whether brevity of expression, due to small screens and keyboards limiting the amount and type of information that can be displayed, lead to superficiality of communication and lack of real engagement with issues.

Finally, will the "filter generation"—learners who multiprocess and multitask using multiple media—learn how to think critically and communicate effectively while using mobile digital tools?

### *Key Points for Effective Practice*

- Match the mobile device to the learning objectives.
- Design activities which are interactive, allowing a two-way flow of information.
- Investigate the hardware, software and bandwidth of the learners before planning and developing the activity.
- Keep pages to 40 kilobytes or less for online resources. The magic number appears to be about 15 seconds for the maximum time users will wait for a page to load.
- Keep fonts simple. San serif fonts like Arial and Helvetica are easier to read on screen. Arial is a very common font that will probably be available on most devices.
- Use moblogs (mobile weblogs) for field work and contexts where students are distributed. Each student can add descriptions from their own location.
- Use PDAs for remote students to contribute data to form a single project.
- Build activities in which students interact with each other, not just with the teacher e.g. sharing and commenting on each other's projects).

## Selected References

Average Student Possessions Worth £2,650. (2011, August 8). Retrieved from http://www.guardian.co.uk/money/2011/aug/08/average-student-possessions-nus-endsleigh

Johnson, L., Smith, R., Willis, H., Levine, A.. & Haywood, K. (2011). *The Horizon Report: 2011 edition* (p. 8). Austin, TX: New Media Consortium.

Koole, M., McQuilkin, J. L., & Ally, M. (2010). Mobile learning in distance education: Utility or futility? *The Journal of Distance Education, 24*(2),59–82.

Rajasingham, L. (2011). Will mobile learning bring a paradigm shift in higher education? Education Research International. Retrieved from http://www.hindawi.com/journals/edu/2011/528495/

Rodrigo, R. (2011). Mobile teaching versus mobile learning, Educause Quarterly, 34(1). Retrieved from http://www.educause.edu/EDUCAUSE+Quarterly/EDUCAUSEQuarterlyMagazineVolum/MobileTeachingVersusMobileLear/225846

Tech-Savvy Students Regularly Carry £1,165 Worth of Gadgets With Them Every Day. (2011, August 10). Retrieved from http://www.endsleigh.co.uk/Media/Pages/Students-take-nearly-%C2%A33000-worth-of-possessions-to-university.aspx

Welcome to mixable @ Purdue University. (n.d.). Retrieved from http://www.purdue.edu/mixable

## Institution: Purdue University, Indiana, USA

*How It Works in Practice.*    In 2010, Purdue released "Mixable"—a web and mobile application that is able to take the existing applications that students know and integrate them with the university systems in a seamless navigation. It makes use of Facebook, Twitter and Dropbox, and allows students to set status updates, microblog, document share and bookmark. Students can choose to join any of the classes within their current programme, and will be connected to other students who have already joined. Using one input box for all posts—the student is able to read a continuous stream of posts both internal and external to the university. As posts are made, Mixable examines them for references to external media or websites. Media, such as images or video, are automatically embedded as thumbnails within the system, and links to websites are screen-captured and compiled into a list of bookmarks. Another clever aspect of Mixable is that it does not store media locally, and automatically transfers it to a student's Dropbox account, which can then be accessed anywhere and does not affect the memory capacity of the mobile device. Mixable also provides access to podcasts of lectures which can then be listened to on the move.

*Lessons Learned.*    Mixable provides a simple way of connecting students and their courses through a virtual medium they already know and understand. It allows for greater interaction of faculty and students. There are ways to monitor access and integrate with digital gradebooks in order to facilitate assessment. Whilst still being piloted, initial results have found the application to be extremely useful for engaging students in greater communication with their peers and with faculty in an environment they use regularly. However, at this stage the application is not being used for assessment within programmes, and it will be interesting to see if this invasion of personal and social space is welcomed by students.

### Selected Reference

Bowen, K. (2011). Mixable: A mobile and connected learning environment. *EducauseE Quarterly, 34*(1). Retrieved from http://www.educause.edu/EDUCAUSE+Quarterly/EDUCAUSEQuarterlyMagazineVolum/MixableAMobileandConnectedLear/225849

## RESOURCE: ONLINE FORUMS

Online forums are also commonly referred to as computer conferences, web forums, message boards, discussion boards, (electronic) discussion groups, discussion forums, bulletin boards.

A forum is essentially a website composed of a number of threads. Each thread entails a discussion or conversation in the form of a series of posts written by the members. These threads remain saved on the forum website for future reading indefinitely or until deletion by a moderator. Most forum software allows more than one forum to be created. Threads in a forum are either flat (posts are listed in chronological order) or threaded (each post is made in reply to a parent post).

A forum administrator typically has the ability to edit, delete, move or otherwise modify any thread on the forum. Administrators also usually have the ability to close the board, change major software items, change the skin, modify the board, ban, delete, or create members. Moderator privileges are often able to be delegated to other forum members, for example, to students. Forums, unlike wikis, do not allow people to edit other's messages. The moderator or administrator is able to remove messages in case they contravene institutional regulations.

Unlike blogs, forums typically allow anyone to start a new discussion (known as a thread) or reply to an existing thread. While many blogs allow other students to post comments in reply, the number of people who can create entries is normally very limited, and the range of viewpoints and beliefs on a blog is also limited. When blogs are used on a course as well as online forums, students may experience a conflict regarding where to post their reflections or comments.

## The Educational Challenge

Designing engaging and effective online activities is not always easy, it takes time and effort on the part of educators, and while some generic types have begun to emerge in the literature, they are not always applicable across all disciplines.

Creating a sense of community amongst learners is a delicate matter, and the necessary trust can be undermined by one student posting unpleasant messages or just being overly boisterous in their responses. It is important to establish rules of engagement or "netiquette" within a forum and make sure that participants follow this. There is no doubt that when a sense of community has developed, students feel that they learn more and benefit more from studying the course.

Online discussions can easily become disjointed, with points being made in isolation from others and questions that have been posed, never being answered. Perhaps worse, a forum can often remain superficial. Effective course design and good online moderating can help, but neither can guarantee high quality discussion.

Obtaining equable participation from all students is the ideal, but it is rarely reached. There are too many extenuating circumstances which account for the fact that most online forums are dominated by a sub-set of the students, though messages may be read by many more.

## Strengths of the Resource

1. It is convenient in time and place. Flexibility and convenience for the learner are paramount especially if they have other commitments. Online forums are accessible 24/7 and are not time-bound and therefore can be used on international programmes where synchronous communication may be prohibitive due to time zone differences.
2. Compared with face-to-face discussion, it is more equable—especially for quieter students. More students participate online possibly because, compared with traditional classroom settings, it minimizes fear and intimidation in front of colleagues.
3. Details of the discussion remain usually throughout the course. One can backtrack and reread a message.
4. The asynchronous nature allows time for a considered response. This leads to a more profound discussion of ideas than is usual in a face-to-face tutorial.
5. Online forums allow the more reflective student the opportunity to participate. In general students are more likely to express opinions and comment on each other's remarks than they would be in a lecture.

6. The lecturer is seen as a moderator, one of the group, rather than a teacher. Nevertheless, for many students, online teachers are more accessible than those in face-to-face lecture courses.
7. Online forums allow for discussion with students from other class groups.
8. The teacher can reply once to a query and all students can benefit. Online forums can also reduce time spent on other administrative course management duties, as a teacher can post up general information points.
9. Online discussion provides an opportunity for students to rehearse information and to formulate their thoughts, which is ideal practice for assessment.

### Potential Disadvantages

In many ways, the advantages of online forums are also disadvantages.

1. The asynchronous nature of the medium provides flexibility, but also requires more motivation and self-discipline from students to log on and participate. It is all too easy for busy students to put off interacting online.
2. While the text-only nature of the communication benefits shy students or those who do not normally participate in face-to-face discussions, many others find online forums off -putting because they are unable to read face-to-face nuances such as body language. Similarly, some students find written communication more challenging and therefore the medium becomes frustrating as they cannot get their point across as clearly as they might do verbally.
3. The support for reflective messages means that there is no immediacy of response. Similarly, it is difficult to get an indication of depth of feeling in an online response.
4. Some students resent the fact that even the non-contributors get to benefit through reading messages.
5. While threading of messages is usually helpful, discussion threads can become confused, allowing discussion to go off -track.
6. The permanency of the record is also a disadvantage in that some students are reluctant to post a message knowing that it will remain throughout the course.
7. Collaborative work becomes very difficult to bring to a conclusion when some students have not contributed. It is difficult to interpret silence!

## Key Points for Effective Practice

- Create a collaborative community spirit by requiring shared activities between students and teachers, ensuring constructive criticism, maintaining motivation, and providing assessment tools with timely feedback. Provide students with a clear idea about when postings will be read and responded to, or they will lose interest and feel their contribution is going unnoticed.
- Design activities which require students to make identified contributions as this reduces the issue of just a minority being involved in the forum. Set individual or collective tasks that encourage all student participation.
- Technical support services must be made available to train and provide ongoing support for both learners and instructor.
- Provide related links and resource listings to support discussions.
- Quantity of forum postings alone is not an adequate indicator of community development. SNAPP software allows a teacher to see a map of all interactions for a forum within a discussion board within VLEs—represented as a social network diagram. Forums exhibiting a high volume of communication traffic do not necessarily equate to the establishment of a strong sense of community, or indeed a high quality discussion. However, SNAPP allows one to identify at-risk students (those who are not contributing), clarify who the key information brokers are within a class, and assess activity intervention before and after to see the effect it has up on student engagement. However, forums exhibiting a greater percentage of learner interactions (learner-learner and learner-content) demonstrate a stronger sense of community.

## Selected References

Charthouse International Learning Corporation (1998) Fish!: catch the energy, release the potential VHS video, Burnsville, MN: Author. http://www.charthouse.com/content.aspx?name=home2

Groves, M., & O'Donoghue, J. (2009). Reflections of students in their use of asynchronous online seminars. *Educational Technology & Society, 12*(3), 143–149.

Kaur, M. (2011). Using online forums in language learning and education. *Student Pulse, 3*(3). Retrieved from http://www.studentpulse.com/a?id=414

Nelson, L. (2010). How to use electronic forums to improve group communication. *E- how.com.* Retrieved from http://www.ehow.com/how_6338777_use-forums-improve-group communication.html#ixzz10k19bcQj

Shachar, M., & Neumann, Y. (2010). Twenty years of research on the academic performance differences between traditional and distance learning: Summative meta-analysis and trend examination, *Journal of Online Learning and Teaching, 6*(2), 146-154.

SNAPP (Social Networks Adapting Pedagogical Practice). (n.d.). Retrieved from http://www.snappvis.org/
What is SNAPP? (n.d.). University of Woolongong. Retrieved from http://research. uow.edu.au/learningnetworks/seeing/snapp/index.html

### Institution: University of the Highlands and Islands, Management School, MSc Leadership and Management (MLM). Inverness, UK

*How It Works in Practice*   The MLM is a totally online programme for students wishing to enhance their leadership skills. Within module spaces, students are assigned a module instructor who engages with the students through a discussion board and chat room facility within Blackboard. Collaborative and individual activities are at the core of the course design method, and tutors are very experienced at encouraging online interactivity. In particular, the programme team have developed a model of interaction which has been very well received by students. Structured around the motivation at work framework of Fish! (Charthouse International, 1998), the same principles of Play, Be There, Make Their Day and Choose Your Attitude, can be applied well to teachers within the online learning environment.

**Play**—Use humour, games, and incorporate films and popular culture into activities.

**Be There**—Maintain a consistent presence within the forum and provide regular feedback to students and inform them as to when you will be looking at posts.

**Make Their Day**—Provide phatics and salutations, vocatives and inclusive pronouns to make students feel valued and part of a community.

**Choose Your Attitude**—Approach online learning forums with the view that they are as equally valid as face-to-face interaction, and be positive in all your interactions.

The students are mostly in full-time employment as supervisors and managers, and the quality of discussion in the online forums is generally very high, though not all students participate equally. There are always champions of the online discussions who post regularly and others who merely lurk or who do the minimum. On the whole, those who contribute more, benefit more from the modules.

*Lessons Learned.*   Simply providing the opportunity to interact does not guarantee good interaction; most learners need a structure and a task within which to orient their contributions.

Students using English as a second language may not be as articulate and as willing to take part in online interaction as mother tongue users.

Grammatical and spelling mistakes are an accepted fact of online interaction, even amongst English speakers, and comprehensibility is the major focus in reduced bandwidths not correctness.

Integrating some real-time events, using audiographics, Google or text-based chat, is welcomed by many students, especially when organised by students for project work or self-help.

Archiving messages regularly helps to move students on to the next unit or activity.

The time taken to participate in online interaction, especially collaborative activities needs to be factored in to the overall student study time (and probably means a reduction in the amount of material to be studied).

The schedules of busy professional people who are attracted to this programme mean that holidays, family crises, sudden job commitments etc. are a major hindrance to regular, sustained participation in group activities.

For additional information on the University of the Highlands and Islands, Management School, MSc Leadership and Management see http://www.managementschool.uhi.ac.uk/cpd/programme/116/sector /4/MSc-in-leadership-and-management.

## RESOURCE: PHOTO SHARING

Photograph sharing is the publishing or transfer of a user's digital photographs online, thus enabling the user to share them with others (whether publicly or privately). This functionality is provided through both websites and applications that facilitate the upload and display of images (see www.flickr.com and www.picasa.com). The term can also be loosely applied to the use of online photo galleries that are set up and managed by individual users, including photoblogs (see www.blipfoto. com). While photoblogs tend only to display a chronological view of user-selected medium-sized photos, most photo sharing sites provide multiple views (such as thumbnails and slideshows), have the ability to classify photos into albums as well as add annotations (such as captions or tags) and comments. Some photo sharing sites provide complete online organisation tools equivalent to desktop photo-management applications.

Flickr is currently the most popular site for photo sharing and, like other web 2.0 applications, has added features from other tools to make an online community platform. For example, the addition of tags, allowing browsing of photos by categories, has fuelled its popularity, and the service is widely used by bloggers as a photo repository. It also has a lesser-known feature that has many potential uses for teaching and learning: the ability to add annotations to an image. Another feature is the facility for setting up groups—either public, public (invitation only), or completely private. Every group has a pool for sharing photos and a discussion board for talking.

Flickr and several other sites provide rapid access to images tagged with the most popular keywords. Because of its support for user-generated tags, Flickr repeatedly has been cited as a prime example of effective use of folksonomy. It was also the first site to implement the use of tag clouds, which are a visual depiction of content tags used on a website. The more frequently used tags are depicted in a larger font or otherwise emphasised, while the displayed order is generally alphabetical. Thus finding a tag is possible by either alphabet or by popularity. Selecting a single tag within a tag cloud will generally lead to a collection of items that are associated with that tag.

Flickr also allows users to categorise their photos into sets or groups of photos that fall under the same heading. However, sets are more flexible than the traditional folder-based method of organizing files, as one photo can belong to one set, many sets, or none at all. Flickr's sets represent a form of categorical metadata rather than a physical hierarchy. Sets may be grouped into collections, and collections further grouped into higher-order collections. Images can be posted to the user's collection via email attachments, enabling direct uploads from many camera phones and applications with email capabilities.

Privacy can be managed by setting each photo according to one of the following:

- *Privacy level*, which determines who can see the image;
- *Usage license*, so copyrights are protected;
- *Content type*, flags photos as either photos, artwork/illustrations, or screenshots;
- *Safety level*, so other members only see images within their specified comfort zones.

### The Educational Challenge

Flickr contains imagery that can be used in every aspect of teaching to help develop visual literacy skills, and in the process, help students understand intellectual property rights, while contributing greatly to a host of learning applications. Every subject area can be enlivened by the appropriate use of images.

Flickr clustering allows clustering of ideas so that a particular word can be clustered in numerous ways. This feature can be the focus of a useful educational game whereby students list all the related tags (categories) that they can think of for a particular concept. Then, using the clustering facility, they analyse the different ways the word has been used by people to tag different concepts. This type of inference thinking helps to broaden the students' thinking and helps them to think in terms of connections instead of one isolated term. They have to compare and contrast tags.

### Strengths of the Resource

Though there are many ways of using images currently within web-based teaching material, Flickr is a lightweight and simple tool that people can use to quickly add images to their courses.

Flickr has increasingly been adopted by many web users as their primary photo storage site, especially members of the weblog community. In addition, it is popular with Macintosh and Linux users, who are often locked out of photo-sharing sites because they require the Windows/Internet Explorer setup to work.

Staff members who have a blog often prefer to host their personal photos on sites such as Flickr, Picasa and/or Blipfoto rather than on their institutional website.

### Potential Disadvantages

Photo sharing is open to the problem of inappropriate and sexual images being easily available. While some people feel that this rules out many photo-sharing sites for educational use, others think that a better approach is to discuss the issue directly with students. It helps them to think critically about something that is going to be a commonplace experience for them on the Internet. Despite the use of filters, students are going to encounter material that adults deem inappropriate. It is the job of educators to teach them how to deal with that. And unfortunately, blocking sites does not teach students what they need to know.

### Key Points for Effective Practice

- Use the notes facility of Flickr to encourage students to comment on an image, prompted by specific questions from the instructor. The students can then actively engage with the image and think about and discuss specific aspects.

- Devise activities for students to create their own image sets and slideshows, and to make presentations to their peers. They can either use their own photos or take advantage of Flickr's tagging system to find images to use as content.
- Develop activities in which students have to browse tags and set requirements to analyse how they have been used.

## Selected References

Flickr: Teaching and Learning Possibilities. (n.d.). Retrieved from http://ltc.umani-toba.ca/wiki/index.php?title=Flickr

Flickr vs Google: Educational Application Analysis. (n.d.). Retrieved from http://edu-withtechn.blogspot.com/2006/10/flickr-vs-google-educational.html

Education Podcast Reflections. (n.d.). Retrieved from http://booruch.libsyn.com/index.php?post_id=103547

Pedagogical uses of Flickr. (2009). Retrieved from http://sites.wiki.ubc.ca/etec510/Pedagogical_Uses_of_Flickr

### Institution: Fashion Institute of Technology, State University of New York, New York City

*How It Works in Practice.* This is an online course for distance students who use the commenting function in Flickr to add hot-spot annotations to an image. Once an image has been published on Flickr, users can draw hotspots on the image and then attach a note to those hotspots. Whenever a user moves the cursor over any of the hotspots, the annotations appear. In this case, the subject is art history and Flickr allows students to annotate famous paintings by attaching layers of notes and markings directly on the image. If asked to find the symbolism in a 15th-century Flemish painting, students can create boxes around the portions of the painting they want to talk about and put comments on the picture. Other students can then mouse over the same picture and see the annotations or pull the mouse back and see the entire painting. The process can make grading and evaluating students a bit more complex, but this is a minor drawback because the visual dimension provides a more interesting, fun and useful way to learn. It breaks down the classroom walls and creates an entirely new collaborative experience for distance students.

*Lessons Learned.* "The problem when you teach online is that you can't, for example, point to a part of a painting in the way you would in a face-to-face classroom," one instructor says. "So it occurred to me that I could use Flickr's annotation function to have students engage more directly with the work of art itself."

In addition to the use of Flickr, students enrolled in the e-learning courses have access to the other online services: bookstore, library services, online library, technology support, tutoring (for additional information see http://www3.fitnyc.edu/historyofart/bigideas/caa%20 article.pdf).

## RESOURCE: PODCASTING

A podcast is an audio file which can be downloaded and listened to either on an iPod or MP3 player for mobile study or a computer or lap-top for location-based study. Podcasting commonly refers to "any soft-ware and hardware combination that permits automatic downloading of audio files (most commonly in MP3 format) for listening at the user's convenience" (Gormley & Tooher, 2009, p. 4). Video podcasts (some-times abbreviated to vidcast or vodcast) are also possible and useful for referring to visual material or for accompanying PowerPoint slides. A blogcast is a blend of two tools—blogging and podcasting. The blog contains associated text and makes the podcast able to be indexed by search engines.

The term podcasting is a combination of iPod (Apple Computer's portable media player) and broadcasting. As with the term radio, pod-casting can refer to either the content or the process. Anyone with access to the Internet and the capability of playing audio files on a com-puter or any portable media device can listen to podcasts.

### The Educational Challenge

Podcasting represents an exciting challenge in that it empowers stu-dents to create content and take part in authentic learning projects. In other words, students can be active learners, not passive consumers of information. There are uses of podcasting for assessment, as part of e-portfolios and as collaborative projects. For example, students can conduct oral histories and create podcasts which are then used to pres-ent their work. Other examples involve students creating reports, his-torical interpretations, or scientific narratives.

Universities can make podcasts of special lectures, cross-cultural exchanges, guest speeches or other events, and make these widely available to students. A number of institutions are using podcasts of all lectures as a way of providing access for certain kinds of disabled stu-dents, and incidentally for all students as a method of review or access to missed lectures. For distance or distributed institutions, podcasting offers a way of providing a richer environment than text for remote students. Podcasts can be used to provide lecture content, thereby freeing more time for discussion.

Research has also indicated that educators have experimented with podcasting as a way to expose students to additional course content in engaging formats. They have created course podcasts that are mock radio programmes, case studies, and interviews with national and international figures (Cheetham. Ackerman, & Christoph, 2009).

The ready availability of podcasts on the Internet provides a resource for teachers to add global perspectives to their teaching through adding podcasts to their reading lists.

### Strengths of the Resource

- The ability to listen to material multiple times;
- Flexibility and portability (when and where to listen);
- Audio resources for blind and distance education students;
- Varied opportunities for student-generated content;
- Relatively low cost, low-barrier tool for both students and teachers;
- Easy to create and access;
- Ideal for short pre-class listening segments; for example, to address students' preconceptions;
- Good use of "dead time" while travelling or even walking between classes.

Compared with written text, the spoken word can influence both cognition (adding clarity and meaning) and motivation by conveying directly a sense of the person creating those words. Audio is an extremely powerful medium for conveying feelings, attitudes and atmosphere.

Listening to an iPod or similar device in public is now common practice and hence socially acceptable. These devices have a tremendous consumer appeal that works to their advantage, particularly for younger students who may be impatient with traditional forms of teaching and learning. Smart phones now incorporate MP3 and MP4 features and also can allow students to access VLE apps directly to their location. For distance students, the strength of podcasting lies in the potency of voice communication, which cuts through the dense text of the Internet and offers a human connection. Tutors, professors, and librarians are using podcasting for myriad training and learning situations, for example, podcasts of academic journal digests, and vodcasts demonstrating how to use software and operating systems.

## *Potential Disadvantages*

- The shortcomings of audio in general appear to be in the area of providing complex or detailed information that needs to be heavily processed, logically deconstructed, committed to memory, or otherwise requires a great deal of concentration.
- It is less good at conveying detail and facts, in that we do not remember facts and figures from audio as easily as general opinions and arguments.
- Unlike text, audio is hard to browse and hence is a less efficient use of study time than text.
- Copyright is a potential issue if podcasts are available outside institutional firewalls. Searchability is also potentially problematic as numbers of podcasts increase. Likewise, where should podcasts be archived, and who should support this? Although increasingly universities are either placing podcasts within their own VLE or within iTunes itself.
- In higher education, podcasting has been widely identified with recording lectures and then uploading them as podcasts. Unfortunately, this single use of podcasting in higher education has seemed to become its identity. This perspective needs to be changed quickly, otherwise podcasting will become just another dissemination medium.
- If a transcript of the podcast is called for—and it usually is, both for deaf students and for students who request it for easier access or review—this adds to the workload in preparing a podcast, although relatively cheap software is available that can convert speech to text.

## *Key Points for Effective Practice*

1. A podcast must be professional and compelling—not the equivalent of shaky home videos. Nevertheless, good podcasting is about the message, the content, not the technology, which should be transparent.
2. Podcasts are great for conveying passion, personality and a limited amount of content. Use text instead if there is a lot of material to cover. Ten minutes maximum per podcast is suggested.
3. Like all technologies, podcasting should supplement and enhance, not replace. The aim should be to more deeply engage the student with the concepts of the course, not to convey basic course material.
4. Tips for keeping the learners' attention include: alternating speakers, surprising turns in the conversation, changing the pace, relating the topic to learners' experience.

5. Devise relevant, authentic, and fun projects for students to make their own podcasts. Integrate with assessment if possible.

### Selected References

Cheetham, J., Ackerman, S., & Christoph, K. (2009). Podcasting: A stepping stone to pedagogical innovation, *EDUCAUSE Quarterly (EQ)*, 32(4). Retrieved from http://www.educause.edu/ero/article/podcasting-stepping-stone-pedagogical-innovation

Gormley, P., & Tooher, M. (2009). Introduction to podcasting: From pilot to mainstream,

Galway, Ireland: Staff Development Workshop, National University of Ireland. King, K., & Gura, M. (2007). *Podcasting for educators*. Greenwich, CT: Information Age.

Morrissey, J. (2012), Podcast steering of independent learning in higher education, *All Ireland Journal of Teaching and Learning in Higher Education (AISHE-J)*, 4(1), 1-7. http://ojs.aishe.org/index.php/aishe-j/article/view/60/45

Salmon, G., Edirisingha, P., Mobbs, M., Mobbs, R., & Dennett, C., (2008). *How to create podcasts for education*, Maidenhead, UK: Open University Press.

### Institution: National University of Ireland, Galway

*How It Works In Practice.*   John Morrissey, a lecturer at the National University of Ireland, used podcasting to steer his students through a final year module on the VLE entitled Contemporary Geopolitics. Morrissey found podcasting to require minimal technical know-how, and the results could very quickly be achieved with little equipment—laptop/desktop, a microphone and sound recording and editing software. Audacity, free sound and recording software, is available online. Therefore, podcasting can be seen to have a high value but low cost (Salmon, Edirisingha, Mobbs, Mobbs, & Dennett, 2008).

Morrissey (2012) found that podcasting was a useful educational tool for three main reasons:

1. prompting independent "deep learning";
2. enabling "constructive alignment" of learning outcomes; and
3. giving effective "student feedback."

Podcasting was used as prompts to provide an overview of each topic within the 12- week programme; to talk through the assessment; provide assessment feedback of a general nature; and guidance on exam preparation. Each podcast was no more than 10 minutes in length.

*Lessons Learned.*   The students found the exam and assignment preparation and feedback podcasts most useful and they accessed it often. However, the re-capping of key concepts was also found to be invaluable. The students found the prompt to further reading of value too. Overall, the use of podcasts allowed for a more innovative approach to engaging students in their learning, and while it did not appeal to all learners, it provided another mechanism whereby differing learning styles can be accommodated.

## RESOURCE: RSS FEEDS

Really Simple Syndication (RSS) is a set of web feed formats used to publish frequently updated content such as blog and wiki entries, news headlines, or podcasts. The RSS feed contains either a summary of the content from the associated site or the full text. This explains the alternative meaning of RSS—Rich Site Summary. The value of RSS feeds is that they make it possible for people to keep up-to-date with their favourite websites in an automated manner rather than having to check them manually. In this sense, RSS feeds could be called a "personal newspaper."

The popularity of blogs and wikis has led to the increased use of RSS feeds; however, they can be used to deliver a great variety of content and even media types. RSS content is read using either a feed reader or an aggregator. The user subscribes to a feed by entering the feed's link into the reader or by clicking an RSS icon in a browser that initiates the subscription process. The reader checks the user's subscribed feeds regularly for new content, downloading any updates that it finds.

In many ways, RSS answers the question of how to filter and organise the vast amount of information on the web. Internet users tend to settle on preferred sources of information, whether news sites, blogs, wikis, or other online resources that regularly update content. RSS allows users to create a list of those sources in an application that automatically retrieves updates, saving considerable time and effort. RSS feeds can be offered at varying levels of granularity, further enhancing users' ability to specify exactly what information they want to receive. For example, a college or university might offer one RSS feed for the institution's main news page, sharing information that concerns the institution broadly, and other feeds focused on the college of arts and sciences, the history department, or research being conducted by a professor of European history. Users can subscribe to feeds independently, tailoring the content they receive to their unique interests and needs. There are even feeds that aggregate other feeds.

Growing numbers of online resources offer RSS functionality. Because applications such as browsers and operating systems increasingly support RSS, the technology has the potential to become the primary vehicle through which users interact with the Internet.

An RSS file will typically display the most recent content of a website, usually 10 items or so, updated whenever a new item is added. An aggregator will check a large number of individual RSS files, returning to a given site once an hour or so. Consequently, when new material is published to a news site or weblog, it is very quickly picked up and distributed.

Though most readers use RSS by turning to an aggregator website, many others use applications known as *headline readers.* A headline reader performs the same function as an aggregator, but is a stand-alone application that usually resides on the reader's own computer (though some are stand-alone websites). Desktop readers frequently divide the screen into three panes and show

- a list of RSS feeds to which a reader subscribes;
- a list of titles from the currently selected feed;
- the text of the currently selected item.

### The Educational Challenge

Finding suitable news feeds is relatively easy; in many cases websites will advertise that they have available RSS news feeds and will also provide addresses, instructions and examples of their use. In addition, there are directories of news feeds to find a suitable feed for a particular subject area.

Students involved in cutting edge research projects can use RSS to monitor news and search engines for specific keywords (like nanotechnology or coldfusion) by creating search feeds. Any time a mention of the keyword phrase occurs in a news piece the item will appear in the search feed. Furthermore, collaborative projects using online tools with a distributed team can use RSS feels to notify each other of new contributions to the site.

Students writing papers or doing research papers on specific topics can create search feeds, so that each time that topic is mentioned they receive notification in their custom search feed.

### Strengths of the Resource

For users of RSS feeds, the most commonly expressed benefit is convenience. RSS headline readers automatically flag new items, so users need not search through a number of websites looking for new content.

Additionally, content is displayed first as a summary description, allowing users to browse quickly through numerous items. RSS readers also provide users with more choice and control because they can determine whether or not to subscribe to a given feed. And unlike e-mail newsletters, which RSS feeds most resemble, the feeds do not contain spam or viruses.

The strength of RSS is its simplicity, flexibility, and utility. Although RSS is not the semantic web originally dreamed of in the laboratory, it is currently the closest example and provides some of the benefits of the original dream.

A particular strength of RSS is that it effectively nullifies spam, which is an increasing problem with e-mail. Furthermore, users can easily opt-in and out of feeds that provide content of interest or importance. Compared with the relative difficulty of unsubscribing from e-mail lists, RSS feeds bring control back into the hands of the end-user. Experience has shown that RSS feeds in education are particularly attractive for use on mobile devices, where the speed, convenience, and adaptability of the message is easily accessed.

### Potential Disadvantages

To take advantage of RSS feeds, users must locate online sources they trust, which can be a time-consuming task. Even if a site is deemed reliable, it may not offer RSS feeds. Moreover, relying totally on RSS feeds reduces the serendipity that comes from browsing websites and finding unexpected resources.

Not all content is appropriate for RSS, and users need to set up their feeds with care by selecting sites which are frequently updated.

While there are no inherent accessibility problems with the RSS file format, the method by which an RSS feed is displayed does have accessibility implications. A wide range of applications exist that aggregate and display. How accessible they are will be dependent on the application themselves, the operating system on which they run, and, if applicable, the assistive device being used.

### Key Points for Effective Practice

1. Use the many how to manuals, such as the one listed in the Selected References, to get started.
2. Search for sites useful to your subject matter.
3. If you have 20 to 30 students posting their work to a wiki, blog, Flickr or other site, instead of checking all 30 sites, you can subscribe to

their RSS feeds using an aggregator and view it all from the one place.

4. Encourage students to set up their own feeds, particularly when working on collaborative projects.

### Selected References

*A Quick Start Guide for Educators.* (n.d.). Retrieved from http://weblogg-ed.com/wp-content/uploads/2006/05/RSSFAQ4.pdf

De Maio, C., Fenza, G., Gaeta, M., Loia, V., Orciuoli, F., & Senatore, S. (2012). RSS-based e-learning recommendations exploiting fuzzy FCA for knowledge modelling. *Applied Soft Computing, 12,* 113-124.

Kyrnin, J. (n.d.). What is RSS? Retrieved from http://webdesign.about.com/od/rss/a/what_is_rss.htm

Lan, Y-F. & Sie, Y-S. (2010). Using RSS to support mobile learning based on media richness theory. *Computers in Education, 55,* 723-732.

### Institution: Athabasca University, Canada: Combining RSS with Blogging Software

*How It Works in Practice.* In 2001, Athabasca University's Centre for Distance Education made RSS conversions of all of its online materials that require occasional updating. Twenty courses, involving syllabi, assignment pages, and faculty bios, were installed at a private account on Blogger.com, using a common template developed for the Centre's website. Each page was made accessible to the faculty member responsible for its upkeep. Instead of having to send updated information to a programmer, the faculty member sends it directly to the web, without needing to touch any of its page code. The Centre set up a virtual server to receive these updates, in order to avoid compromising the file transfer passwords of the University's secure server.

*Lessons Learned.* The result was an immediate increase in departmental speed and job satisfaction. For the webmaster responsible for maintaining the online course sites, the update process for each teaching semester was reduced from two weeks to a single day. For the individual faculty members, the amount of time spent on the updates was the same, though they now had ownership of them, rather than having to refer hack editing work to the media team. For the editing and programming mediators, the result has been an easing of their workload, and the ability to concentrate on developing new course design methods (for additional information see, http://technologysource.org/article/blogging_as_a_course_ management_tool/).

## RESOURCE: SECOND LIFE

Designed by Linden Lab in California and first opened to the public in 2003, Second Life (SL) is a 3-D multi-user virtual environment. It is a user-defined world, owned by its residents, in which people explore, communicate, and do business. Second Life has over 18 million accounts registered, and between 30,000 and 70,000 daily users. More surprisingly, Second Life supports a fully integrated marketplace in which transactions involving millions of Linden dollars, which can be bought with US dollars, take place. The residents create and retain intellectual property rights on their own virtual goods and services. It is possible to sell one's virtual goods and services on "real" sites such as eBay, and Second Life has produced a number of millionaires as a result of its virtual economy.

Given these components, it may not appear initially to have significant educational potential. However, the ease with which users generate content appears to be a particular draw for Second Life in a range of educational projects, especially business and marketing programmes. Each user creates an avatar and personalises it to represent them in this virtual world. Avatars walk, fly and gesture, and may resemble the user's real-world appearance or appear very different. Avatars can communicate by local and group chat and by Global Instant Messaging (IM), share files and documents, and now by voice at local and IM levels. This kind of virtual presence can help the development of community especially for distance education. Second Life is not a game. It has no goal, and most resources are not restricted. Characters move through space or breathe water, and they never age or die. Massively multi-user virtual environments such as Second Life are a new type of collaborative workspace.

Adepts are convinced of the future applications of this first example of a mass market virtual reality. In fact, many see Second Life as taking web 2.0 into web 3.0 or even web 3.D! Businesses are seeing the potential of some of the broader applications for Second Life. For example, IBM uses SL to host virtual conferences and test new concepts with customers. However, it should be noted that, although numbers of daily users continued to rise from inception to 2010, according to the Second Life Grid Survey (2011, 2012), the numbers have plateaued and even fallen, which might suggest the popularity of Second Life could be diminishing.

### The Educational Challenge

Second Life provides a unique and flexible environment for educators interested in distance learning, computer-supported cooperative work, simulation, new media studies, and corporate training. Using Second Life as a supplement to traditional classroom environments also provides new opportunities for enriching existing curricula. For distance education, Second Life offers an opportunity to weave in real-time activities.

Besides improving the quality of distance learning, educators are finding that Second Life is a good way to introduce international perspectives. Students from around the world can join in discussions and work on team projects. Unlike online forums, students in Second Life cannot "lurk." Their presence is visible to all. The quality of interaction in Second Life is what distinguishes it from online forums and online games—it does not replace face to face communication, but it is more engaging than text-based communication.

Second Life provides an opportunity to use simulation in a safe environment to enhance experiential learning, allowing individuals to practice skills, try new ideas, and learn from their mistakes. The ability to prepare for similar real-world experiences by using Second Life as a simulation has unlimited potential! Many predict that real and virtual worlds will merge, and we will become used to the "Metaverse" as a part of our everyday life. More and more people will work in virtual worlds. Instead of frustrating hours in traffic jams to reach the workplace, work will take place in a virtual office, perhaps located on the other side of the world.

### Strengths of the Resource

The wide availability, global reach, and low barrier to entry are the essential qualities that make it a useful educational tool. It offers opportunities to use simulation and the immersion experience is very powerful. Students can develop informal spaces in which they can interact socially, and also create communities of practice.

Synchronised discussions appeal to both extrovert and introvert learners as confident students can get instant feedback from each other and tutors; and more shy students are able to "read" transcripts of chat before responding.

Educators can create virtual worlds which are far more "realistic" than text books and case studies. It allows students to make "real" mistakes without "real" consequences.

Private islands provide users the ability to create secure intranet spaces with restricted membership for students and faculty. Islands can also open up to be accessible to everyone logged in to SL. This has the potential to be of extreme benefit to professionals located anywhere in the world who can collaborate on projects and also create spaces where students from different locations can meet and interact.

There is a "Help Island" with volunteer mentors to help students navigate, change their avatar's appearance, learn how to build, and so on.

### Potential Disadvantages

While Second Life is relatively easy to use, without a solid foundation, students can struggle while trying to acquire the navigational skills necessary to complete assignments. Frustration can lead to disengagement and then it is hard to encourage students to re-engage. The benefit of being entirely user-driven has the disadvantage that it depends entirely on users to make it a learning experience. It is essentially a blank space. It requires a competent instructor to create spaces and activities which will retain student engagement and this can be very time-consuming.

The technological requirements of SL rely on a certain level of bandwidth and computer capability which may not be available to all students—particularly those in remote areas.

SL does require collaboration and working with peers and this might not be suitable for all types of students, who may actually have chosen distance learning precisely because it affords them a certain amount of anonymity.

When made available, SL is an external resource within most educational establishments, and as such, if there are technical issues with the site, then there is a reliance on an external body to rectify and this can mean that students and lecturers are not able to use SL effectively. It is recommended that any use of SL as an educational tool also has alternative teaching opportunities within internal virtual learning environments.

The appropriateness of some Second Life content for students is an issue. As with the web itself, there is a range of seedy activity available to users: gambling, stripping, and virtual prostitution are easy to find if you look for them. Partially because of that, Linden Lab has set up a teen version of the world, known as Teen Second Life. There is also an issue of the informality and possibly inappropriate design of avatars that could be considered offensive by other users.

## Key Points for Effective Practice

- There are many tutorials and Second Life support material available to help students become proficient users.
- Second Life provides an opportunity to think outside the box, to practice the true constructivist principles, and to empower students to learn rather than be taught.
- Instructor training, presence is needed for it to be truly effective.

## Selected References

Baker, S. C., Wentz, R. K., & Woods, M. M. (2009). Using virtual worlds in education: Second Life® as an educational tool. *Teaching of Psychology, 36*(1), 59–64.

Buckless, F., Krawczyk, K., & Showalter, S. (2012). Accounting education in the Second Life world. *CPA Journal, 82*(3), 68–71.

Cargill-Kipar, N. (2009). My dragonfly flies upside down! Using Second Life in multimedia design to teach students programming. *British Journal of Educational Technology, 40*(3), 539–542.

Robbins, S., & Bell, M. (2008). *Second life for dummies*. London: Wiley.

Rudestam, K. E., & Schoenholtz-Read, J. (Eds.). (2010). *Handbook of online learning* (2nd ed.). Thousand Oaks, CA: Sage.

Second Life and Education. (n.d.). Retrieved from http://secondlife.onmason.com/second-life-education/

Second Life for Education. (n.d.). Retrieved from http://wiki.secondlife.com/wiki/Second_Life_Education

Second Life Grid Survey—Economics Metrics. (2011, 2012). Linden Lab. Retrieved from http://www.gridsurvey.com/economy.php

## Institution: North Carolina State University, Raleigh: Masters of Accounting (MAC)

*How It Works in Practice.* North Carolina State University (NC State) used Second Life to provide office hours for two courses, a cost accounting simulation, a financial accounting research case, and an inventory observation audit simulation. The latter was used to teach auditing to undergraduate and graduate accounting students in 2010 and 2011.

The NC State's accounting department used Second Life to develop and host an inventory observation audit simulation for use in the undergraduate and graduate auditing courses.

Students were provided with traditional audit documentation for a hypothetical beer manufacturer, including:

- a physical inventory observation programme;
- a memo discussing a client's physical inventory observation process;

- the client's inventory count instructions for count teams; and
- the client's inventory count worksheet.

Students were required to "visit" the beer company's warehouse and observe inventory in various forms through SL. The students were able to work in teams at times, which suited all members, and really experience carrying out an inventory.

*Lessons Learned.*   While most students enjoyed the experience of using Second Life as it provided realistic opportunities to learn in a safe environment, all experienced some problems with using the system. The accounting department realised that it is vital to discuss SL with users early and often. Inform students of minimum computer specifications to allow SL to work on their machines. Encourage users to create appropriate avatars that resemble themselves and can be recognised by other members of the student group. Ensure students are provided with multiple opportunities to engage with SL so they see it as an integral part of their learning and not merely a time-consuming addition.

NC State found that they had made assumptions about the confidence students would have in using SL. However, results showed that students required far more support and encouragement than originally thought; this could be a barrier to effective use if not tackled appropriately.

However, overall, the accounting department at NC State believes they have only just scratched the surface in terms of uses for Second Life both in terms of educational and training opportunities and business ventures.

## RESOURCE: SOCIAL BOOKMARKING

In a social bookmarking system, users store lists of Internet resources that they find useful. These lists are accessible either to the public or to a specific group, and other people with similar interests can view the links by category, tags, or even randomly. Some allow for privacy on a per-bookmark basis. Users categorise their resources by the use of informally assigned, user-defined keywords or tags. Most social bookmarking services allow users to search for bookmarks which are associated with given tags, and rank the resources by the number of users which have bookmarked them. Many social bookmarking services also have implemented algorithms to draw inferences from the tag keywords that are assigned to resources by examining the clustering of particular keywords, and the relation of keywords to one another.

The increasing popularity of social bookmarking and the growth of competitor sites has led to services extending their facilities to offer more than just sharing bookmarks, such as rating, commenting, the ability to import and export, add notes, reviews, e-mail links, automatic notification, feed subscription, web annotation, and creating groups and social networks. Since the classification and ranking of resources is a continuously evolving process, many social bookmarking services allow users to subscribe to web feeds (see RSS) based on tags, or a collection of tag terms. This allows subscribers to become aware of new resources for a given topic, as they are noted, tagged, and classified by other users.

Social bookmarking sprang mainly from academic roots and a personal desire to share links and bookmarks with like-minded individuals. Collaborative bookmarking has arisen predominantly from the organisational desire to glean information or knowledge from workers with the hope of storing and retransmitting that knowledge to other workers, particularly at the time that the knowledge or information is needed. Collaborative bookmarking is as much about linking people together as it is about linking people to relevant websites.

Tags are one-word descriptors that you can assign to your bookmarks. They are like keywords but are non-hierarchical. You can assign as many tags to a bookmark as you like and easily rename or delete them later. Tagging can be a lot easier and more flexible than fitting your information into preconceived categories or folders.

Collaborative tagging is regarded as democratic folksonomy metadata generation, i.e., rather than an individual controlling the metadata or tags about an article or other content, metadata is generated by both the creator and consumers of the content. This caters to the long tail of search terminology by deliberately introducing minority keywords and removes the restriction placed on the content of metadata by a controlled vocabulary. Although a collaborative tagging system is more likely to generate meta-noise (i.e., superfluous metadata), this adds to the usefulness of the metadata as it continues to cater to the "thin end" of the long tail of system users.

## The Educational Challenge

There are a number of ways in which social bookmarking can be useful in teaching and learning. Groups can set up a network to share resources they find over a period of time working on a joint project. Experts can share their bookmarks with novices. Individual students can share their resources with their peers. Managing the mass of information on the Internet is extremely difficult and social bookmarking is a simple way for sharing the burden.

Social bookmarking is an ideal tool for research as it allows the user to keep track of all source materials and commentaries found online. The researcher can even tag the bookmarks with asterisks to indicate quality or usefulness.

In browsing the web, users finding a podcast they want to mark for later listening, can simply add it to their bookmarks.

Users of del.icio.us, a popular social bookmarking site, can save interesting websites and add a bit of commentary to create a lightweight link-log. This can then be added to the user's blog or website.

### Strengths of the Resource

Ease of use is again an important feature of social bookmarking, as it is with most of the other web 2.0 tools described in this book. An additional benefit is that the user's bookmarks can be accessed from any machine, whether at home, at work, in a library, or on a friend's computer. There is nothing to download or install.

Bookmarks can be shared publicly, so your friends, co-workers, and other people can view them for reference, amusement, collaboration, or anything else. Similarly, users can find other people who have interesting bookmarks and add those links to their own collection. Additionally, as people bookmark resources that they find useful, resources that are of more use are bookmarked by more users. Thus, such a system will "rank" a resource based on its perceived utility. This is arguably a more useful metric for end users than other systems which rank resources based on the number of external links pointing to it.

Social bookmarking has several advantages over traditional automated resource location and classification software, such as search engine spiders. All tag-based classification of Internet resources (such as websites) is done by the users, who understand the content of the resource, as opposed to software which algorithmically attempts to determine the meaning of a resource. This provides for semantically classified tags, which are hard to find with contemporary search engines.

### Potential Disadvantages

There are drawbacks to tag-based systems:

- There is no standard set of keywords (also known as controlled vocabulary).

- There is no standard for the structure of such tags (e.g., singular vs. plural, capitalization, etc.).
- Mistagging takes place due to spelling errors.
- There are tags that can have more than one meaning.
- There are unclear tags due to synonym/antonym confusion.
- Some users provide highly unorthodox and "personalised" tag schemas.
- There is no mechanism for users to indicate hierarchical relationships between tags (e.g., a site might be labelled as both *cheese* and *cheddar*, with no mechanism that might indicate that *cheddar* is a refinement or subclass of *cheese*).

Social bookmarking can also be susceptible to corruption and collusion. Due to its popularity, some users have started considering it as a tool to use along with search engine optimization to make their website visible. The more a web page is submitted and tagged, the more chances it has of being found. Spammers have started bookmarking multiple times the same web page or each page of their website using a lot of popular tags, hence obliging the developers to constantly adjust their security system to overcome abuses.

## Key Points for Effective Practice

- Use a folksonomy-based tool for research and take advantage of the insights of other users to find information related to the topic you are researching, even in areas that are not obviously connected to the primary topic.
- Develop activities for students in which they have to consider how information is or should be classified.
- Consider a course-based site that provides selected reading, week by week, for classes or cohorts studying a particular programme.

## Selected References

Behan, A., & Boylan, F. (2009). Harnessing developments in technology and merging them with new approaches to teaching: A practical example of the effective use of wikis and social bookmarking sites in 3rd level professional education. *Articles*. Paper 4. Retrieved from http://arrow.dit.ie/beschspart/4

Farwell, T. M., & Waters, R. D. (2010). Exploring the use of social bookmarking technology in education: An analysis of students' experiences using a course-specific Delicious.com account. *Journal of Online Learning and Teaching, 6*(2), 398–408.

Hammond, T., Hannay, T., Lund, B., & Scott, J. (2005). Social bookmarking tools (1), a general review. *D-Lib Magazine, 11*(4). Retrieved from http://www.dlib.org/dlib/april05/hammond/04hammond.html

Iskold, A. (2006, September). The social bookmarking faceoff . *Read/WriteWeb,*. Retrieved from http://www.readwriteweb.com/archives/social_bookmarking_faceoff.php

### Institution: Dublin Institute of Technology: Course on Geomatics

*How It Works In Practice.* The teacher establishes a social bookmarking site to enable the class or subgroup to share references to resources. These resources may be useful websites as well as direct links to specific journal articles relevant to the course and/or group project. The students within each group must collaborate to create an informative wiki in which each individual student adds a contribution to the group project. The resources added to the social bookmarking site are able to be shared by all group members, who can also add their own favourite resources. Allowing each member of the group to share all the resources enables research initiated by one member of the group to be continued by others in a manner that is efficient and relatively seamless.

*Lessons Learned.* Some students may not be aware of the techniques of social bookmarking, so it will be necessary to give a brief outline on how to establish and manage the site. Some guidelines may also be advisable on the establishment of common tagging procedures (e.g., no plurals or use_of_underscoring to make phrases, etc.) Some users have created one account for an entire class, with a common user-name and password—others have encouraged students to use their own accounts that will remain with them longer than the duration of the course. The use of common tags, e.g., "week one" to structure the collection of bookmarks is advisable.

## RESOURCE: SOCIAL NETWORKING

Social networking sites, such as MySpace and Facebook, have become incredibly popular with young people almost overnight. They offer an interactive, user-submitted network of friends, personal profiles, blogs, groups, photos, music, and videos internationally. There are many such sites, some more specialised than others and some very much more popular than others. MySpace.com was an extremely popular, general social networking site that allowed members to set up unique personal profiles that could be linked together through networks of friends. It overtook Google as the most visited site in the United States in 2006, however, since then its numbers have declined, and, in 2008, MySpace was overtaken by Facebook in terms of numbers of worldwide users. Similar to MySpace, Facebook members can view each other's profiles, communicate with old friends and meet new friends on the service, share photos, post journals and comments, and describe their interests. People may then elect to join one or more participating networks, such as a high school, place of employment, or geographic region.

When logging into Facebook, one reaches one's homepage on which is a newsfeed of all the comments or "status" messages from all the "friends" you have. This can be filtered in terms of most recent or top stories, and you can choose to have a newsfeed that only includes status of your "favourite" friends. There is also an instant messaging or chat service, and one can choose to be on or offline; the service will show if you are available to chat or not. Interest groups, ranging from religion and politics, to lovers of cake or a particular genre of music, can be created by anyone, and you can decide who is able to join or if it can be made open to anyone. There is also a private messaging service where one can send messages that will not be seen by anyone other than the respondent. Also there is a "poke" facility. This tells a friend that you have poked them and acts as a way of letting people know you are thinking of them or that you want to attract their attention without having to send any text. Your own "profile" pages can be customised to say as little or as much about you as you would like. Privacy settings are now quite complicated but do mean that, if done correctly, that initial scares about public access have been allayed as various filters ensure that your profile can remain locked down and only accessible to those who you choose.

Facebook, which was originally developed for college and university students, but has since been made available to anyone with an email address, has grown enormously and currently has over 800 million members. It is the second most popular website after Google. Facebook's success is one that has attracted considerable interest. According to Fogg and Eckles (2008), Facebook contains the three essential components of behavioural action: motivation, ability and trigger. As more people heard of Facebook, it became the place to be to communicate with others, and not being "connected" in this way might mean you were missing something. Whilst some of the tools on Facebook are still relatively complicated for the novice user, increasingly the software designers are making it more and more user-friendly. Finally, in terms of the trigger, Facebook is readily available on one's phone or PC, and you can be alerted when you have been sent a message, someone wants to be your friend, or you are tagged in a photo. Smart phones are now able to provide a constant newsfeed of everything that is happening in your world—combining world news through news websites like the BBC, world gossip and thoughts and exactly what your friends and family are up to through Twitter—at any given moment.

## *The Educational Challenge*

The rationale for using social networking in education is that teachers have a responsibility to give students skills in how to cope with the virtual relationships and to understand what friendship means in the new social culture created by the web 2.0 environment. It is a well-known fact that the social areas of forums used in higher education receive more messages and visits than do the educational conferences. Since the introduction of educational forums in the 1990s, educators have begun to realise that social communication is an important aspect of learning.

Another rationale for the use of social networking in education is the opportunity it provides for student creativity, both in self-presentation through profiles, and in artistic presentation through photos and music additions to their profiles. In short, the use of social networking in education is an acknowledgement of the social change this phenomenon has spawned. As with the social forums in educational conferencing, networking sites give students the feeling of belonging and the chance to explore their own identity.

## *Strengths of the Resource*

As with other web 2.0 tools, ease of use explains much of their success. Social networking is an asynchronous tool and has many of the same advantages as educational forums: allows flexible access and keeps a written record of communications. With social networking, virtual connections often lead to real, face-to-face connections.

Many observers claim that these types of networks are ingrained in Internet practice now and are here to stay, though the formats will change. The essence of them is the idea of joining online communities and being able to participate in them.

## *Potential Disadvantages*

The volatility of the youthful user base means that social network sites are unusually vulnerable to the next "new new" thing. As quickly as users flock to one trendy Internet site, they can just as quickly move on to another, with no advance warning.

On a more serious note, there is evidence of teachers and employers viewing the profile of a student or prospective employee and seeing a very different persona, which may have negative consequences.

Finally, social networking has become an addictive pastime for many young people as they keep monitoring their site for new activity or comments. Students can do this during lectures and seminars, and whilst most educational institutions now encourage the use of laptops and tablets in the classroom, ensuring students are "learning" and not just catching up with friends, is a difficult task. However, recent research has indicated that the effect of using Facebook by students has a negligible effect on grade point averages (GPA), either positively or negatively (Junco, 2012a).

While social networking is an extremely important medium for Internet users today, there is concern that using this "space" for educational purposes is blurring certain boundaries that students would like to keep separate. However, a recent study found that only 15% of students would feel that their personal space was being invaded if faculty were to use Facebook for educational purposes (Roblyer, McDaniel, Webb, Herman, & Witty, 2010). Moran, Seaman, and Tinti-Kane (2011) found that 77% of faculty uses social media and 60% of faculty reported using social media in class. However, only 4% of faculty surveyed reported using Facebook in class. Interestingly, this may suggest that students are more comfortable with the educational use of Facebook than are their instructors.

While remaining free to users, social networking sites use advertising revenue, however the sheer volume of advertising on sites such as Facebook can be distracting and not appropriate for certain users.

### *Key Points for Effective Practice*

- Rather than blocking students from using social networking in the classroom, teach them how to discern when, where, and for what purpose technology may be appropriate or inappropriate.
- Offer opportunities for students:
    - to discriminate content on social network sites,
    - not to accept profiles at face value,
    - to realise that in addition to one's peers, others—marketers, university authorities, law enforcement personnel can and do access profiles.
- Provide opportunities for discussion about profiles—how to construct them and what it means to "present" oneself online.

- Use social networking as a means to communicate and interact with students and guide them to other sources of information that contain more "academic" content.
- Make use of the Facebook in Education page and downloads in order to see how social networking can best be used for your purposes.
- Meet the students where they are, rather than trying to make them come to you. Instructor disclosure and presence has a positive correlation on student engagement, and this, in itself, is hugely important to academic achievement (Junco, 2012b). Therefore, using Facebook to interact with students at a semi-personal level is advantageous.

### Selected References

Fogg, B. J., & Eckles, D. (Eds.). (2008). *Mobile persuasion*. Stanford, CA: Stanford Captology Media.

Facebook in Education. (n.d.). Retrieved from http://www.facebook.com/education#!/education

Junco, R. (2012a). Too much face and not enough books: The relationship between multiple indices of Facebook use and academic performance. *Computers in Human Behavior, 28*(1), 187-198. Retrieved from http://reyjunco.com/wordpress/pdf/JuncoCHBFacebookGrades.pdf

Junco, R. (2012b). The relationship between frequency of Facebook use, participation in Facebook activities, and student engagement. *Computers & Education, 58*(1), 162-171. http://blog.reyjunco.com/pdf/JuncoFacebookEngagementCAE2011.pdf

Moran, M., Seaman, J., & Tinti-kane, H. (2011). Teaching, learning, and sharing: How today's higher education faculty use social media Babson Park, MA: The Babson Survey Research Group. Retrieved from http://www.pearsonlearningsolutions.com/educators/pearson-social-media-survey-2011-color.pdf

Roblyer, M. D., McDaniel, M., Webb, M., Herman, J., & Witty, J. V. (2010, June). Findings on Facebook in higher education: a comparison of college faculty and student uses and perceptions of social networking sites. *The Internet and Higher Education, 13*(3), 134–140.

### Institution: Melbourne Metropolitan University, Melbourne, Australia

*How It Works In Practice.* In a study to ascertain how first year psychology students used Facebook, and how it could be used to improve overall student engagement, it was found that while the site was used for academic exchanges with peers, this was mostly in the form of asking for help or advice, or a copy of notes, rather than any form of academic debate. University-based groups were prevalent and used for connecting students on the same courses, but also for recreational pursuits and merely to find out about things going on around the campus. The 392 respondents to a questionnaire were also assessed in terms of their personality traits, to ascertain how traits might influence Facebook usage.

*Lessons Learned.* Students with higher extroversion scores are more likely to have more friends on Facebook and belong to more groups. They interact with their friends through instant messaging and update their status regularly. Those with high neuroticism scores also have many friends, but do not interact as much. They use Facebook as a means to keep in touch with what people are doing but without actually having to engage with them. More introverted students had less friends and also did not engage very much, and also said less about themselves on their profile pages. This suggests that personality traits are significant in how students use Facebook, and therefore any attempt to use it as an educating tool needs to take this into account. Social interaction in a uniform sense is not a given.

While some students use Facebook constantly and it is a distraction in class, others are able to tune in and out of it with ease. Again, finding the balance here is an important element in making sure that some students are not "too" engaged, whilst others do not engage at all. Also those who score highly in social engagement may score very low in academic engagement, and vice versa, so this may mean targeting different students with different forms of interaction.

There is a complete lack of control over what Facebook looks like for instructors—they can play no part in its construction, and therefore have to make content fit the tool, and it is not necessarily fit for purpose. At least within a VLE, there is more scope for designing activities and dealing with different types of personality and engagement than there is within a social networking site. However, VLEs should interface with Facebook to make the student's path to all connections seamless.

The research indicates that Facebook may not provide the necessary attributes to encourage greater academic student engagement, and that Twitter may be a more fruitful tool as it is designed to be concise and to provide a constant information flow in a way that Facebook does not. Twitter is less about social interaction per se, and more about exchanging information and knowledge, which is more congruent with successful learning.

### Selected Reference

Wise, L. Z., Skues, J., & Williams, B. (2011). Facebook in higher education promotes social but not academic engagement. In G. Williams, P. Statham, N. Brown, & B. Cleland (Eds.), *Changing demands, changing directions. Proceedings ascilite*

*Hobart 2011: Concise Paper* (pp. 1332–1342). Retrieved from http://www.ascilite. org.au/conferences/hobart11/procs/Wise-full.pdf

## RESOURCE: TWITTER

At its simplest, Twitter is a blogging and online social networking service—sometimes called microblogging because the messages that can be sent by users are restricted to no more than 140 characters. Small files with short messages, web links and/or individual images can be shared, either with another individual user, or among a group of "followers." The number of followers may be restricted to a small personal community—such as students on a course—or a very large number, perhaps following a journalist or celebrity. The messages (called "tweets") can range from insubstantial items in which users post their current thoughts (such as "I am tired") to very focused messages relating to a specific topics (such as commenting on a presentation, programme, or conference). Users can send tweets from their computer, laptop or, more commonly, from their mobile phone, and it is this latter innovation that has seen the number of active users rocket to over 140 million in less than six years since its creation. The ease of use of Twitter means that users range from children to busy professionals, covering multiple languages and almost every conceivable subject of conversation. Twitter users can prefix key words with a hashtag "#" or personal user names with the "@" tag to cluster messages around specific themes or people. The real-time nature of Twitter has given it an immediacy for following events and emergency news stories "as they happen" and as such Twitter has been associated with the reporting of popular civil unrest (e.g., the "Arab Spring") where broadcasting by conventional channels can be difficult.

### *The Educational Challenge*

As a means of communication, Twitter has been used for recommending reading materials to the student body, highlighting course relevance (links to breaking news stories) reminders of events (e.g., seminars) and academic tasks (submission of assignments, reminders of overdue library books). Examples range from participating by posting questions and comments online during a face-to-face class and/or academic conference, to sharing this experience with students/colleagues who are distributed or at a distance remote from the campus. A course-specific account can be created to follow the activities throughout the academic year and communications between students (peer-to-peer) can be encouraged as well as group communication with the teacher. Some experience indicates that quieter (and new) students might feel more comfortable tweeting their questions rather than speaking in front of the class. Student participation in the Twitter group can encourage the feeling of being involved in a learning community, and this fits well with social constructivist ideas of pedagogy and student support. Twitter has the potential to collect feedback from students in real time and to suggest ways in which students can improve their learning experiences.

### Strengths of the Resource

The ease of use is a key strength of this application, and although Twitter offers multi-platform access, the choice of the mobile phone as the preferred access device for Twitter gives this communications tool great flexibility and a potentially almost ubiquitous presence. The demands for concise expression in the messages encourages frequent posting, and the medium is ideal for drawing attention to key points and for giving real-time guidance. The medium encourages free-flowing discussion, so, when clearly focussed on a topic (e.g., a class presentation), there are good opportunities for wide student participation and fostering a learning community with a high level of social presence. The application also has a high potential to enhance interpersonal relations between students and faculty and to encourage the continuation of learning beyond the classroom activities. The ability to rapidly develop a conversation thread enables students to project their own personality and values into the group and exploit the learning benefits of a supportive community of inquiry.

### Potential Disadvantages

A major criticism is that the limitation to 140 characters can "dumb-down" the message to the level of trivia, so some training to encourage concise expression may be necessary, although posting links to personal blogs and further sources of reading or viewing can moderate the difficulty. The immediacy of Twitter tends for it not to be read in the same way as email, so instructors need to be aware that students may not read the message immediately, or may overlook the message if they have a time-gap between the times they check access. The "Twitter feed" constantly updates tweets, and an important message can disappear very quickly if a student is "following" lots of people. The largely informal nature of Twitter communications may mean that the application is best used for learning support to students rather than for teaching, although, when used to direct students to further learning resources, this division may get rather blurred. Like many other online applications, there are background concerns of the possibilities of addiction and overload when users embrace the network communications aspect overeagerly, but as with other applications the remedy is in setting out clearly at induction the netiquette and the discipline required for effective use.

### Key Points for Effective Practice

- The use of Twitter needs to be relevant and meaningful for students—keep the discussion focussed on a specific issue common to the group (e.g., a particular course, or even a particular lecture during that course).
- Utilise the strength of the immediacy of the application to give "just-in-time" advice, guidance, and direction to relevant resources as particular issues surface.
- Encourage the regular participation of all students to foster a vibrant community of inquiry with common interests. Encourage users to write concisely but informatively. Consider extending the core group to include relevant practitioners and professionals to add experience and diversity.

### Selected References

Aspden, E. J., & Thorpe, L .P. (2009). Where do you learn?: Tweeting to inform learning space development. *EDUCAUSE Quarterly*, *32*(1). Retrieved June 11, 2012, from http://www.educause.edu/ero/article/where-do-you-learn-tweeting-inform-learning-space-development

Dunlap, J. C., & Lowenthal, P. R. (2009). Tweeting the night away: Using Twitter to enhance social presence. *Journal of Information Systems Education*, 20(2). Retrieved June 11, 2012, from http://patricklowenthal.com/publications/Using_Twitter_to_Enhance_Social_Presence.pdf

Kesmit3 (2009). The Twitter experiment: University of Texas, Dallas. YouTube. Retrieved June 11, 2012, from http://www.youtube.com/watch?v=6WPVWDkF7U8

McNeil, A. (2010). Twitter in higher education—Case studies of practice, University of Kingston. Retrieved, June 11, 2012, from http://www.scribd.com/doc/27156556/Twitter-HE-Case-Studies

Ramsden, A. (2009). *Using micro-blogging (Twitter) in your teaching and learning: An introductory guide* [Discussion paper]. University of Bath. Retrieved June 11, 2012, from http://opus.bath.ac.uk/15319/1/intro_to_microblogging_09.pdf

Wheeler, S. (2009). Teaching with Twitter. Retrieved June 11, 2012, from http://steve-wheeler.blogspot.com/2009/01/teaching-with-twitter.html

### Institution: Lock Haven University, Lock Haven, Pennsylvania

*How It Works in Practice.* There are a number of good examples of Twitter being used in education—from primary schools through to university level—but while many of these have documented their experiences, there has been little in the way of large-scale systematic research on the application. One systematic study by Junco, Heibergert, and Loken (2011) investigated the link between student engagement (with desired institutional outcomes) and the final grade of the students, at Lock Haven University. Two groups were studied, a control group and one using Twitter to continue conversations not able to be explored fully in class; to encourage Twitter students to participate in asking questions; to stimulate discussion on course reading; for class reminders and organising study sessions, etc. The twitter engagement also included both optional and required assignments that involved carrying out a task and reflecting upon the required reading/viewing. The results concluded that Twitter had a positive effect on student engagement and was an educationally relevant tool to consider for higher education courses.

*Lessons Learned.* The expectations and the ground-rules of use need to be clearly articulated at the start of the course. Probably the best way to engage students is to introduce social networking through Twitter as an optional extra to draw attention to new course resources, then draw-in the more technology-resistant, or less proficient students through clearly showing the advantages of belonging to the learning community. Some motivating interest can also be added by the inclusion of "guest tweets" from noted experts and/or celebrities who can add some fun as well as some opinions to the conversations. It is probably also a good idea to "back-up" the conversations (and any answers, mentions of resources, etc.) to another archive (e.g., a VLE) so as not to disadvantage students who prefer not to use Twitter, or to ensure important information is not lost in a feed. Reports on some experiences of using Twitter have suggested that incorporating Twitter-derived information into formative assessments may encourage students to value the application and to engage more enthusiastically with its possibilities. However, as with many of the technology applications in this book, best results are achieved when the technology introduction is linked to sound pedagogical direction and when there is enthusiastic participation by faculty staff.

*Selected Reference*

Junco, R., Heibergert, G., & Loken, E. (2011). The effect of Twitter on college student engagement and grades. *Journal of Computer Assisted Learning, 27,* 119-132. Retrieved on 13 June 2012 from http://onlinelibrary.wiley.com/doi/10.1111/j.1365-2729.2010.00387.x/pdf

## RESOURCE: VIDEO MESSAGING

There are a range of tools for easy videoconferencing and file sharing amongst a small group of people on the web. Windows Messenger is one example and FlashMeeting, designed by the Knowledge Media Institute at the Open University, is another. There are a growing number of software products that allow video as well as audio connections to enable short synchronous communications (e.g., Facetime, ConferenceMe, or Movi). One of the benefits of these systems is that they are very easy to use from a computer, iPad, iPod, or mobile phone over the web and do not depend on expensive equipment, support staff or installations. In this sense, they are more equivalent to instant messaging than to videoconferencing. As with other web 2.0 tools, it is hard to find a term to describe these tools generically. This is partly because they are evolving so quickly and adding the features and functionalities of other tools, and partly because some names of specific tools come to stand for the whole activity; for example, iPods and podcasting. In this case, what we have called video messaging has characteristics of desktop videoconferencing, of white-boarding, of instant messaging, of Voice over IP (VOIP), and of streaming video. As soon as one tool becomes popular, other very similar ones spring up overnight.

### The Educational Challenge

These tools are ideal for small group tutorials and seminars where students are geographically distributed. Of course, they are real-time tools, but in the case of FlashMeeting at least, it is possible to record and play back a session. This is obviously ideal for students who are unable to join the real-time session. Most of these tools allow only one speaker at a time, thus eliminating any overlaps and confusions. However, the other participants in the group who are not broadcasting may send text messages. FlashMeeting also includes other ways to communicate, such as shared URLs, emoticons, and voting (all things that have little impact on the bandwidth), that can be used while the main broadcast is streaming. The later versions of FlashMeeting also include whiteboard and file upload/download features.

Flashmeeting is already being extensively used by schools in Europe, the United States, and Asia, as it is free to use and offers a secure environment. FlashMeeting is ideal for pupils practicing their language or communications skills and for joint project work in many curriculum areas both on campus and in distributed classrooms.

### Strengths of the Resource

Video messaging is a cost effective way of bringing an international partnership to life as it relies on a basic webcam rather than expensive purpose-built video conference equipment. Video interactions are much richer and more complex than text-only ones, particularly in individual desktop contexts where a number of other parallel communication forms and activities can be freely used alongside the audio-visual channel, in support of, or even antagonistic to it. For example, students can ask questions via instant messaging, or use text chat rooms, shared browsing, virtual whiteboards, and so on, whilst others are speaking over the main video channel.

### Potential Disadvantages

Some of these tools are blocked by firewalls (e.g., Netmeeting), but FlashMeeting has been designed to be firewall-friendly. Broadband is necessary for a video connection, so some students accessing from home will be disadvantaged if they do not have a high speed connection.

### Key Point for Effective Practice

• Devise peer-to-peer activities that benefit from real-time interaction, so that students can experience both receiving and initiating live video.

### Selected References

Instant Messaging Gets the Picture. (n.d.). Retrieved from http://www.pcworld.com/article/id,113025-page,1/article.html

Video Messaging. (n.d.). Retrieved from http://www.zdnet.co.uk/tsearch/video+messaging.htm

### Institution: A Well-Respected Course on Animation Operated by a Prominent U.S.-Based Company

*How It Works in Practice.* Over a six-month-period a group of international students studying animation attended 99 live, online study group events amounting to around 120 hours of live broadcast meeting time. Some meetings were very large, with up to 34 participants, but the average was 10 students. These events were entirely self-organised, policed and managed by the student community. Some students emerged as natural mentors, and the group exhibited substantial supportive, mutually facilitative roles. The use of video meetings on this course was not part of the original design, but was instigated by one of the students. Despite the lack of formal course support for the activity, students operated the events very successfully, providing peer support for each other.

*Lessons Learned.* The contrast between formal and non-formal models of learning is highlighted by this example. With the advent of newer web technologies that enable the Internet learner to seek content and assistance outside a formal program of learning, modes of non-formal work and learning are becoming increasingly interesting.

No external incentives, positive or negative, were provided to the students for the use of this system, and yet over the six-month sample period something like 100 different students spoke online to each other for 120 hours, with 27 of them attending more than 10 different events. They managed this substantial community themselves, taking on appropriate roles within meetings as required and supporting each other's work. Overall, the surprisingly symmetrical patterns in the log data clearly support the users' subjective experience that the events are remarkably peer-to-peer, and shared very evenly within this large community. Even without formal external drivers the students formed and managed a powerful learning model.

It may well be that the subject, animation, is particularly well suited to peer-critique learning, and indeed it does seem that this substantial community has made strikingly good use of it. The students said in interviews, and demonstrated through each event, that live online meetings are extremely powerful in helping them with their work in this non-formal, at-a-distance learning context. The analysis of the log data also clearly illustrates a substantial and longitudinal mutual support and shared use of each other's time and effort.

*Selected Reference*

Peter Scott, P., Quintero, L., Quick, K. & Linney, J. (2007). Symmetrical support in FlashMeeting. Retrieved from http://kmi.open.ac.uk/publications/pdf/kmi-07-01.pdf

# RESOURCE: WIKI

Wikis are collaborative, web-based sites for sharing text and other resources. The significant feature of wikis is their open editing function that allows users to jointly create the resource. The information on a wiki can be edited by any and all users but can be controlled by allowing/denying password access. Superficially, a wiki may appear not dissimilar to any other web page, but the ease with which the wiki web pages can be edited, the application is very much more versatile than a conventional static web page. The medium deliberately encourages participation in the joint creation of content, and this may take place either by revising existing text or by adding links to other web pages (within the wiki or to external websites) to extend the information provided. Through the participation of many authors constantly adding and revising information, the wiki can be effectively self-policed to reduce misinformation through inaccuracy or malicious intent. The rapid growth of Wikipedia, the free, online, multi-lingual encyclopedia, has helped to popularise wikis as an effective tool for generating and sharing large amounts of complex knowledge. The wiki has given real substance to the shift of the web towards web 2.0—towards an online environment in which users are encouraged to contribute and interact with other users rather than be the passive recipients of static information. Another web 2.0 characteristic of wikis is that they encourage a different attitude to information: whereas print suggests that information is fixed and authoritative, wikis create an environment in which information is seen to be fluid and flexible (perhaps even unfinished) and, even more importantly, communally constructed and owned.

## The Educational Challenge

Wikis allow asynchronous peer-to-peer interaction, and, with the convergence of digital media, a wiki can include images and sound, as well as text. There are several crucial aspects of wikis that would seem to make them ideal for use in an educational environment. First of all, wikis are subject driven rather than time driven and can be adopted as repositories of information on specialist areas of interest, such as an academic course, a research group, or a corporate organisation with participating workers scattered across the globe. The fundamental premise of wiki construction is a belief in the shared construction of knowledge, and this is consistent with a constructivist pedagogy and a focus on encouraging learner-centred content rather than teacher-generated content that students are expected to read and digest. Wikis are very flexible in being able to adapt how information is organised, so that new pages can be added, the layout changed, and sections deleted by interacting to reach a common consensus. Most wikis will allow users to compare the current version of the text with previous versions in order to refine the text and also will enable each amendment/addition to be traced to individual users. This facilitates wikis being used to build collaborative projects while enabling the contribution of individual students to be credited.

Because of their potential for dispersing disinformation, wikis offer an ideal opportunity for educators to help students gain the skills to differentiate and make their own judgements regarding the accuracy of information.

### Strengths of the Resource

Wikis enable the users to generate web pages easily and to alter/amend the text in collaboration with peers to create a mutually agreed version that is commonly accessible. Information is not fixed (as in print) but flexible and changeable to meet the needs of the community of users. Wikis can be closed (only an agreed group of users can change the text) or open (allowing any registered password-holder to change text). Generally, a wiki requires very little technical skill or training to use it effectively, thereby allowing the users to concentrate on the content and the context rather than be distracted by the technology. The resource encourages users to work in groups, to develop peer-to-peer generation of information, and to contextualise knowledge by linking text to other relevant resources. The ease and accessibility of the resource encourages wikis to be utilised for building common agendas, problem-solving, brainstorming and creating complex reference lists of hyperlinked information. The medium is ideal for creating group cohesiveness and commonly agreed definitions or information sources among online communities. Wikis allow the structured organisation of resources, as well as asynchronous editing and participation by geographically distributed users, and can link with other digital resources including image repositories and e-portfolios.

## Potential Disadvantages

Some critics have argued that the ease of access to wiki editing and the unmonitored open environment may lead to a very low level of content and no contextual relevance. There has been an extended debate relating to the accuracy of wiki contents, but educators have argued the importance of using the opportunities of this medium to educate learners to make their own judgements regarding the accuracy of information. The potential complexity of a site that has many authors requires care in the construction of the navigation to ensure that users are able to locate and extend the information in a systematic manner and without repetition. The organic nature of wiki development may mean that some pages appear to be fragmentary or unfinished as the context is re-worked and re-edited.

## Key Points for Effective Practice

- Although wikis lend themselves to collaborative writing by groups of users, this requires a clear focus and an element of self-discipline.
- Unlike traditional forms of writing, wikis offer the ability to trace comments and receive feedback from other users and link simply with other digital sources of knowledge. BulletAs with other educational resources, a little bit of pre-planning and some clear guidelines on its use can really help students to make the best use of the wikis.
- The flexibility of the wiki can allow users to create some very effective, dynamic knowledge bases and to share these widely for further comment. These can range from the trivial (a shopping list or "to-do" list) to the very complex (a personal e-portfolio) or the activities of an interdisciplinary research group.
- One particularly valuable use of a wiki is for a group to think about how information is organised, especially in a large or complex area, and to consider how to present it in small, hyperlinked chunks.

## Selected References

Beach, R., Anson, C., & Kastman Breuch, L-A. (2008). Teaching writing using blogs, wikis and other digital tools. Norwood, MA: Christopher-Gordon. Retrieved from http://digitalwriting. pbwiki.com

Holtman, L. (2009, January). Using Wikis in the teaching of a short course on the history and philosophy of science. *International Journal of Instructional Technology and Distance Learning*. Retrieved from http://www.itdl.org/journal/jan_09/article03.htm

Konieczny, P. (2007, January). Wikis and Wikipedia as a teaching tool. *International Journal of Instructional Technology and Distance Learning*. Retrieved from http://www.itdl.org/Journal/Jan_07/article02.htm

Lee, J., & Bonk, C. J. (2009, June). Exploring the use of wikis for the improvement of English writing skills: Research, reflections, and recommendations. *International Journal of Instructional Technology and Distance Learning*. Retrieved from http://www.itdl.org/Journal/Jun_09/article02.htm

Parker, K. R., & Chao, J. T., (2007). Wiki as a teaching tool. *Interdisciplinary Journal of Knowledge and Learning Objects, 3*. Retrieved from http://www.ijklo.org/Volume3/IJKLOv3p057-072Parker284.pdf

Wheeler, S., Yeomans, P., & Wheeler, D. (2008). The good, the bad and the wiki: Evaluating student-generated content for collaborative learning. *British Journal of Educational Technology, 39*(6), 987-995.

### Institution: Western Cape University, Bellville, South Africa

*How It Works in Practice.*   Using a free wiki provider (a wiki farm) or internal wiki software, a site is established to which users (potential readers, contributors, and editors) are directed. A loose structure and hierarchy of headings is established around a pre-agreed on subject or project, and users are encouraged to collaborate to contribute and amend text and/or images to build a commonly agreed narrative. The nature of the work and the potential for interdisciplinarity means that users do not need to be co-located or sharing information in real time, but allows a repository of information and links to be built up as different areas of the project progress at different speeds. Wikis have been used to encourage students to individually research good examples and supplementary reading around course themes then to share this with their peers. Other uses include collaborative writing and peer review or assessment of student work. Some institutions (e.g., Cape Western Reserve University) have established a wiki that can be accessed and edited by every member of staff, thereby creating an evolving resource on every aspect of the life and work of the university.

*Lessons Learned.*   The uses and potential of wikis are endless, but this flexibility can itself be a problem, so for the best results a wiki should have transparently clear navigation (and/or a "how-to-use" guide) as well as a clearly defined purpose from the outset.

Having established some simple hierarchy of layout to launch a wiki, it is best to populate it with a few simple examples of text, images, links and so on to set the tone and encourage others to contribute.

Although wikis can be used as a one-way application to express ideas, they work best when there is open, multiple authorship around a central theme, so initial ideas should be clearly expressed (e.g., "This wiki is about …") and users prepared that their contributions to the wiki might subsequently be edited or deleted as the wiki evolves.

Advertising of the wiki's central theme should not be too specific because this might discourage contributors from thinking creatively and might restrict their contributions to a relatively narrow area that soon runs out of steam.

Regenerating enthusiasm for a wiki can be injected through instructor contributions strategically placed to keep students involved in the wiki; user engagement will rise and fall over time.

Because the wiki is flexible, contributors should be encouraged to modify what others have written, if it is relevant, and to add pages/sections of their own as the wiki grows and becomes a wider repository of useful information on the central theme and on its various subdivisions of knowledge.

### Selected References

University of Calgary Wiki. (2011). Retrieved from http://wiki.ucalgary.ca/page/Main_Page

Case Western Reserve University. (2011). Retrieved from http://wiki.case.edu/Main_Page

## RESOURCE: VIDEO CLIPS AND YOUTUBE

Launched in December 2005, YouTube provides users with the opportunity to upload their own videos and watch others in a standard format which is accessible to anyone with Internet availability. Initially seen as a way for people to share their home video, quickly it became apparent that this could be an excellent way of reaching large new audiences. As a result, YouTube has launched music groups and created "stars." Businesses have recognised the potential of this medium and advertise alongside "viral" (extremely popular) uploads. Some have even created their own "viral" videos. The top ten most watched video clips of 2011 achieved more than 285 million hits worldwide—very sizable target market. Of those top ten, the number one slot was taken by a talking dog, with a flying cat and a spoof of the British Royal wedding also in the running. Kevin Allocca, YouTube's trend manager, explains that the site unites cultures and countries as cute babies, talking animals and clever advertising seem to be popular regardless of what language we speak (Thornhill, 2011).

YouTube allows the posting of copyrighted works but removes them once the copyright holder objects. In 2011 YouTube istarted to roll out over 100 professionally produced channels as part of a wider strategy for increasing the amount of time people spend on the site. Providing a plethora of channels on every subject imaginable is just one of the ways

YouTube is growing from a site for amateur video sharing to one which rivals and exceeds the popularity of television audiences.

## The Educational Challenge

This medium can enrich the learning experience of students by providing video material to accompany their textbooks, in-class documentaries and course lectures. In December 2011, YouTube launched YouTube EDU, an area of the site which offers free access to all educational material it holds, but without users being able to reach the rest of the site, thereby providing safe and secure educational resources. The EDU site is split into resources available for primary and secondary schools, universities and colleges and also there is a section entitled life-long learning.

While YouTube was initially and still is conducive to web 2.0 approaches to devise activities in which students create the content, there are now also excellent lectures from professors at prestigious universities throughout the world, most notably MIT, Harvard and The Open University, thereby allowing students to learn from not just their own instructors. However, instructors are also encouraged to upload their own material as content for the site and offer the lecture experience to online students.

Finally, the web's shift from a tool of reference to one of collaboration presents teachers with some rich opportunities for e-learning by encouraging students to create videos as part of their assessments.

## Strengths of the Resource

Unlike more static and limited media, such as PowerPoint, plus the decorative course web page, video and audio sharing help professors be more creative and ambitious in the classroom. Video sharing with classmates on the social front is easy, fun, and rising in participation. Particularly with the increasing use of Smart Phones, which can record and upload videos, it is now possible to share such information immediately. Education using multimedia and other visual aids has always been a strengthening component of many subjects' curriculum, and today's educators are taking steps to incorporate the Internet and media-based tools to improve participation and learning. Class projects that involve presentations or directions on how to do something could be enhanced with video uploading. With the increasing number of online educational programmes being developed, YouTube clips provide a reliable and informative medium for encouraging learning. Virtual learning environments such as Blackboard and Moodle are able to embed YouTube code easily so that students can access clips directly from their learning resources, thereby ensuring that they do not have to go through the YouTube interface, which can have advertisements and, occasionally, obnoxious comments.

The act of "hunting" for potentially useful clips is seen as an important part of the learning process in which students can actively be involved in acquiring their own resources for discussion. In terms of "time shifting" and "space shifting," YouTube allows students to view clips at any time and from any location (Trier, 2007).

## Potential Disadvantages

Infringements of copyright are a potential disadvantage of video sharing, although steps are being taken, for example, by Google, which has bought YouTube, to address the problem. Nevertheless, good educational material can be made available, legally, on YouTube and other such services. As with other web 2.0 tools, it is incumbent on teachers to raise the issue of copyright with students and thereby encourage, enhance, and empower critical thought.

Another unfortunate aspect of YouTube popularity is the misuse made of it by students' videoing lectures without permission and uploading clips of their instructors doing less than appropriate things in the classroom.

There is also the issue of availability. Some videos are only made available for short periods of time and then disappear. The quality of some homemade videos can be very poor and hard to watch. Also, some videos may not be appropriate for students to view and should therefore be vetted thoroughly before suggesting they be used for teaching purposes.

## Key Points for Effective Practice

YouTube is not vital to achieve effective learning in the classroom, however it is an excellent resource, which, when used appropriately, can enhance the overall learning experience of students.

- YouTube simply makes more resources available to teachers than ever before, and facilitates engaging and active learning.
- Rather than use up valuable time in class watching a film or video clips, such media can be assigned to students as homework in the same way that reading is assigned. However, to make it work, faculty should keep in mind that the best way to deliver this content in a controlled manner is through a VLE.

## Selected References

YouTube Edu. (n.d.). Retrieved from http://www.youtube.com/education

TED Ed Lessons Worth Sharing. (n.d.). Retrieved from http://ed.ted.com/

Using YouTube Videos in Education. (n.d.). Retrieved from http://www.techforschools.com/handouts/youtubeineducation.pdf

Thornhill, T. (2011, December 20). Mail online. Retrieved from http://www.dailymail.co.uk/sciencetech/article-2076652/YouTube-videos-2011-Rebecca-Black-trumps-Ultimate-Dog-Tease.html

Trier, J. (2007). "Cool" engagements with YouTube. *Journal of Adolescent & Adult Literacy, 50*(5), 408–412.

## Institution: Hunter College School of Nursing (SON)
## City University of New York, New York

*How It Works in Practice.*   Dr. Sharoff is an Associate Professor at the City University of New York in the Hunter College School of Nursing (SON). She is the Coordinator of Simulation and Learning Resources for the SON. As an early adopter of technology within the nursing curriculum, Dr. Sharoff has used YouTube clips for her students to learn about pathophysiology, pharmacology, obstetrics, paediatric nursing and medical/surgical nursing. She has also provided students with undergraduate curricula concepts, as well as more theoretical postgraduate material. Students are required to watch the clips and comment in groups through the VLE. YouTube videos can provide a visual portrayal of ailments, procedures and treatments in a safe and non-confrontational. The opportunity to discuss what they have seen helps students develop their critical understanding.

*Lessons Learned.*   Sharoff (2011) argues that the application and uses of the millions of videos available on YouTube are only limited by faculty and student creativity and imagination. Being able to provide visual examples of health practice is an excellent way to engage and encourage learners. Also, by using assessment methods which require students to upload their own clips (data protection and privacy rights permitting) helps students to develop their technological skills.

## Selected Reference

Sharoff, L. (2011, August 17). Integrating YouTube into the nursing curriculum. *OJIN: The Online Journal of Issues in Nursing, 16*(3). Retrieved from http://www.nursingworld.org/MainMenuCategories/ANAMarketplace/ANAPeriodicals/OJIN/TableofContents/Vol-16-2011/No3-Sept-2011/Articles-Previous-Topics/YouTube-and-Nursing-Curriculum.aspx#Trier07Part1

## RESOURCE: VIDEO CHAT

Although Internet telephony, or Voice-over IP (VoIP), had existed for some time, Skype was the first to make it a massively popular tool, no doubt because it offered unlimited free calls between online users, wherever they are in the world. Now there is a plethora of free-to-download video chat sites such as ivideochat, faceflow, Googletalk, and ichat. However, Skype is still the most popular video chat site and has almost reached generic term status. Once the user has logged in, they can locate other users on a central register and take part in an audio or video call across the Internet. A recent survey found that 37% of Internet users aged between 12 and 17 regularly used a video chat service (Lenhart, 2012).

Video chat is a form of peer-to-peer network, although these are based on an ethic of participation, collaboration, responsible sharing and the contribution of content for others to enjoy. Video chat users are sharing conversations and expanding their social networks through both its voice application and instant messenger (IM) function. It is, in some ways, like having email, IM and a high-quality phone connection combined in one programme, which operates over the Internet through peer-to-peer networks.

Most video chat software is free and installs easily, and then with an Internet connection the calls using the system are free, and calls to others not on the system are normally very low cost. Video chat has offered individuals the opportunity to connect in real time using video and audio, anywhere in the world.

### *The Educational Challenge*

Educational uses are many and varied:

- One-to-one support for remote graduate students;
- Authentic interactions with native speakers for language teaching ;
- Integrating a multicultural perspective through global interaction;
- Useful research tool for telephone interviews or feedback from students;
- Possibility of keeping video chat office hours especially for remote students;
- Opportunities for inviting guest expert speakers into an online course.

Using video chat as a tool within the classroom also can allow for group interaction, particularly now through Skype. Skype premium offers group screen sharing which allows up to 10 students to collaborate on a presentation. Also, group video calling allows, again, up to 10 students to have a shared call in real time to discuss an issue or to have a small tutorial session. Skype also offers free file-sending, allowing users to send documents of any size to their peers. Also, with the more accepted uses of Skype such as video and voice calling, this allows interaction between classmates to discuss assessments, work on reports and also practice language skills.

Skype in the classroom offers teachers and students the opportunity to interact with other like-minded individuals and to collaborate on multi-cultural and multi-disciplinary content to enhance their learning and teaching. Skype has partnered with a number of institutions and organization as a way for schools to bring outside experts into their classrooms. Some of the programmes offered include: a Penguin young readers group to connect authors and readers; live interaction with educators and musicians from the New York Philharmonic; and live interactive projects between children and staff of the Science Museum, London, featuring the "punk science resource."

### Strengths of the Resource

The most obvious strength of video chat is that calls are free to other users within a site. Furthermore, the sound quality keeps the high and low tones of sound, whereas telephones and other VoIP software/hardware may clip out those parts of speech. This makes video chat particularly valuable for language learners.

As with other real-time technologies, video chat communications offer immediacy and opportunities for direct feedback. Large files can be exchanged, and groups of individuals are able to interact. Although hardly a web 2.0 use of the tool, one-to-many audio lectures can be given to remote students. Finally, Skype allows you to expand your list of contacts and indicates when others in your social network are available to chat.

### Potential Disadvantages

Video chat, like most other network applications, has risks as well as benefits. While initially there appeared to be a risk of network security with the use of peer-to-peer architecture, this has now been fully resolved. Internal administration of IT networks within universities does not always allow for the uploading of software to individual machines, without administrator rights. This means you may need to check if your institution approves the use of video chat and how this can be uploaded to your machine.

A feature of video chat that may be very welcome to its users is that all communications are encrypted end-to-end between the two communicating clients. However, within Skype, it may be desirable to prevent telephone conversations from being tapped, the encryption also applies to all other Skype activities such as file transfer and chat. This means that any filtering or protection for the user or their PC that is implemented on the organisation's firewall or network will be unable to inspect files or other content transferred to the Skype client. Skype effectively provides an encrypted tunnel through the firewall that could be used for attacks against the client's PC and any other networked devices it can connect to in turn. Users and PCs must therefore be able to protect themselves against inappropriate or malicious content including viruses and other malware, or even attacks against the Skype system itself, without any assistance from other systems.

Skype, for example, uses quite a bit of memory, possibly 120 MB, and it is important that students be aware of this if running it on their home PC where memory space may be limited.

Although video chat will work over a dial-up connection, it can be very slow, and often video cannot be enabled without a time delay or connection failure. Broadband provides a better and more efficient connection but only where users can receive at least 2 mbps, as anything less than this can cause the same connectivity issues as dial-up. This could represent a disadvantage for remote students with a slow broadband speed or no broadband connection at all.

Finally, whilst video chat is excellent for synchronous conversation, this can become difficult through online learning if attempting to communicate with a group of students in different time zones. Video chat needs to be managed carefully to ensure a parity of experience, both in terms of accessibility and functionality.

### Key Points for Effective Practice

- Encourage students to use video chat for peer-to-peer contact, where appropriate.
- Engage a guest expert to add a real-time input to a course.
- Make use of Skype in the classroom to share best practise.

### Selected References

Skype in the Classroom. (n.d.). Retrieved from http://education.skype.com/

Chat face to face with family and friends. (n.d.). Retrieved from https://www.google.com/chat/video

Science Museum, London. (n.d.). Retrieved from http://education.skype.com/partners/15-science-museum-london

Lenhart, A. (2012). Teens and online video. Pew Internet and American Life Project Washington, DC: Pew Research Center. Rertrieved from http://pewinternet.org/Reports/2012/Teens-and-online-video.aspx

The 'Granny Cloud' Uses Skype to Educate Children in India. (n.d.). Retrieved from http://thenextweb.com/apps/2011/01/18/the-granny-cloud-uses-skype-to-educate-children-in-india/

### Institution: Lews Castle College, University of the Highlands and Islands, Stornoway, Scotland

*How It Works In Practice.*   The undergraduate degree programme in Sustainable Rural Development is a fully online course with teacher support that is delivered from the main teaching campus on the Isle of Lewis in the Scottish Hebrides to students remote from the campus or located throughout Europe. In addition to discussion boards and other asynchronous digitised resources on the VLE the tutors use instant messaging and Skype to offer some element of intimacy and synchronous short discussion sessions with the remote students. Students need to have broadband Internet access and are given guidance in the relatively simple task of downloading the proprietary software, but are thereafter able to make free calls to other users, including instructors and fellow learners. An icon can be set on the desktop of the remote student by the teacher to indicate when she or he is available to receive calls. If a student would like to discuss a particular item on the course, a call can be placed to the instruction simply by clicking a button. If the call is accepted, both teacher and student can have voice, video live image, and live text chat in any (or all) combinations.

Usually the sessions are fairly short (5–10 minutes) similar to a phone call rather than a set "lecture" and are used to raise questions, clarify points, or put across a particular point of view. The chat sessions can be recorded and archived for future reference.

The inclusion of video allows the participants to see each other in real time while they are talking and allows facial cues that greatly increase the sense of intimacy over simple telephone conversation. Pre-arranged mini-conference calls of three or four people can be used to have a group discussion on particular points that have a relevance to more than one learner.

*Lessons Learned.*   Keep the sessions short and focussed; the novelty of the situation sometimes encourages participants to become immersed in the discussion and, if this is not properly directed, can tend to ramble a bit. The teacher should set some time aside for receiving incoming

Skype calls and make this time known to the group of learners. The teacher should set his or her "online status" icon to indicate availability for calls (e.g., available, busy, or away) to avoid unwanted distractions by incoming callers.

Use the Skype sessions to deal with individual problems and questions in order to add value to the other components of the course learning resources. This is especially important when not all students in the course have access to Skype, so the Skype contact should be regarded as an option for students rather than a mainstream method of communication. In this case, students without Skype can opt for other methods of personal communication—instant messaging, telephone, or other means that suit their needs better.

If the online chat facility is used, save the conversation at the end and archive as it evidence of the activity that can be called upon in future to help reflection, supervision, and other issues.

## *Selected References*

University of the Highlands and Islands. (n.d.).What is sustainable development. Retrieved from http://www.sustainabledevelopmentonline.co.uk/

# 5

## CONSTRAINTS ON COURSE DESIGN

In this chapter we discuss a wide range of problems that can occur in course design using social networking tools. We have divided the discussion into three sections—issues related: to students, to teachers or academics, and to educational institutions. Of course, this division is rather arbitrary as the three are intimately connected, so these categories are used simply to provide structure to the chapter.

Perhaps the most significant factor, which affects all three parts of the triad, is the degree of unresearched, overblown and unsubstantiated claims currently being made about the effect that these tools will have on education in general and young learners in particular. So much web 2.0 literature focuses on the potential of these tools to:

- Provide anytime, anywhere learning;
- Allow students to become publishers, teachers, creators;
- Give access to vast amounts of content;
- Increase students' opportunities to interact with other students, teachers and experts;
- Extend learning to the traditionally excluded, to the disabled and to the global community.

The list could go on, and most of these "potentialities" are perfectly accurate. The more relevant issue is whether any are being actualised! There is no guarantee that these tools are wanted or desirable or without other insuperable barriers just because they allow these facilities.

The kind of enthusiasm that web 2.0 has generated is not unique; in fact it is common to most social initiatives, particularly those related to education. The problem is that it creates unreasonable expectations and an inevitable backlash. Already we see many commentators objecting to the very category web 2.0, downplaying its importance and innovatory qualities. Whether it is new, different, merely evolutionary, what the web was originally meant to be, or all of these, the fact is that it is a force to be reckoned with in education. This requires research, experimentation and an open mind, but not a gung-ho attitude.

## ISSUES FOR STUDENTS

While many commentators have written about the readiness of the young to use web 2.0 tools and the effects this is having on their perceptions of learning (e.g., Oblinger & Oblinger, 2005; Prensky, 2001a, b), there is also evidence that some students do not welcome e-learning, much less the use of web 2.0 tools for education. Although this may well change with time, it will probably take considerably longer than the enthusiasts currently assume. Kirkwood and Price (2005), for instance, note that online access remains problematic for some students and access from work or public machines is frequently not adequate for the kinds of online activities that web 2.0 tools require.

> Access to ICT is rarely ideal and unrestricted: learners often need to share computing and communication facilities with others. Course design should reflect this and not be over-dependent upon ICT.
> Getting access to and downloading remote resources can be very time-consuming when working via a dial-up network: in certain circumstances such activities will not be sanctioned. p. 271)

Kirkwood and Price (2005) point to another student issue: the blurring of the distinction between full-time and part-time study, such that many of the constraints that used to be unique to part-time, distance students are now faced by those ostensibly engaged in full-time study—namely, combining employment with study (p. 258). This means that lack of time and the need for flexible study patterns are major considerations for course designers.

The degree to which young learners are using web 2.0 tools masks another student issue: the need to provide training for those, possibly a small minority, who are not skilled in the use of a range of software that might be used on formal courses. This creates problems for course design, in that it is necessary to cater to novices as well as to provide stimulating and challenging activities for the very experienced users. In terms of the kind of training required, there are further headaches:

novices (whether students or tutors) want personalised, just-in-time training opportunities, not formalised, standardised courses at a time convenient to the providing institution. Despite the fact that commentators have been predicting for nearly 20 years that training will no longer be required as software becomes more intuitive and more widely used, every evaluation study still cites training as a continuing requirement (e.g., Weyers, Adamson, & Murie, 2004). Related to technology training is the need for training in information literacy. Recent research in a *Horizon Report* notes:

> Contrary to the conventional wisdom, the information literacy skills of new students are not improving as the post-1993 Internet boomlet enters college. At the same time, in a sea of user-created content, collaborative work, and instant access to information of varying quality, the skills of critical thinking, research, and evaluation are increasingly required to make sense of the world. (New Media Consortium, 2007, p. 4)

Guinee and Eagleton (2006) have observed students taking notes from online sources and have discovered that they tend to copy large blocks of text rather than paraphrasing for future reference. When they come to use the material, they have lost track of the distinction between their own words and material copied from other sources. Furthermore, they do not assess the quality of the ideas copied, nor do they try to produce a synthesis from the materials they have copied. In short, they have the technical skills to find, cut and paste information, but not the pedagogical literacy skills to make it their own.

Several studies seem to indicate that students want only a moderate amount of new learning tools to be used on formal courses (e.g., Kvavik & Caruso, 2005) and most students are very strategic in their use of these tools. For example, Kear (2004) found that:

> Students will participate in a discussion forum if they see sufficient benefits for the time invested—and there are different kinds of benefits for different students. Some students will only take part if the course assessment gives them marks for doing so. Some will take part because they gain information and help from others, which supports their learning. Others value interaction for its own sake, and gain support and motivation from other students in the forum. (p. 162)

Students continue to value face-to-face teaching, though it is unclear whether they simply say this in response to questionnaires, regardless of whether they actually attend, or whether they equate face-to-face with value for money, or whether they are suspicious of online forms of learning.

Course design must, therefore, address two aspects of the student perspective:

1. The need to keep the student workload very much in mind—there is evidence that overloaded courses lead to surface-level learning, and that activities and online interaction are much more time-consuming than is usually acknowledged.
2. The need to plan every aspect of the course for strategic learners— that is, every element must deliver "learning value for time spent".

These are both difficult elements to judge accurately when designing a course because there is a large unpredictable element in online learning. Having the honesty to admit that some element has not worked, as well as the perceptiveness and resources to change it are the best ways of approaching the problem.

## REFLECTION AS A LEARNED SKILL

The expanding use of e-portfolios and blogging in higher education has uncovered another shortcoming of many students: the misunderstanding of, or inability to, reflect on their learning. Yet the practice of reflection has become a prominent tool for learning in recent years. One definition of it is the following:

> Reflection is a form of mental processing that we use to fulfil a purpose or to achieve some anticipated outcome. It is applied to gain a better understanding of relatively complicated or unstructured ideas and is largely based on the reprocessing of knowledge, understanding and possibly emotions that we already possess. (Moon, 2005, p. 1)

Successful uses of e-portfolios in higher education inevitably ascribe a key role to reflection in the design of the course. As the definition suggests, structuring the practice of reflection transforms it into a learning experience. For example, the teacher may provide prompts to help students connect their reading with the core issues of the course. The affective dimension of reflection is also an important part of the process and one with which students may well need guidance. They may need encouragement to use the first person in their reflective writing and to acknowledge the significance of feelings in the learning process.

One very effective way of structuring reflective activities is to relate them to the learning objectives of the course. Documents, project plans and an annotated bibliography might also be organised around the objectives along with the reflective pieces of work. Frequent feedback may be required to prompt students to think further about issues, and to consider other perspectives.

Reflection is not something to be carried out only at the end of an activity or learning experience. Reflection should be a continuous process throughout the study period. At the beginning of a course, it is useful for students to reflect on what they do not know, what they would like to learn and how they want to go about it. Students might then work in small groups to identify useful resources to address their knowledge gaps. They might also form larger discussion groups to evaluate the resources they have found. Students might be required to keep a learning journal throughout the course in which they record their thoughts, observations, feelings and questions. It is up to the teacher or tutor to direct students' attention to other resources or to further questions. This process is facilitated by e-portfolio software which allows the student to share parts or the whole of the growing portfolio with named people.

Many students will need help in understanding what reflection means in an academic context. For this reason it is useful to provide examples of reflective writing and to build an activity around them by asking students to evaluate what learning is being gained through the reflective process. One of the barriers to learning through reflection is that students rely on formulaic responses to reflection exercises. This may be prevented by studying examples of authentic reflection and by the teacher referring to the examples if students appear to be floundering.

Reflection is an essential feature of a deep approach to learning. However, it is inappropriate and unnecessary on a course whose aim is to impart a large corpus of information for students to digest and then reiterate in the exam at the end.

> Reflection seems to be a part of the kinds of learning in which learners try to understand material that they encounter and to relate it to what they already knew. Relating new material to what one knows already may mean reflecting on what one knows and modifying it (deep approach). Reflection does not seem to have a role in the learning in which learners try just to retain new information without creating deep links with the new ideas (surface approach). Reflection will also be involved in the process of representing learning—when, for example, a learner's

understanding is tested in a format that demands reprocessing
of the ideas (e.g. an essay). It is less or uninvolved in an approach
that requires reiteration of the responses in the same format as
the original knowledge. (Moon, 2005, p. 2)

An example of an activity that helps students to relate new material
to what they already know is called a "critical incident diary", which
works very well in e-portfolio software. This involves students describing instances of learning over a period of about a week. Examples might
include solving a problem, encountering a new idea, resolving a conflict or enjoying a novel experience. The purpose in writing about these
instances is, first of all, to observe them, second, to be able to describe
them and, finally, to consider what was learnt from them: if the learning
can be related to course issues, so much the better.

Should reflection be assessed? This is a question which divides practitioners down the middle. Some say that it is not appropriate to "grade
people's feelings." Others contend that it will only be valued by students
if it does contribute to their final grade. What is obvious is that the
teacher needs to think carefully about how to assess the reflective component of the course. Three factors are critical:

- The reflective activities need to be directly related to the learning
  outcomes of the course.
- They need to be appropriate to the level and content of the course.
- Students need to receive adequate preparation and feedback from the
  teacher about the reflection process.

If these guidelines are followed, assessing the reflective element of
an e-portfolio or blog can contribute to students' intrinsic motivations
for learning.

Herrington and Oliver (2002) describe the method they used to
encourage reflection on a graduate level online course. This involved a
learning journal and a continuous process of reflecting on their work.
However, the central feature of the process was their use of an authentic
task, chosen by the student, as the focus of the work:

It is entirely up to the student to propose a task that suits their
own particular circumstances, with the proviso that their work
is informed by current literature, and that they consciously
reflect on the process as it is happening. (p. 317)

The other significant aspect of the process was that students had
access to a variety of online resources and supports; for example, a list

of books and relevant texts, links to online journal articles on reflection, and a website which helped students structure their reflection on the task. The authors note that a complex task requiring decision making and reasoning is required in order that students appreciate the need for reflection.

At an undergraduate level, a number of practitioners recommend dual entry procedures to support students in understanding the nature and value of reflection (Hatton & Smith, 1995). So, for example, in the first column students might describe a learning experience or summarise an issue from the course material; in the second column, they might write a critical reflection on the experience or issue. In this way students learn to distinguish between description and reflection, and are empowered to consider their own thoughts and feelings about their learning.

The aim of developing reflective learners is to encourage students to be more self-aware and self-critical; to be honest about themselves, and open to criticism and feedback. An e-portfolio with structured reflective processes and mentoring by the teacher can instil these qualities in students. Activities which require students to be objective in weighing up evidence or encourage them to be open to different approaches and prepared to try them, fit well within an e-portfolio framework. Ultimately, this method of teaching helps to develop independent lifelong learners. Nevertheless, many students are resistant to reflecting on their own learning and it will require course design skill on the part of the teacher to instil it. Many studies report findings that suggest students are task-focused and outcome oriented and that they find it difficult to understand the need for reflection (e.g., Mitchell, 2002).

## ISSUES FOR TEACHERS

Ever since the introduction of online learning in the early 1990s, there have been reports about the ways in which technology changes faculty roles because it changes their workload and responsibilities. The change is usually regarded as more work for the same pay and recognition. This perception on the part of teachers has four related elements: workload, promotion, skills, and intellectual property rights.

### 1. Workload
Parker's (2003) analysis of over 100 articles concludes that it is intrinsic rewards that motivate most teachers to develop innovatory, online elements in their courses: personal satisfaction, flexible scheduling and reaching non-traditional students. Using new technologies and developing new ideas also enter the equation. Maguire's (2005) study shows

that if the necessary extrinsic rewards are offered, such as decreased workload, release time, stipends and technology support, then the usual barriers are more easily overcome. Workload and time requirements are difficult to measure, which perhaps explains contradictory evidence from studies claiming that moving to online teaching takes more time and those which show that it does not. Sammons and Ruth (2007) conclude that:

> Time requirements are difficult to measure, as they are dependent on the subject, number of students, instructor skills, type of technologies used in the course, and course quality, but the clear finding is that for most full timers the conversion to online mode is a significant user of previously discretionary time. Regardless of whether the workload actually increases, certainly the pace of work and the working style change. The time spent teaching online may not actually be greater, but the "chunking" or flow of tasks online is different. (p. 12)

Nevertheless, there is some evidence that the amount of interaction with students actually increases. Because of the individualized nature of e-mail communication, interactions are more numerous and personalized than in many traditional courses (American Association of University Professors [AAUP], 2002). For some faculty, the increase in student-teacher interaction may be viewed as a disincentive, for others it acts as an incentive.

Faculty members also complain about changes in the scale of their teaching, and this is linked to government and university-level policies and efforts to save money. They often report increasing staff workloads, first year transition problems and problems arising from the increasing diversity of students. Although generally critical of pushes for flexible delivery through the use of Internet-based technologies, these new modes of delivery are acknowledged as the most obvious way to deal with the larger student numbers. However, many faculty members continue to express reservations about more flexible modes because, although they are an obvious response to larger student numbers, they are not viewed as solutions to problems caused by these large numbers. They fear that online solutions will diminish community involvement on campus, personal contact, self-development and one-to-one contact.

In addition to the increasing number of students, there is an increasing diversity of students. Changes noted in the student population include the more diverse language and educational background of students, the more diverse experience and skills of students and more diverse student circumstances. The increase in diversity of students' language and educational background was linked to the growing number of international students and to government and university level policies on widening participation (Lynch & Collins, 2001). In theory, web 2.0 tools should help to address the problems created by the increasing diversity of student backgrounds and experiences: choice, personalisation, flexibility and student-centred approaches are all hallmarks of web 2.0 tools. In any case, one-size-fits-all lectures are less and less effective for the changing student population.

## 2. Promotion

As we noted in chapter 1, the nature of scholarship is changing due to web 2.0 and other technologies. The traditional processes of recognition and promotion act as a barrier to faculty venturing into the web 2.0 environment. The 2007 *Horizon Report* notes:

> Academic review and faculty rewards are increasingly out of sync with new forms of scholarship. The trends toward digital expressions of scholarship and more interdisciplinary and collaborative work continue to move away from the standards of traditional peer-reviewed paper publication. New forms of peer review are emerging, but existing academic practices of specialization and long-honored notions of academic status are persistent barriers to the adoption of new approaches. Given the pace of change, the academy will grow more out of step with how scholarship is actually conducted until constraints imposed by traditional tenure and promotion processes are eased. (New Media Consortium, 2007, p. 4)

An example of this new form of scholarship is given by Weller (2007b) who explains the benefits of blogging and justifies it as an academic activity:

> My main aim was to get across the idea that keeping a blog is both an academically valid activity and also really beneficial for the individual.... For me I would say the two strongest points are that it provides a useful means of engaging with technology, a base camp in the online world as it were, and that of all the academic activity I engage in, blogging is the one I probably enjoy the most (apart from having drinks in a bar at a conference in Hawaii, say, which is also quite nice). It is where a lot of the stuff you came into academia for in the first place, but has been eroded by increased administration, workloads and formal metrics (casts disapproving look at RAE), still persists—for example,

lively debate, creativity, new ideas, good humour, collegiality, the progressive development of half-formed concepts through dialogue, etc. (Weller, 2007b)

Related to the issue of promotion is the perception that using these tools will de-professionalise the faculty role. As content is increasingly available online and particularly in open-content sites (e.g., the Open Learn website by the Open University http://www.open.ac.uk/open-learn/home.php), some academics see their traditional role as content experts being undermined. Chisholm (2006) notes:

> Faculty who use commercial course management software become almost invisible ... this invisibility contributes to the illusion that the twenty-first century instructor is a generic, easily replaceable part in a larger Automated Education Machine.

Instead of seeing web 2.0 tools as an opportunity, some see it as a threat to their traditional ways of working, their well-established view of their curriculum and their notions of teaching and learning. They perceive that their role as teachers will be diminished as the role of technology increases, even though most studies suggest that the role of the teacher will change but not necessarily diminish. While it is true that the nature of the interaction with students becomes computer-mediated, the quality of interaction often improves—moving from question and answer to genuine discussion and debate.

## 3. Skills

Lack of the necessary skills to use web 2.0 and other online tools is a recurring theme in the literature on inhibitors to innovation in education. There are two aspects of this skill shortage: lack of experience with the technology and lack of understanding about how to use it for learning. Many teachers are worried about developing online courses on their own time with few institutional resources. Without assistance from instructional designers or graphic designers, faculty may feel that the task is too daunting (O'Quinn & Corry, 2002). Wilson (2001) found that faculty frequently expressed inhibitions about not possessing the necessary and progressive technological savvy or having the requisite technical support for themselves (Bower, 2001; Pachnowski & Jurcyzk, 2003; Rockwell, Schauer, Fritz, & Marx, 1999).

Technical skills need to be offered by the institution, although they may best be acquired through personal practice, collegial interaction or one-to-one sessions with friends. The same applies to pedagogical skills, which include:

- **Online community building:** Academics have to learn how to welcome, encourage, support, and control students in an online environment. They also have to encourage intra-class participation (e.g., introducing and connecting students).
- **Designing online activities:** Academics need to be able to design learning activities that can effectively be carried out online.
- **Discussion forum:** There is a wide range of skills to learn to facilitate an effective online discussion. These include discussion activity design and set-up, discussion introduction and close-down, discussion moderation, and assessment of contributions.
- **Information literacy:** Academics have to develop skills to help students find and manage information (McSporran & Young, 2004).

Academics have always seen themselves as content experts not media experts. Online learning is increasingly demanding a different set of skills.

## 4. Intellectual Property Rights

Many faculty members see the move from face-to-face teaching to online learning as a loss of their rights over their teaching material. Open Content initiatives by universities are an obvious example, but even material posted in the institutional VLE may be considered the property of that institution. Chisholm (2006) notes:

> Teachers can lose their intellectual property when they upload course materials to course-management programs. In a 2000 article published in the *Atlantic Monthly*, Eyal Press and Jennifer Washburn reveal that many teachers who develop courses on WebCT and similar systems lose the rights to their material after they post it, thereby enabling the vendor or the university to sell the material to an online school or to hire an adjunct to "redeliver" the same material for considerably less money. Many universities have rewritten their faculty handbooks or intellectual property agreements so that the university or the course-management system owns the course material. Their doing so is part of a larger effort to turn faculty work into a currency that retains its value long after a teacher graduates or is laid off.

Chisholm (2006) argues that faculty who knowingly or unknowingly give up ownership of their course materials contribute to the erosion of intellectual freedom, and that freedom is compromised when individual course material is distributed to others as part of a standardized curriculum initiative. Furthermore, distance education courses are often treated by universities like inventions, with the result that the university treats them more like items for which they own the patent and for which they will return a portion of the royalties to the faculty member. This is in contrast to the traditional classroom where the faculty members have the full rights to publish their materials and all royalties return to the faculty member (Estabrook, 1999).

These perceptions and attitudes are clearly at odds with the social changes happening on the web regarding what is often termed *the gift culture*, the notions of user-generated content and the evidence from research on socially constructed knowledge.

## KNOWLEDGE ACQUISITION THROUGH ONGOING DISCOURSE

Knowledge acquisition is not a stand-alone entity but rather is constructed over time through social engagements and ongoing discourses within cultural contexts and value systems. Based on assumptions of social constructivist theory, an individual acquires knowledge only through his or her engaged social activities. When members of a community get together and interpret a world as their shared world, they form a set of beliefs and culture, and, over time, knowledge about their world. In this social negotiation process or zone of proximal development (ZPD), students contribute to and learn from each other's pragmatic knowledge while adjusting to a group consensus on a topic (B. Kim, 2001; Vygotsky, 1978).

Influenced by knowledge acquisition theories, many learning theorists have begun to connect learning theories with brain research. Existing studies look at the complex and interconnected nature of the brain and how the mind constructs meaning. Brain researchers examine how the brain seeks meaning through different patterns and why instructions should be designed with the process of reflective inquiry that allows students to connect problems directly to their lives (Gibson & McKay, 1999). Since learning is influenced not only by new information but also by emotion and personal biases, "the need for social interaction … is somewhat like the weather. [It is] ongoing and the emotional impact of any lesson or life experience may continue to reverberate long after the specific event" (Caine & Caine, 1991, p. 82). Accordingly, knowledge acquisition in an online environment has to embed activities that allow students to frequently reassess their knowledge in response to new developments of predicted or unpredictably new knowledge created through social engagements. In designing an online course, the question is how to design a curriculum that allows students to connect and reflect on literature and personal experiences, and to acquire new knowledge through social engagements and ongoing discourses.

It is generally recognised that technologies are first used by enthusiastic early information technology (IT) adopters, later by mainstream users, and eventually by late adopters (McGovern, Pannan, & van der Kraats, 2001). While some elements of online learning have been mainstreamed, web 2.0 uses are still in the early adopter phase. Long-standing tensions regarding online learning have still not been resolved and remain barriers certainly for the late adopters, if not even for those who follow immediately behind the early adopters.

## ISSUES FOR INSTITUTIONS

Marginson and Considine (2000) outline a significant change in the governance of educational institutions over the last few years. Although they write about the Australian context, their comments are widely applicable:

> Universities are no longer governed by legislation: they are more commonly ruled by formulae, incentives, targets and plans. These mechanisms are more amenable to executive-led re-engineering than are the deliberations of a council or an academic board, and less accessible to counter-strategies of resistance. They also fit with management-controlled tools such as soft money budgets, commercial companies, temporary institutes for research or teaching, fund-raising and marketing campaigns, all drawn together in a complex web of accountability tied only to the senior executive office. (p. 10)

These changes mean that the culture of institutions has to reflect the new imperatives, and there is considerable resistance to this cultural change. Some have referred to it as the commoditization of knowledge and the "student as customer" approach to learning. What web 2.0 approaches have led to, according to some, is the "cult of the amateur". Keen (2007) has written a book with this title in which, apart from a number of rants and provocative statements, he points out the downside of mass amateurization:

- The lines between fact and opinion, informed expertise and amateurish speculation are wilfully blurred.
- History has proven that the crowd is not often very wise, and he cites slavery, infanticide, the Iraq war and the disastrous Tulip-mania that swept the Netherlands in the 17th century.

- Because web 2.0 celebrates the "noble amateur" over the expert, and because many search engines and websites tout popularity rather than reliability, it is easy for misinformation and rumours to proliferate in cyberspace.
- The democratized web's penchant for mashups, remixes and cut-and-paste jobs threatens not just copyright laws but also the very ideas of authorship and intellectual property.
- Blogs and wikis are decimating the publishing, music and news-gathering industries that created the original content those websites "aggregate."
- Other commentators agree about the spread of amateurisation,
- though not all are so caustic. Coates (2003), for example, pinpoints weblogs as the leading tool in the process:

> Weblogs are becoming the bridge between the individual and the community in cyberspace—a place where one can self-publicise and self-describe but also learn, debate and engage in community. In other words, weblogs are not only a representative sample of mass amateurisation, they're becoming enmeshed in the very structures of information-retrieval, community interaction and media distribution themselves. Weblogs are now facilitators of mass amateurisation.

Poore (2006) takes a more measured approach and one more geared to the educational implications of amateurization for the course designer:

> Web 2.0, and the changes to thinking about education it signifies, is a frightening prospect for many. There is, of course, the fear of being technologically left behind. And then there is the fear that many students "won't know anything anymore". But the latter, at least, is not quite true … students will just need to know different things. And if those "things" are the higher-order skills of analysis, critique and evaluation, then that is surely a good thing, and new ways of learning need to be embraced. It's our job as teachers to make sure, however, that students don't simply become overwhelmed by what's out there in cyberspace, and that we focus instead on using our own critical skills to lead them safely through Web 2.0.

Downes (2007) has an even more optimistic view:

It may be that the resulting socialisation of teaching and learning, if it occurs, will go hand in hand with less prescriptive, target-driven and centralised policy. Looking back five years from now, I suspect the apotheosis of mechanistic, e-learning "content delivery" systems will coincide with the peak of target-driven, test-based education policy, and what follows will be more personal and aimed towards a broader set of personal development goals in both technology and pedagogy. The personalisation agenda is not only about interface options and learning styles, but the whole experience of how, what and with whom we learn. (pp. 9–10)

No doubt there are many who are more pessimistic about the possible demise of policy-driven education.

Another aspect of this amateurisation of education is the view of some academics that course design using web 2.0 tools is simply a form of pandering to students and "dumbing down" the content of courses. Many critics of current student attitudes have pointed to students' inability to make their educational activities a true priority (Crone & MacKay, 2007); their need for someone else to provide structure, direction, and praise; and their inability or unwillingness to engage deeply with concepts and ideas. A particularly strident attack comes from Gorman (2007):

> There is a present danger that we are "educating" a generation of intellectual sluggards incapable of moving beyond the Internet and of interacting with, and learning from, the myriad of texts created by human minds over the millennia and perhaps found only in those distant archives and dusty file cabinets full of treasures unknown. What a dreary, flat, uninteresting world we will create if we succumb to that danger!

The opposite argument to the pandering claim is that if education providers fail to engage with the way students interact and exchange ideas, they risk becoming irrelevant. Between these two extremes lies the route of engaging with their tools and discourse while at the same time directing them to an educational outcome.

For educational institutions, these issues raise a number of concerns around policies and practices in the following areas:

- Learning managements systems or virtual learning environments (VLEs),

- Staff development,
- Assessment processes.

## VIRTUAL LEARNING ENVIRONMENTS

Regarding institutional VLEs, Attwell (2007) points out:

> The major implementations of educational technology have been not to encourage such networking and creativity but to manage learning and to isolate networks. Learning Management Systems are WSYWYG—they do what they say, manage learning. Systems have been developed as a "walled garden," to perpetuate the isolation of the school from the wider outside community.
>
> We tend to recreate with new technologies older social forms of organisation. Thus we talk of the virtual classroom or the virtual university, attempting to recreate and preserve the old paradigm of education with new technical forms. Even in Second Life, a multi-player 3D virtual world, universities have been investing heavily in buying islands to recreate in 3D form their building and classrooms.

In short, Attwell (2007) implies that institutions are not grasping the implications of web 2.0 changes. His reference to the "walled garden" raises a particularly contentious and complicated issue for universities and other educational institutions: in order to control activities, aggregate blogs and in some cases, provide protection from predators, many institutions have chosen to keep all educational material and interaction behind a firewall. Of course, this practice negates some of the main benefits of social networking: the opportunity to extend and develop interactions with people outside the limited group of peers on one's course. Anderson (2007), commenting on blogs in particular, says:

> Motivation is arguably the most important task of the teacher. Those that really want to learn usually do. Closed blogs tell students that they are engaged in "school" work that by definition is removed from their real world of family, personal interest and employment. Many find it much harder to engage with energy when the context is alien and removed from their real existence.

In terms of protection of students, commentators talk about moral panic and evidence this by noting that there are more studies of sexual predators on sites like MySpace than actual proven instances. Hine (1999, cited in Boyd 2006b) notes: "Moral panics are a common reaction to teenagers when they engage in practices not understood by adult culture. There were moral panics over rock and roll, television, jazz and even reading novels in the early 1800s" (pp. 104-105).

## STAFF DEVELOPMENT

The second issue facing institutions is the need to understand the nature of the requirement for staff development, given the impact of the Internet in general and web 2.0 in particular. It is well known that most innovative efforts in higher education today are the product of individual faculty members working alone, with the use of innovative approaches and materials restricted to individual courses. Bates (2005) referred to this as the Lone Ranger phenomenon:

> Teachers work individually creating their own Web-based materials.... They are essential in most institutions for getting Web-based learning started. They are usually very enthusiastic, and put in a great deal of their own time on developing the materials.... This model of Web-based development fits well with the autonomy of the individual teacher ... Lone Rangers are usually self-taught, not just in the use of technology but also in course design. (p. 164)

Bates (2005) goes on to list the many problems with this model: quality issues, workload for the individual (and possible burnout) and scalability. In short, he concludes, Lone Rangers are amateurs, not professionals. Teamwork is imperative in designing, supporting and presenting online courses. However, has web 2.0 thinking changed the model yet again? Waller (2007), in his article entitled "Are We All Learning Designers Now?", reflects on the process of course design thus:

> I used to explain that to create a good piece of instruction you needed at least three people, each from different disciplines. The subject matter expert (SME) is the person who knows a great deal about the subject in hand and may have already delivered face to face courses in the same vein. They will know how to test individuals on their knowledge and proficiency of the subject once the course has ended. To be able to transfer the knowledge, especially using technology, an instructional designer must look at the material that the SME supplies and work out a way that will make the technology assisted version just as good if not better than the "chalk and talk" variety. There will be few people who can do both of these roles. Lastly a programmer will

> interpret what the instructional designer says and convert it into graphics, assessment tests or flash animations or whatever else is required. Again, few people exist who can do any two of these roles let alone all three. But is this all now old hat?

He points to the range of rapid content production tools now available which allow anyone, regardless of experience, to create a learning program. He cites the call to cede control of learning to the learner. Nevertheless, he concludes that the evidence of "death by podcast" courses and "let them get on with it blogs and wikis" clearly show the need for better course design. In fact, he thinks that a disproportionate amount of the process of offering courses should be devoted to designing them.

What does all this mean for institutions trying to support academics in designing innovatory courses? The answer is not a monolithic training programme for all staff, but rather a multi-facetted approach with a wide range of strategies and types of staff development. Some examples include:

- Case studies could be developed from within the institution of successful uses of innovatory course designs.
- Communities of practice should be encouraged, both inter- and intra-institution.
- Opportunities for sharing and re-using resources might be encouraged and supported through banks of teaching resources.
- Rewards or time allowances for academics wishing to develop innovatory course material.
- Seminars and workshops led not just by early adopters, but also by less enthusiastic users.

It will take time for institutions to adjust to web 2.0 and the many changes it might bring, but all the while, web 2.0 applications will continue to evolve, making the process of change much more complicated. Web 2.0 is a potentially disruptive technology because of its potential to change the model of higher education from institution-controlled, teacher-centric, to a more student-centred model.

## ASSESSMENT PROCESSES

A third area of contention for institutions, and one in which they have created problems for themselves, is that of assessment. Most educational institutions remain rigidly tied to the idea of developing and assessing individual attainment. Obviously, assessment is connected with accreditation and quality assurance—two very important elements in educational institutions' decreasing armoury of weapons against the onslaught of social perceptions of an over-priced, ivory-tower, feather-bedded profession. Against the onslaught of web 2.0, individual assessment is increasingly problematic, however. Plagiarism detection software is the usual institutional response. On this subject, Weller (2007b) blogs:

> My feeling though is that plagiarism is a symptom of old-fashioned assessment techniques, and to put effort into plagiarism detection is to miss the point. What a plagiarism susceptible system reveals is an unhealthy emphasis on content and an old-fashioned world-view. If you assume that all content is freely available (not necessarily true, but let's go with it as a starting point), then if you ask students to create content then of course they're going to lift bits from various sources, whether intentionally or unintentionally. There is an argument that the assessment method is going contrary to the connectedness of the modern world here, although acknowledging others is always good practice. But my point is that if we took this as a base assumption we would devise different assessment methods. There is nothing about the conventional exam or essay that is an absolute measure of academic quality—in fact you can view these as administrative conveniences based on the face to face, physical constraints of education. Finding ways of perpetuating them by "catching" plagiarism to me just demonstrates a lack of imagination.

While the idea that we should enable each individual to develop to their full potential is laudable as a social goal, knowledge and creativity in a web 2.0 world are dependent on engagement within wider social networks. How can this be developed within education systems based on individual attainment? Despite the fact that many studies show that learning takes place in a much wider context than the formal classroom, education systems remain wedded to attainment against a narrow curriculum of formal knowledge. Informal learning is hardly acknowledged, much less fostered and facilitated. Critical to such an understanding is a basic need to shift thinking from "learners engaging with institutional provision and procedures" to "the institution engaging with the learner." This would imply that institutions have to recognise the new cultures of learning and networking, and engage with those cultures.

Yet that involves a profound change in institutional practice and procedures, curriculum organisation, and pedagogic approaches.

Individual achievement acts as a substantial barrier to collaboration, reflection and feedback, and to project based group work. Stiggins (2004) distinguishes between the assessment *of* learning and assessment *for* learning. The assessment of learning seeks to discover how much students have learned as of a particular point in time. Assessment for learning asks how we can use assessment to help students learn more. Moving to assessment for learning would allow the introduction of wider forms of assessment including group, peer and self-assessment. Of course, there is an issue as to how much learning is actually taking place through participation and engagement in social networking sites, but the aim should be to understand and improve this activity, not exclude it.

## ASSESSMENT 2.0

Some leading edge practitioners are beginning to talk about how web 2.0 tools can be embedded into assessment. They view the tools as offering a rich environment for finding, capturing, describing, organising and sharing evidence for assessment purposes. Elliott (2007) gives a specific example:

> For example, when undertaking an assessment, a student could use Live Search to search the world wide web for relevant information, subscribe to a number of RSS feeds using Bloglines to monitor appropriate websites, and check Wikipedia for appropriate articles. Relevant web pages could be saved using Furl or parts of web pages could be grabbed using Clipmarks. Google docs and spreadsheets could be used to pull together this information into an initial report, which can be stored online using Box.net. The whole project can be coordinated using a dedicated home page created using Netvibes, which would include RSS feeds, calendars, instant messaging, e-mail and a range of additional "gadgets" relevant to the assessment task. Throughout this process, students can learn from one another by sharing their discoveries through such services as Furl and Clipmarks, which permit students to subscribe to one another's archives—or rate archived material to identify the most relevant information.

Elliott (2007) goes on to suggest ways in which issues of authenticity and ownership of the evidence can be assured—by examining the email messages, forum contributions, and blog posts for authorial tone and literacy, or by using Skype for remote oral questioning of learners

**Table 5.1**

| Assessment of learning | Assessment for learning |
| --- | --- |
| Purpose of portfolio prescribed by institution | Purpose of portfolio agreed upon with learner |
| Artifacts mandated by institution to determine outcomes of instruction | Artifacts selected by learner to tell the story of their learning |
| Portfolio usually developed at the end of a class, term or program—time limited | Portfolio maintained on an ongoing basis throughout the class, term or program—time flexible |
| Portfolio and/or artifacts usually "scored" based on a rubric and quantitative data is collected for external audiences | Portfolio and artifacts reviewed with learner and used to provide feedback to improve learning |
| Portfolio is usually structured around a set of outcomes, goals or standards | Portfolio organization is determined by learner or negotiated with mentor/advisor/teacher |
| Sometimes used to make high stakes decisions | Rarely used for high stakes decisions |
| Summative—what has been learned to date? (Past to present) | Formative—what are the learning needs in the future? (Present to future) |
| Requires extrinsic motivation | Fosters intrinsic motivation—engages the learner |
| Audience: external—little choice | Audience: learner, family, friends—learner can choose |

*Source:* Barrett (2006)

to assess whether the learner actually understands what has been submitted. Elliott also includes an analysis of a wide range of web 2.0 tools suggesting their applicability for various assessment types: summative, formative, individual, peer and group.

Barrett (2006) examines e-portfolios by comparing their use as assessment of learning versus assessment for learning as she shows in Table 5.1.

It is evident from this list that long-held learning beliefs about assessment and established educational methods must be reshaped in order to incorporate the benefits of web 2.0.

## CONCLUSION

Course designers need to exploit the skills students have developed outside formal education without pandering to their desire for instant gratification or shallow thinking. They must see their role as expanding, not contracting because content is no longer the primary requirement. In short, they are not being asked to abdicate their authority, but rather to channel it in a different direction. Courses which exploit web 2.0 technologies and approaches can also be challenging and demanding if they require critical thinking skills and develop knowledge rather than mere information management.

For students, the tools may change, but the real work of analysis, synthesis and deep level engagement with ideas, should not. For institutions, there may well be a sea change that requires re-thinking many sacred cows such as control, authority and ownership. This change does not signal the death-knell of formal education any more than the growth of libraries did. Libraries have existed as long as universities; the web is a somewhat different form of library—full of learning potential, and requiring, not undermining, universities as a means of actualising the potential of learners.

# 6
## POSTSCRIPT

Since the first edition of this book, there have been rapid advances in both the world of digital communications and in its application to education. In particular, the growth of social networking has transformed the way that an entire generation makes links with peers and communicates their ideas to the wider world. It would be unwise to try to predict the scenario in a further five or ten years, almost certainly it will be wrong, but there are some interesting features to note.

## COLD STARTS

Slowly there is a realisation that although students may use technology in their own lives (or they may not), there needs to be an explicit recognition of the requirement to provide instruction on software applications before learners start to use them on educational courses. The fast-changing pace and the almost ubiquitous access to communications technology has somehow implied that because so many people use this technology, they will know *how* to apply this technology effectively for education and learning. There are contrasting views on this; some educators point out that their students have shown a reluctance to engage with social networking media in their academic courses because they prefer to keep their work and private lives separate—a place where they can interact with peers without the presence of their teachers or tutors; others have argued that because people already have a preference for different ways of communicating digitally, there are benefits for the students to bring the technology that they use to the course, rather than switching to institutional applications—such as is practiced on Massive Open Online Courses (MOOCs), which we will come to later in this chapter.

As we indicated in earlier chapters, the new applications are frequently championed by the "early adopters" who, by self-definition,
tend to be technophiles. What follows is frequently a search for ways
to deploy this new application, within education, without first estab-
lishing the strengths, weakness, and "affordances" that the technology
will permit. Some uses will perhaps hit the mark and have a transforming effect on the ability to provide educational resources for a given
subject, and new ways of engaging learners, but other uses have been
shown by experience simply to demonstrate rather clumsy attempts to
simulate "online" versions of standard face-to-face pedagogy. It comes
as little surprise that educational technologists wring their hands in
despair when they see innovative applications being used for inappropriate purposes. The end result may be something counter-productive
for learning, turning an activity that should be stimulating and informative into a frustrating mess of confusion where students focus on
coping with the technology rather than engaging with the content.

We need to assess the merits of the technology for educational purposes and to then (re)design courses to use the potential of the application and remain pedagogically sound. This may be easier said than
done, and there will be some period of time before sufficient evidence
is produced through trial and error to make an informed assessment.
Many web 2.0 educational technologists are realising the potential of
social media for the educational market and are helping with this process by developing specific areas for pedagogical purposes—e.g., Skype
for tutorials, YouTube EDU as a surrogate classroom, and Facebook for
Education is a student support tool, but these are really in their infancy.
It will be enlightening to see if these provide a more enhanced learning
experience for the participants, or merely another marketing tool. In the
meantime, it should not be assumed that the students (guinea pigs) who
are trialling the new technology will be able to, or indeed want to, make
full use of the application through pure intuition. A number of online
educators report that when they provide an induction programme with
clear instructions and technical guidance at the start of a course, they
frequently get greater student buy-in and greater student satisfaction
with the use of the technology. The hope is that this will lead to high levels of student engagement and retention, with a focus on the subject matter (content and context) rather than on the media of communication.

A good example of this that has come to the fore over the past few
years is the use of Facebook in education. While there are obvious concerns over Internet safety when dealing with younger students, there
are an unspecified number of degree courses that incorporate Facebook
links in some aspects of the course. The open and informal nature of

this social medium has been both praised and criticised by academic staff and, while it is currently unlikely that Facebook will be widely adopted for direct tuition purposes, there is a recognition that it may provide a valuable social support role for distributed students who are remote from the campus and from each other. There is still a need, however, to induct students into the appropriate use (subject matter, language, online etiquette, etc.) of Facebook, for example, as a tool for educational support, as opposed to being a place to simply swap tales with close friends. Similarly, while Twitter was barely heard about when the first edition of this book was published, the phenomenal rate of customer adoption has been suggested by some to be a potential means of the mass distribution of educational information. While attention may recently have been centred on the cult of celebrity tweets, which many might regard as "media trivia" rather than education, and while potentially every new communications technology has the scope to perform some educational function, we are still in the very early stages of exploration. Academic colleagues are currently experimenting with Twitter to feed a running commentary of conferences, or to circulate their thoughts (particularly web links to more detailed information in articles and blogs) to specialist "thematic groups" where other colleagues can "follow" current developments as they happen. It remains to be seen if this is a flash in the technological pan or a lasting platform for educational social networking. What should also be recognised is that, in the same way or not, everyone likes to communicate through social networking. However, not all individuals will like or use this method of communication when combined with education. Secondly, even though there are large numbers of students using these sites, they use them in different ways and, this will affect how they might gain from its use in education. Faculty must consider the sorts of technologies they use and how these will be interpreted by the student body— both in terms of competence and psychological profile.

The use of applications such as Facebook, Twitter, and the almost countless other networking technologies (e.g., Google Docs) leads to several other key issues for discussion.

## WHO HAS CONTROL?

As the educational power of online communities of practice becomes increasingly recognised as both a teaching and a support network, new ethical and technical issues come to the fore. For example, many institutions have attempted to create their own online social networks for staff and students to use, in an attempt to reinforce the identity "brand" of their institution. While some of these have been moderately success-ful, they have also raised questions as to why we should create a new social network for students when so many students already use net-works such as Facebook as their first choice. Conversely, many univer-sity courses have utilised "closed" areas of Google-mail or Facebook to provide an online social forum for their students, but these have been criticised from a number of technical and ethical aspects (e.g., the provision of data back-up, support services, privacy of correspon-dence, ease of access, etc.). Again, the issue is raised that students may feel that institutions using Facebook (and other such applications) for educational purposes would be an invasion of their privacy and would prefer the different areas of their lives to be kept separate. Using a sep-arate site requires the student to log-in to an application that might not be quite as functional or exciting as their private social network, but may have other benefits. Incentivising students to become, and remain, active in institutional sites has had a mixed response. Is it bet-ter to invest in separate IT services, or to "go to where the students are" and utilise customised third-party providers? This is not intended to be a comprehensive review of the subject, but simply to raise aware-ness in an educational context of the issues of this fast-changing sec-tor. External hosting of institutional services, whether university email, student records, support communities, or any of the other traditional; campus-based services, has its pros and cons. A certain critical mass of external hosting may improve the efficiency and cost structure for the university, but at the loss of operational control and the ability to provide fine-grained customisation of the services. In the trend of the convergent nature of new technology, some universities are developing apps that allow institutional networks to aggregate different commu-nications tools, internal and external, into one continuous feed to link personal and institutional messages on one site.

These issues are not restricted to educational practice, of course, and there has been an enormous amount written and spoken about the influence of social networking in journalism, music, fashion, and in society in general. There is a subtle but important difference, how-ever, between these and the use of social networks for education. While "the wisdom of crowds" might provide a revolutionary method of news gathering, or creating articles on Wikipedia, through opportunities for mass participation in the creative process, the communications gener-ally do not pretend to be unbiased. They seek to provide an alternative report, to push a particular product, or publicise a particular topic. It is technically possible to pre-select certain news channels, on certain themes, by certain writers, so that we only ever read the news that we want to see and that we know we will agree with. We can select never to see a contradicting opinion or a topic that we consider to be unpleasant. Education, on the other hand, seeks the diversity to examine an issue from several different, challenging, often contradictory angles, and to make sense of these contradictions by reliance upon impartial evidence. In using social software for education, we want to have diverse ideas and we want to share these ideas, but we also want to be able to trust the information.

## OPEN FOR EDUCATION

Another significant trend over the past decade has been a growing movement to share digital resources over the Internet, and, although education is currently only a small proportion of this activity, there are signs that the concept is increasing in significance. The open source movement is part of this enhanced desire to share digital materials, as is the global interest in open educational resources (OER), but despite the interest from universities, colleges, and schools, the main drivers towards sharing have largely been purely recreational leisure motivations through applications such as Flickr and Blipfoto (photographs), YouTube (video clips), and audio files (music, radio programmes, podcasts) for downloading. Of course, these resources also have the potential to be used for educational purposes, but in most cases this was not the primary objective.

By contrast, open educational resources are specifically designed to be shared for educational purposes, and, although the standard definition of OER is "digitised materials offered freely and openly for educators, students and self-learners to use and reuse for teaching, learning and research" (Organisation for Economic Co-operation and Development [OECD], 2007 p. 10), in practice this definition covers a very wide area. With numerous clarifications, a refined definition of an OER is considered to be:

> digitised materials offered freely and openly for educators, students and self-learners to use and re-use for teaching, learning and research. Such resources are accumulated assets that can be enjoyed without restricting the possibilities of others to enjoy them. This means that they should be non-rival (public goods), or that the value of the resource should be enlarged when used (open fountain of goods). Furthermore, to be "open" means that the resources either provide non-discriminatory access to the resource or can also be contributed to and shared by anyone. (OECD, 2007, p. 38)

Despite the huge growth in the creation and availability of OER (often hosted collaboratively through iTunes, Academic Earth, YouTube, or TED). there have been substantially fewer examples of the systematic re-use of OER by educators and institutions in the creation of new programmes. It seems that there is still a reluctance among academics to use educational resources that are "not made here." In contrast, students and learners of all sorts seem to have no such inhibitions. Following the Open Courseware developments by MIT, where the lecture notes and audio recordings of full courses have been made freely available on the web, a number of top universities have also moved in this direction. The Open University (UK) have made available hundreds of free courses on their Openlearn website, and, more recently, under the Stamford Udacity initiative, have started to make high quality, free, open-access courses available to anyone with an Internet connection. This is a fundamental shift in academia, from the universities being the "gatekeepers" to access knowledge to a world where individual academics, and also non-academic experts, can share their resources—articles, images, even data sets—with potentially limitless networks of individuals who essentially co-create the interpretations and build upon the work of others for free. With the move towards open access journals, and with some research funders insisting that the results (and even the raw data) of their funded research must be freely available to the public in such journals (*Guardian*, 2012), there is a definite trend towards public transparency and more open academic collaboration.

This permeability and ecology of inter-linked applications is what has been termed the architecture of participation (O'Reilly, 2004) and is critical for the realisation of networked learning. Faced with this sea change in the availability and relevance of knowledge, Siemens and others have attempted to address the connectedness (of ideas and of technology) and the disposability of knowledge, by running Massive Open Online Courses (MOOCs; Cormier, 2010). Central to this idea is that rather than have an educator design a complete course that students are required to learn, the MOOC provides a learning structure through which a large number of individuals can link freely, contribute their own knowledge and their questions, and through a structured process of interaction can direct their own learning experience (Rheingold, 2011). The "course" is therefore constructed mainly by the participants, who in turn gain different rewards from it according to their own frameworks and expectations. This is entirely consistent with the points made in earlier chapters relating to the attention economy (Gold Haber, 1997, 1998) in which, from the complex mass of available information, it will be the few pieces of information that have the ability to attract our attention that we place the highest value.

## DIGITAL SCHOLARSHIP

This leads us on very nicely to another concept that is gaining recognition—increasingly academics are placing their thoughts, their ideas, and their written articles in online spaces rather than (or as well as) in the format of the printed journal. Only reluctantly, however, are academic institutions giving recognition to online scholarship with regards to academic reputation and career promotion—perhaps because the new technologies are "fast, cheap, and out of control", whereas the institutions have a strong vested interest in being the elitist gatekeepers of more restrictive traditional means of knowledge dissemination. Weller (2011) has explored this in detail and is an excellent source.. The ability of academics and scholars to spread their ideas via digital resources to unspecified individuals who can then aggregate, re-mix, and re-use these resources in different situations, is a powerful, disruptive, and potentially liberating innovation for education. The extent to which we can make these resources free, or at least a common public service, is tantalising, but certainly, as academics, we should actively seek opportunities to use digital technology to construct new spaces for learning in a similar way to that which Oldenburgh (1995) described "third places" (after work and the home) as meaningful centres of social interaction and social learning.

The increasing ability of everyone to become not simply a consumer, but a creator (or co-creator) of information and to share this easily in digital format that enables easy aggregation and re-purposing, is a powerful driver for open education. Weller (2011) notes that already we are seeing academics gain wider recognition from their blog site or You-Tube clip than from an article on the same subject in a printed journal. Already we notice that of the many tens of thousands who are following the free courses available on the web from trusted university sources, only a tiny percentage are actually studying these for a formal credit. The notion of "life-long learning" (for fun or for continuous professional development) is merging hand-in-hand with the realisation of the academic expert as an international star with a global audience for their ideas.

## COMMUNITY OF INQUIRY

Finally, the concept of social networking is critical to the notion of a community of inquiry (and also a community of practice) where people come together, and, through their interaction, create a discourse that builds understanding through social constructivism. The three necessary components of the community of enquiry are: the teaching presence, cognitive presence and the social presence.

While we can achieve all three in face-to-face pedagogy, we have been trying, with varying degrees of success, to achieve the third—social presence, in the online learning environment. In our efforts to address this, we have turned to these social networking technologies as the panacea to cure some of the problems of retaining student engagement in the online environment. We might not have got the content right, but the media does appear to have advantages if used appropriately. Research indicates that where students feel that instructors are interacting with them in a trusting environment, on a regular basis, their levels of engagement are enhanced. Similarly, where students feel they are able to communicate with peers and use them as a support network, they, too, develop greater critical thinking skills. It may be that the use of social networking in education does not simply require adaptation of the technology, but a continued drive towards learning practise which views the relationship between the individual student, their peers, and the tutor, as being of equal importance. This cycle of support and inquiry is one where learning communities reside. The contemporary higher education institution is one in which each member of the cycle is capable of providing knowledge, support and problem solutions in a community of enquiry. Social networking technologies provide a mechanism to enhance and sustain these communities, but only if all three types of "presence" are addressed.

Communities of enquiry are developing to have many functions—some for peer-to-peer support, for sharing information and problem-solving, or for exploiting a distributed model of gathering user inputs. To some extent this new, more open model of collaboration is impeded by existing "traditional" ideas of the solitary researcher and restricted publication for specialists in peer-reviewed journals, but as we have seen these attitudes are also changing. On the other hand, the issue of having confidence in "trusted sources" will be crucial at all levels of sharing communities, from students' discussion class assignments to international researchers making their data and ideas available for others to work on before they themselves have published their results. In both cases a shared understanding of the process of education and a common vision of the value of education is a unifying community factor.

In online education, there is frequent discussion about what technology "will allow" educationalists to do with their courses and their students. This technological determinism, this view of assuming that technology shapes the way that we work and interact with other humans, can be a very negative perspective. In this book we have tried to show that it is the cultural attributes of individuals that shape the way that technology is used in our society, and that we should first look at the people, the culture, and the pedagogy of the individuals we want to educate. Only after that, should we seek the most appropriate technology to facilitate the learning interchanges. However, it is going to be used in the future, digital social networking has already transformed our understandings of the purpose, the structure, and the very nature of higher education.

# REFERENCES

Allen, I., & Seaman, J. (2006). Making the grade: Online education in the United States. Retrieved December 12, 2007, from the Sloan Consortium website http://www.sloan-c.org/publications/survey/pdf/making_the_grade.pdf

Allen, M. (2004). *Assessing academic programs in higher education.* Bolton, MA: Aker.

American Association of University Professors (AAUP), Special Committee on Distance Education and Intellectual Property Issues. (2002). *Suggestions and guidelines: Sample language for institutional policies and contract language.* Retrieved December 12, 2007, from http://www.aaup. org/AAUP/issues/DE/sampleDE.htm

Anderson, C. (2006, July 14). People power. *Wired Magazine.* Retrieved December 12, 2007, from http://www.wired.com/wired/archive/14.07/people.html

Anderson, P. (2007). *What is Web 2.0? Ideas, technologies and implications for education.* Retrieved December 12, 2007, from http://www.jisc.ac.uk/media/documents/techwatch/tsw0701b.pdf

Aspden, E. J., & Thorpe, L. P. (2009). Where do you learn?: Tweeting to Inform Learning Space Development. *Educause Quarterly, 32*(1). Retrieved June 11, 2012, from http://www.educause.edu/ero/article/where-do-you-learn-tweeting-inform-learning-space-development

Attwell, G. (2007). Web 2.0 and the changing ways we are using computers for learning: What are the implications for pedagogy and curriculum? *elearning Europa.* Retrieved December 12, 2007, from http://www.elearningeuropa.info/files/media/media13018.pdf

Baker, S. C., Wentz, R. K., & Woods, M. M. (2009). Using virtual worlds in education: Second Life® as an educational tool. *Teaching of Psychology, 36*(1), 59-64.

Barrett, H. (2006). *Authentic assessment with electronic portfolios using common software and Web 2.0 tools.* Retrieved December 12, 2007, from http://electronicport folios.org/web20.html

Bates, A. (2005). *Technology, e-learning and distance education* (2nd ed.). Abingdon, UK: Routledge.

Behan, A., & Boylan, F. (2009). Harnessing developments in technology and merging them with new approaches to teaching: a practical example of the effective use of wikis and social bookmarking sites in 3rd level professional education. *Articles.* Paper 4. Retrieved from http://arrow.dit.ie/beschspart/4

Beldarrain, Y. (2006). Distance education trends: Integrating new technologies to foster student interaction and collaboration. *Distance Education, 27*(2), 139–153.

Bloch, M. (n.d.). Web 2.0, mashups and social networking—What is it all about? Retrieved December 12, 2007, from http://www.tamingthebeast.net/articles6/web2-mashups-social-network.htm

Blood, R. (2002). *The weblog handbook: Practical advice on creating and maintaining your blog.* Cambridge, MA: Perseus Books Group.

Boettcher, J. (2007). Ten core principles for designing effective learning environments: Insights from brain research and pedagogical theory. *Innovate Journal of Online Education, 3*(3). Retrieved December 12, 2007, from http://innovateonline.info/index.php?view=issue&id=18

Bonk, C., & Graham, C. (Eds.). (2006). *The handbook of blended learning.* San Francisco: Wiley.

Boud, D. (1995). Assessment as learning: Contradictory or complementary? In P. Knight (Ed.), *Assessment for learning* (pp. 35–48). London: Kogan Page.

Bowen, K. (2011). Mixable: A mobile and connected learning environment. *Educause Quarterly, 34*(1). Retrieved form http://www.educause.edu/EDUCAUSE+Quarterly/EDUCAUSEQuarterlyMagazineVolum/MixableAMobileandConnectedLear/225849

Bower, B. (2001). Distance education: Facing the faculty challenge. *Online Journal of Distance Learning Administration, 4*(2). Retrieved from December 12, 2007, http://www.westga.edu/~distance/ojdla/summer42/bower42.html

Boyd, D. (2006a). Social network sites: My definition. Retrieved December 12, 2007, from http://www.zephoria.org/thoughts/archives/2006/11/10/social_network_1.html

Boyd, D. (2006b). Identity production in a networked culture: Why youth heart. The role of networked publics in teenage social life. In D. Bucking-ham (Ed.), *Youth, Identity, and Digital Media* (pp. 119–142). Cambridge, MA: MIT Press.

Buckless, F., Krawczyk, K., & Showalter, S. (2012). Accounting education in the Second Life world. *CPA Journal, 82*(3), 68–71.

Caine, R. N., & Caine, G. (1991). *Making connections: Teaching and the human brain.* Alexandria, VA: Association for Supervision and Curriculum Development.

Cargill-Kipar, N. (2009). My dragonfly flies upside down! Using Second Life in multimedia design to teach students programming. *British Journal of Educational Technology, 40*(3), 539–542.

Carlson, S. (2005, October). The net generation goes to college. *The Chronicle of Higher Education, 52.* Retrieved December 12, 2007, from http://chronicle.com/free/v52/i07/07a03401.htm

Casey, J., & Wilson, P. (2006). A practical guide to providing fl exible learning in further and higher education. Quality Assurance Agency for Higher Education. Retrieved December 12, 2007, from http://trustdr.ulster.ac.uk/outputs/flexDeliveryGuide.php

Castells, M. (2001). *The internet galaxy: Reflections on the internet, business, and society.* Oxford, UK: Oxford University Press.

Chau, J., & Cheng, G. (2010). Towards understanding the potential of e-portfolios for independent learning: A qualitative study. *Australasian Journal of Educational Technology, 26*(7), 932–950. Retrieved from http://www.ascilite.org.au/ajet/ajet26/chau.pdf

Cheetham, J., Ackerman, S. & Christoph, K. (2009) Podcasting: A stepping stone to pedagogical innovation. *Educause Quarterly, 32*(4). Retrieved from http://www.educause.edu/ero/article/podcasting-stepping-stone-pedagogical-innovation

Chisholm, J. (2006). Pleasure and danger in online teaching and learning. *Academe Online, 92*(6). Retrieved December 12, 2007, from http://www.aaup.org/AAUP/pubsres/academe/2006/ND/Feat/chis.htm

Cho, H., Gay, G., Davidson, B., & Ingraffea, A. (2007). Social networks, communication styles, and learning performance in a CSCL community. *Computers and Education, 49* (2), 309–329.

Coats, M., & Stevenson, A. (2006, July). *Towards outcomes-based assessment: An unfinished story of triangulation and transformation.* Paper presented at the Association for the Study of Evaluation and Assessment in Education in Southern Africa Conference. Retrieved December 12, 2007, from http://www.open.ac.uk/cobe/docs/ASEASA2006.pdf

Coates, T. (2003). (Weblogs and) the mass amateurisation of (nearly) everything. Retrieved December 12, 2007, from http://www.plasticbag.org/archives/2003/09/weblogs_and_the_mass_amateurisation_of_nearly_everything/

Collis, B. & Moonen, J. (2001). *Flexible learning in a digital world.* London: Kogan Page.

Conole, G., de Laat, M., Dillon, T., & Darby, J. (2006). Student experiences of technologies. Joint Information Systems Committee (JISC) Final Report. Retrieved December 12, 2007, from http://www.jisc.ac.uk/media/documents/programmes/elearning_pedagogy/lxp%20project%20fi nal%20re port%20dec%2006.pdf

Conole, G., Oliver, M., Falconer, I., Littlejohn, A., & Harvey, J. (2007). Designing for learning. In G. Conole & M. Oliver (Eds.), *Contemporary perspectives in e-learning research: Themes, methods and impact on practice* (pp. 101–120). Abingdon, UK: Routledge Falmer.

Cormier, D. (2010). What is a MOOC? Retrieved June 12, 2012, from http://www.youtube.com/watch?v=eW3gMGqcZQc

Crone, I., & MacKay, K. (2007). Motivating today's college students. *Peer Review, Association of American Colleges and University, 9*(1). Retrieved December 12, 2007, from http://www.aacu.org/peerreview/pr-wi07/prwi07_practice.cfm

Cross, J. (2007). Designing a web-based learning ecology. Retrieved December 12, 2007, from http://informl.com/?p=697#more-697

Dailly, H., & Price, S. (2007). *The electronic training needs analysis (ETNA): Vol. 3. Scottish colleges and the provision of learning for the digital generation: An analysis of staff capabilities and training needs.* Edinburgh: Joint Information Systems Committee (JISC) Regional Support Centre for Scotland.

De Maio, C., Fenza, G., Gaeta, M., Loia, V., Orciuoli, F., and Senatore, S. (2012) RSS-based e-learning recommendations exploiting fuzzy FCA for Knowledge Modelling. *Applied Soft Computing, 12,* 113-124.

Deal, A. (2007). Podcasting: A teaching with technology white paper. *Educause Connect.* Retrieved December 12, 2007, from http://connect.educause.edu/files/CMU_Podcasting_Jun07.pdf

Deng, L., & Yuen, A. H. K. (2012). Understanding student perceptions and motivation towards academic blogs: An exploratory study. *Australasian Journal of Educational Technology, 28*(1), 48-66. Retrieved from http://www.ascilite.org.au/ajet/ajet28/deng.html

Dillenbourg, P., & Traum, D. (1996). Grounding in multi-modal task-oriented collaboration. In P. Brna, A. Paiva, & J. Self (Eds.), *Proceedings of the European conference on artificial intelligence in education* (pp. 401–407), Lisbon, Portugal.

Downes, S. (2007). Learning networks in practice. In *Emerging technologies for learning* (Vol. 2). Retrieved December 12, 2007, from the British Educational Communications and Technology Agency, Coventry website http://partners.becta.org.uk/index.php?section=rh&rid=13768

Driscoll, M. (2000). *Psychology of learning for instruction*. Needham Heights, MA: Allyn & Bacon.

Duffy, P., & Bruns, A. (2006, September 26). The use of blogs, wikis, and RSS in education: A conversation of possibilities. In *Proceedings of the Online Learning and Teaching Conference 2006, Brisbane, Australia*. Retrieved from https://olt.qut.edu.au/udf/OLT2006/gen/static/papers/Duffy_OLT2006_paper.pdf

Duffy, T. M., & Cunningham, D. J. (1996). Constructivism: Implications for the design and delivery of instruction, In D. H. Jonassen (Ed.), *Handbook of research for educational communications and technology* (pp. 170–198). New York: Macmillan.

Dunlap, J. C., & Lowenthal, P. R. (2009). Tweeting the night away: Using Twitter to enhance social presence. *Journal of Information Systems Education, 20*(2). Retrieved June 11, 2012, from http://patricklowenthal.com/publications/Using_Twitter_to_Enhance_Social_Presence.pdf

Elliott, B. (2007). Assessment 2.0. Retrieved from Scottish Qualifications Authority's website http://www.sqa.org.uk/sqa/22941.html

Estabrook, L. (1999, April 10). *New forms of distance education: Opportunities for students, threats to institutions*. Paper presented at the Association of College and Research Libraries National Conference, Detroit.

Farwell, T. M., & Waters, R. D. (2010). Exploring the use of social bookmarking technology in Education: An analysis of students' experiences using a course-specific Delicious.com account. *Journal of Online Learning and Teaching, 6*(2), 398–408.

Fogg, B. J., & Eckles, D. (Eds.). (2008). *Mobile persuasion*. Stanford, CA: Stanford Captology Media.

Gagnon, G., & Collay, M. (2006). *Constructivist learning design: Key questions for teaching to standards*. New York: Sage.

Garrison, D., & Baynton, M. (1989). Beyond independence in distance education: The concept of control. In M. Moore & G. Clark (Eds.), *Readings in principles of distance education* (pp. 3–15). University Park, PA: American Center for the Study of Distance Education.

Gibson, S. & McKay, R. (1999) What Constructivist theory and brain research may offer social studies. Retrieved from http://www.educ.ualberta.ca/css/Css_35_4/ARconstructionist_theory.htm

Goldhaber, M. (1998). The attention economy will change everything. *Telepolis*. Retrieved December 12, 2007, from http://www.heise.de/tp/english/inhalt/te/1419/1.html

Goldhaber, M. H. (1997). The attention economy and the net. *First Monday, 2*(4). Retrieved December 12, 2007, from http://www.firstmonday.org/issues/issue2_4/goldhaber/index.html

Gorman, M. (2007). Jabberwiki: The educational response. Part II, Britannica Blog. Retrieved December 12, 2007, from http://blogs.britannica.com/blog/main/2007/06/jabberwiki-the-educational-response-part-ii/

Gormley, P., & Tooher, M. (2009). *Introduction to podcasting: From pilot to mainstream*. Galway, Ireland: Staff Development Workshop, National University of Ireland.

Gourley, B. (2006, September 26). Vice Chancellor's speech to Council. *Open House*, [internal publication of the University].

Groves, M., & O'Donoghue, J. (2009) Reflections of students in their use of asynchronous online seminars. *Educational Technology & Society, 12*(3), 143–149.

*Guardian.* (n.d.). Retrieved from http://www.guardian.co.uk/commentisfree/uk-edition

*Guardian.* (2012). Wellcome Trust joins "Academic Spring" to open up science. Retrieved June 20, 2012 from http://www.guardian.co.uk/science/2012/apr/09/wellcome-trust-academic-spring

Gudmundsson, A., & Matthiasdottir, A. (2004). Distributed learning in the Nordic countries and Canada. *European Journal of Open, Distance and e-Learning (EURODL).* Retrieved December 12, 2007, from http://www. eurodl.org/materials/contrib/2004/Arnor_Gudmundsson.htm

Guinee, K., & Eagleton, M. (2006). Spinning straw into gold: Transforming information into knowledge during web-based research. *English Journal, 95*(4), 46–52.

Habuchi, I. (2005). Accelerating reflexivity. In M. Ito, D. Okabe, & M. Matsuda (Eds.), *Personal, portable, pedestrian: Mobile phones in Japanese life* (pp. 165–182). Cambridge, MA: MIT.

Hall, R., Watkins, S., & Eller, V. (2003). A model of web-based design for learning. In M. Moore & W. Anderson (Eds.), *Handbook of distance education* (pp. 367–376). Mahwah, NJ: Erlbaum.

Hatton, N., & Smith, D. (1995). Facilitating reflection: Issues and research. *Forum of Education, 50*(1), 49–65.

Hemmi, A., Bayne, S., & Land, R. (2009). The appropriation and repurposing of social technologies in higher education. *Journal of Computer Assisted Learning, 25,* 19–30. Retrieved form http://www.malts.ed.ac.uk/staff/sian/pdfs/jcal_paper.pdf

Henderson, L. (1996) Instructional design of interactive multimedia: A cultural critique. *Educational Technology Research and Development, 44*(4), 86–104.

Herrington, J., & Oliver, R. (2002). Designing for reflection in online courses. *Higher Education Research & Development Society of Australia (HERDSA),* 2002, 313–319. Retrieved December 12, 2007, from http://elrond.scam.ecu.edu.au/oliver/2002/HerringtonJ.pdf

Himpsl, K., & Baumgartner, P. (2009). Evaluation of e-portfolio software. [Special Issue on e-portfolios] *International Journal of Emerging Technologies in Learning, 4*(1), 16-22 Retrieved from http://online-journals.org/i-jet/issue/view/51

Hine, T. (1999). *The rise and fall of the American teenager.* New York: HarperCollins.

Holtman, L. (2009, January). Using wikis in the teaching of a short course on the history and philosophy of science. *International Journal of Instructional Technology and Distance Learning.* Retrieved from http://www.itdl.org/journal/jan_09/article03.htm

Howe, N., & Strauss, W. (2000). *Millennials rising.* New York: Vintage Books.

Irlbeck, S., Kays, E., Jones, D., & Sims, R. (2006). The phoenix rising: Emergent models of instructional design. *Distance Education, 37*(2), 171–185.

Jameson, J., Ferrell, G., Kelly, J., Walker, S., & Ryan, M. (2006). Building trust and shared knowledge in communities of e-learning practice: Collaborative leadership in the JISC, eLISA and CAMEL lifelong learning projects. *British Journal of Educational Technology, 37*(6), 949–967.

Jegede, O. J., Gooley, A., & Towers, S. (1996). An Evaluation of the Queensland Open

Learning Network Audiographic Conferencing Professional Development Programs. *Journal of Instructional Science and Technology*, 1(4) Article 2. Retrieved from http://www.ascilite.org.au/ajet/e-jist/docs/vol1no4/article2.htm

Jenkins, H. (2006a). Confronting the challenges of participatory culture: Media education for the 21st century. Retrieved December 12, 2007, from the MacArthur Foundation website http://www.digitallearning.macfound.org/atf/cf/%7B7E45C7E0-A3E0-4B89-AC9C-E807E1B0AE4E%7D/JENKINS_WHITE_PAPER.PDF

Jenkins, H. (2006b). Confronting the challenges of participatory culture: Media education for the 21st century. Retrieved from New Media Literacy website http://www.projectnml.org/files/working/NMLWhitePaper.pdf

Jeong, W. (2007). Instant messaging in on-site and online classes in higher education. *Educause Quarterly*, 1. Retrieved from http://www.educause.edu/ir/library/pdf/eqm0714.pdf

Jochems, W., van Merrienboer, J., & Koper, R. (Eds.). (2003). *Integrated e-learning: implications for pedagogy, technology and organization*. Abingdon, UK: Routledge Falmer.

Johnson, D., & Johnson, R. (2004). Cooperation and the use of technology. In D. Jonassen (Ed.), *Handbook of research on educational communications and technology* (2nd ed.; pp. 1017–1044). Mahwah, NJ: Erlbaum.

Johnson, L., Smith, R., Willis, H., Levine, A., & Haywood, K. (2011). *The Horizon Report: 2011 edition*. Austin, TX: New Media Consortium.

Joint Information Systems Committee (JISC). (2004). *Effective practice with e-learning: A good practice guide in designing for learning*. Bristol: The Higher Education Funding Council for England. Retrieved December 12, 2007, from http://www.jisc.ac.uk/elp_practice.html

Joint Information Systems Committee (JISC). (2005) *Innovative practice with e-learning: A good practice guide to embedding mobile and wireless technologies into everyday practice*. Bristol: The Higher Education Funding Council for England. (pp. 5–56). Retrieved December 12, 2007, from http://www.jisc.ac.uk/uploaded_documents/publication_txt.pdf

Joint Information Systems Committee (JISC). (2008). *Effective practice with e-portfolios*. Retrieved from http://www.jisc.ac.uk/eportfolio

Joyes, G., Gray, L., & Hartnell-Young, E. (2010) Effective practice with e-portfolios: How can the UK experience inform implementation? *Australasian Journal of Educational Technology*, 26(1), 15–27. Retrieved from http://www.ascilite.org.au/ajet/ajet26/joyes.pdf

Junco, R., Heibergert, G., & Loken, E. (2011). The effect of Twitter on college student engagement and grades. *Journal of Computer Assisted Learning*, 27, 119–132. Retrieved on 13 June 2012 from http://onlinelibrary.wiley.com/doi/10.1111/j.1365-2729.2010.00387.x/pdf

Junco, R. (2012a). Too much face and not enough books: The relationship between multiple indices of Facebook use and academic performance. *Computers in Human Behavior*, 28(1), 187–198. http://reyjunco.com/wordpress/pdf/JuncoCHBFacebookGrades.pdf

Junco, R. (2012b). The relationship between frequency of Facebook use, participation in Facebook activities, and student engagement. *Computers & Education*, 58(1) 162–171. http://blog.reyjunco.com/pdf/JuncoFacebookEngagementCAE2011.pdf

Kapp, K. (2006). Gadgets, games and gizmos: Informal learning at Nick.com. Retrieved December 12, 2007, from http://karlkapp.blogspot.com/2006/12/gadgets-games-and-gizmos-informal.html

Karpati, A. (2002). Net generation. Retrieved from http://www.emile.eu.org/Papers1.htm

Kaur, M. (2011). Using online forums in language learning and education. *Student Pulse, 3.03*. Retrieved from http://www.studentpulse.com/a?id=414

Kear, K. (2004). Peer learning using asynchronous discussion systems in distance education. *Open Learning, 19*(2), 151–164.

Keen, A. (2007). *The cult of the amateur: How today's internet is killing our culture*. London: Nicholas Brealey.

Kesmit3. (2009). The Twitter experiment: University of Texas, Dallas. YouTube. Retrieved June 11, 2012, from http://www.youtube.com/watch?v=6WPVWDkF7U8

Kim, A. J. (2000). *Community building on the web: Secret strategies for successful online communities*. Berkeley, CA: Peachpit Press.

Kim, B. (2001). Social constructivism. In M. Orey (Ed.), *Emerging perspectives on learning, teaching, and technology*. Retrieved from http://www.coe.uga.edu/epltt/SocialConstructivism.htm

King, K., & Gura, M. (2007). *Podcasting for educators*. Greenwich, CT: Information Age.

Kirkwood, A., & Price, L. (2005). Learners and learning in the twenty-first century: What do we know about students' attitudes towards and experiences of information and communication technologies that will help us design courses? *Studies in Higher Education, 30*(3), 257–274.

Konieczny, P. (2007, January) Wikis and Wikipedia as a teaching tool. *International Journal of Instructional Technology and Distance Learning*. Retrieved from http://www.itdl.org/Journal/Jan_07/article02.htm

Koole, M., McQuilkin, J. L., & Ally, M. (2010). Mobile learning in distance education: Utility or futility? *The Journal of Distance Education 24*(2), 59-82.

Kvavik, R., & Caruso, J. (2005). *Study of students and information technology: Convenience, connection, control, and learning* (Vol. 6). Boulder, CO: Educause Center for Applied Research, Research Study. Retrieved December 12, 2007, from http://www.educause.edu/ir/library/pdf/ers0506/rs/ers0506w.pdf

Lamb, B. (2007, July/August). Dr Mashup; or, why educators should learn to stop worrying and love the remix. *Educause Review, 42*(4), 12–25. Retrieved December 12, 2007, from http://www.educause.edu/apps/er/erm07/erm0740.asp

Lan, Y-F, & Sie, Y-S. (2010) Using RSS to support mobile learning based on media richness theory. *Computers in Education, 55*, 723-732.

Langenbach, C., & Bodendorf, F. (1997). Learner support in a distributed learning environment: The use of www-based teachware packages. *Information Research, 3*(1). Retrieved December 12, 2007, from http://informationr.net/ir/3-1/paper31.html

LaRose, R., & Whitten, P. (2000). Re-thinking instructional immediacy for web courses: A social cognitive exploration. *Communication Education, 49*, 320–338.

Lea, M., & Nicoll, K. (2002). *Distributed learning. Social and cultural approaches to practice*. London: Routledge.

Lee, J., & Bonk, C. J. (2009). Exploring the use of wikis for the improvement of English writing skills: Research, reflections, and recommendations. *International Journal of Instructional Technology and Distance Learning.* Retrieved from http://www.itdl.org/Journal/Jun_09/article02.htm

Lenhart, A. (2012). *Teens and online video.* Washington, DC: Pew Internet and American Life Project, Pew Research Center. http://pewinternet.org/Reports/2012/Teens-and-online-video.aspx

Livingstone, S., & Bober, M. (2005). UK children go online. Retrieved December 12, 2007, from http://www.york.ac.uk/res/e-society/projects/1.htm

Lohnes, S., & Kinzer, C. (2007). Questioning assumptions about students' expectations for technology in college classrooms. *Innovate, 3*(5). Retrieved December 12, 2007, from http://www.innovateonline.info/index.php?view=article&id=431

Lorenzen, M. (1999). Using outcome-based education in the planning and teaching of new information technologies. *Journal of Library Administration, 26* (3–4), 141–152. Retrieved December 12, 2007, from http://www.libraryinstruction.com/obe.html

Luor, T., Wu, L., Lu, H. &, Tao, Y. (2010). The effect of emoticons in simplex and complex task-oriented communication: An empirical study of instant messaging. *Computers in Human Behavior,* 26(5), 889–895.

Lynch, J., & Collins, F. (2001). From the horse's mouth: Factors inhibiting and driving innovation in ICT education. *Melbourne Studies in Education, 42*(2), 105–130. Retrieved December 12, 2007, from http://www.aare.edu.au/01pap/lyn01093.htm

McConnell, D., Lally, V., & Banks, S. (2004). *Theory and design of distributed networked learning communities.* Paper presented at Networked Learning Conference, Lancaster, UK. Retrieved December 12, 2007, from http://www.networkedlearningconference.org.uk/past/nlc2004/proceedings/symposia/symposium11/mcconnell_et_al.htm

McGovern, J., Pannan, L., & van der Craats, C. (2001, April 22–25). Large-scale delivery of web based university courses: The experience of one science faculty. In A. Treloar & A. Ellis (Eds.), AusWeb01: The pervasive web. *Proceedings of 7th Australian world wide web conference* (pp. 235–246). Lismore, NSW, Australia: Southern Cross University Press. Retrieved December 12, 2007, from http://ausweb.scu.edu.au/aw01/papers/refereed/mcgovern/paper.html

McNeil, A. (2010). Twitter in higher education—case studies of practice, University of Kingston. Retrieved June 11, 2012, from http://www.scribd.com/doc/27156556/Twitter-HE-Case-Studies

McSporran, M., & Young, S. (2004, November). Critical skills for online teaching. *Bulletin of Applied Computing and Information Technology, 2*(3). Retrieved December 12, 2007, from http://www.naccq.ac.nz/bacit/0203/2004McSporran_OnlineSkills.htm

Mader, S. (2006a). Ways to use wiki in education. Retrieved December 12, 2007, from http://www.wikiineducation.com/display/ikiw/Ways+to+use+wiki+in+education

Mader, S. (Ed.). (2006b). *Using wiki in education, the book.* Retrieved December 12, 2007, from http://www.wikiineducation.com

Maguire, L. (2005). Literature review—Faculty participation in online distance education: Barriers and motivators. *Online Journal of Distance Learning Administration, 8*(1). Retrieved December 12, 2007, from http://www.westga.edu/%7Edistance/ojdla/spring81/aguire81.pdf

Marginson, S., & Considine, M. (2000). *The enterprise university: Power, governance and reinvention in Australia.* Cambridge, UK: Cambridge University Press.

Mason, J., & Lefrere, P. (2003). Trust, collaboration, e-learning and organisational transformation. *International Journal of Training and Development, 7*(4), 259–270.

Mason, R., & Rennie, F. (2006). *eLearning: The key concepts.* Abingdon, UK: Routledge.

Matheos, K., & Archer, W. (2004). From distance education to distributed learning surviving and thriving. *Online Journal of Distance Learning Administration, 7*(4). Retrieved December 12, 2007, from http://www.westga.edu/~distance/ojdla/winter74/matheos74.htm

Meyers, C., & Jones, T. B. (1993). *Promoting active learning: Strategies for the college classroom.* San Francisco: Jossey-Bass.

Middlehurst, R. (2002). *Will e-learning have a dramatic effect on the overseas student market?* Paper presented at UUK Policy Conference, The Future of Higher Education: Profits, Partnerships and the Public Good, London.

Mitchell, L. (2002). *Active learning and reflection, higher education academy.* Retrieved December 12, 2007, from http://www.heacademy.ac.uk/resources

Moon, J. (2005). Learning through reflection. *Higher Education Academy guide for busy academics,* No. 4. Retrieved from http://www.heacademy.ac.uk/resources

Morrissey, J. (2012). Podcast steering of independent learning in higher education. *All Ireland Journal of Teaching and Learning in Higher Education (AISHE-J),* 4(1), 1–7. Rertrieved from http://ojs.aishe.org/index.php/aishe-j/article/view/60/45

Motschnig-Pitrik, R., & Holzinger, A. (2002). Student-centered teaching meets new media: Concept and case study. *Educational Technology & Society, 5*(4), 160–172. Retrieved December 12, 2007, from http://www.ifets.info/journals/5_4/renate.pdf

Nelson, L. (2010). How to use electronic forums to improve group communication. *E- how.com.* Retrieved from http://www.ehow.com/how_6338777_use-forums-improve-groupcommunication.html#ixzz10k19bcQj

New Media Consortium. (2007). *The horizon report 2007 edition.* Retrieved December 12, 2007, from The New Media Consortium and Educause website http://www.nmc.org/horizon/2007/report

Niemi, H., Launonen, A., & Reahalme, O. (Eds.). (2002, September 11–14). *Towards self-regulation and social navigation in virtual learning spaces: Proceedings of the European Conference on Educational Research, University of Lisbon.* Retrieved December 12, 2007, from http://www.leeds.ac.uk/educol/documents/00002589.htm

Normand, C., & Littlejohn, A. (2006). A model for analysis and implementation of flexible programme delivery. Quality Assurance Agency for Higher Education. Retrieved from http://www.enhancementthemes.ac.uk/documents/flexibleDelivery/fl exible_delivery_QAA_124.pdf

Notari, M. (2006, August 21–23). How to use a wiki in education: Wiki based effective constructive learning. *Proceedings of the 2006 International Symposium on Wikis* (pp. 131–132). Odense, Denmark. Retrieved December 12, 2007, from http://www.wikisym.org/ws2006/proceedings/p131.pdf

Oblinger, D., Barone, C., & Hawkins, B. (2001). Distributed education and its challenges: An overview. Retrieved December 12, 2007, from American Council on

Education website http://www.acenet.edu/bookstore/pdf/distributed-learning/distributed-learning-01.pdf

Oblinger, D., & Oblinger, J. (Eds.). (2005). *Educating the net generation.* Boulder, CO: Educause. Retrieved December 12, 2007, from http://www.educause.edu/ir/library/pdf/pub7101.pdf

Oldenburg, R. (1995). *The great good place: Cafes, coffee shops, bookstores, bars, hair salons and other hangouts at the heart of a community.* New York: Marlowe & Company

Oliver, M., & Trigwell, K. (2005). Can "blended learning" be redeemed? *E-Learning,* 2(1), 17–26. Retrieved December 12, 2007, from http://www.wwwords.co.uk.

O'Quinn, L., & Corry, M. (2002). Factors that deter faculty from participating in distance education. *Online Journal of Distance Learning Administration,* 5(4). Retrieved December 12, 2007, from http://www.westga.edu/~distance/ojdla/winter54/Quinn54.htm

O'Reilly, T. (2004). *The architecture of participation.* Retrieved June 15, 2012, from http://oreilly.com/pub/a/oreilly/tim/articles/architecture_of_participation.html

O'Reilly, T. (2005). What is Web 2.0? Retrieved December 12, 2007, from http://www.oreillynet.com/pub/a/oreilly/tim/news/2005/09/30/what-isweb-20.html?page=1

Organisation for Economic Co-operation and Development (OECD). (2007) Giving knowledge for free: The emergence of open educational resources. Retrieved June 15, 2012, from Centre for Educational Research and Innovation http://www.oecd.org/document/41/0,3343,en_2649_201185_38659497_1_1_1_1,00.html

Owen, M. (2004). The myth of the digital native. Retrieved December 12, 2007, from http://www.futurelab.org.uk/resources/publications_reports_articles/web_articles/Web_Article561

Pachnowski, L., & Jurczyk, J. (2003). Perceptions of faculty on the eff ect of distance learning technology on faculty preparation time. *Online Journal of Distance Learning Administration,* 6(03). Retrieved December 12, 2007, from http://www.westga.edu/~distance/ojdla/fall63/pachnowski64.html

Pallof, R., & Pratt, K. (2003). *Virtual student: A profile and guide to working with online learners.* San Francisco: Jossey-Bass.

Pan, C-C. (2011). Guidelines, challenges, and recommendations for digital game-based learning. International. *Journal of Instructional Technology and Distance Learning,* 8(4). Retrieved from http://www.itdl.org/Journal/Jul_11/index.htm

Papert, S. (1998). Does easy do it? Children, games, and learning. *Game Developer.* Retrieved December 12, 2007, from http://www.papert.org/articles/Doeseasydoit.html

Parker, A. (2003). Motivation and incentives for distance faculty. *Online Journal of Distance Learning Administration,* 6(3). Retrieved December 12, 2007, from http://www.westga.edu/%7Edistance/ojdla/fall63/parker63.pdf

Parker, K. R., & Chao, J. T. (2007). Wiki as a teaching tool. *Interdisciplinary Journal of Knowledge and Learning Objects,* 3, 57–72. Retrieved December 12, 2007, from http://ijklo.org/Volume3/IJKLOv3p057-072Parker284.pdf

Philip, D. (2007). The knowledge building paradigm: A model of learning for net generation students. *Innovate,* 3(5). Retrieved December 12, 2007, from http://www.innovateonline.info/index.php?view=article&id=368

Poore, M. (2006). Web 2.0 and the future of education. Retrieved from http://eganpoore.wordpress.com/2006/10/29/6/

Poster, M. (1990). *The mode of information. Poststructuralism and social contexts.* Cambridge, UK: Polity Press.

Prasad, D. (2010, December). Launching towards a university-wide implementation of an ePortfolio system. *International Journal of Instructional Technology and Distance Learning.* Retrieved from http://www.itdl.org/Journal/Dec_10/article04.htm

Preece, J. (2000). *Online communities: Designing usability, supporting sociability.* Chichester, UK: Wiley.

Prensky, M. (2001a, September/October). Digital natives, digital immigrants. *On the Horizon, 9*(5), 1–6.

Prensky, M. (2001b, November/December). Digital natives, digital immigrants, Part II: Do they really think diff erently? *On the Horizon, 9*(6), 1–6.

Press, E., & Washburn, J. (2000). Th e kept university. *Atlantic Monthly, 285*(3). Retrieved December 12, 2007, from http://www.theatlantic.com/issues/2000/03/index.htm

Price, M., & Rennie, F. (2005, June). MSc degrees in managing sustainable mountain/rural development at the UHI Millennium Institute. *Planet, 14,* 2–4. Retrieved December 12, 2007, from http://www.gees.ac.uk/pubs/planet/p14/mpfr.pdf

Project Gutenberg. (n.d.). Retrieved from http://www.gutenberg.org/

Rabinowitz, M., Blumberg, F., & Everson, H. (Eds.). (2004). *The design of instruction and evaluation: Affordances of using media and technology.* Mahwah, NJ: Erlbaum.

Rajasingham, L. (2011). Will mobile learning bring a paradigm shift in higher education? *Education Research International.* Retrieved fron http://www.hindawi.com/journals/edu/2011/528495/

Raines, C. (2002). Generations at work, managing millennials. Retrieved December 12, 2007, from http://www.generationsatwork.com/articles/millenials.htm

Ramsden, A. (2009). *Using micro-blogging (Twitter) in your teaching and learning: An introductory guide* [Discussion paper]. University of Bath. Retrieved June 11, 2012, from http://opus.bath.ac.uk/15319/1/intro_to_microblogging_09.pdf

Relan, A., & Gillani, B. (1997). Web-based information and the traditional classroom: Similarities and differences. In B. Kahn (Ed.), *Web-based instruction* (pp. 41–46). Englewood Cliffs, NJ: Educational Technology.

Rennie, F., & Mason, R. (2004). *The connecticon: Learning for the connected generation.* Greenwich, CT: Information Age.

Reynol Junco, R., & Cotten, S. R. (2011). Perceived academic effects of instant messaging use. *Computers & Education, 56*(2), 370–378.

Rheingold, H. (2000). *The virtual community* (Rev. ed.). Cambridge, MA: MIT Press. (Original work published 1998) Retrieved December 12, 2007, from http://www.rheingold.com/vc/book

Rheingold, H. (2002). *Smart mobs: The next social revolution.* Cambridge, MA: Perseus.

Rheingold, H. (2011). George Siemens on Massive Open Online Courses (MOOC's). Retrieved June 20, 2012, from http://www.youtube.com/watch?v=VMfipxhT_Co&feature=related

Robbins, S., & Bell, M. (2008). *Second life for dummies.* London: Wiley.

Roblyer, M. D., McDaniel, M., Webb, M., Herman, J., & Witty, J. V. (2010, June). Findings on Facebook in higher education: a comparison of college faculty and student uses and perceptions of social networking sites. *The Internet and Higher Education, 13*(3), 134–140.

Rockwell, K., Schauer, J., Fritz, S., & Marx, D. (1999). *Online Journal of Distance Learning Administration, 2*(4). Retrieved from http://www.westga.edu/~distance/ojdla/winter24/rockwell24.html

Rodrigo, R. (2011). Mobile teaching versus mobile learning. *Educause Quarterly, 34*(1). Retrieved from http://www.educause.edu/EDUCAUSE+Quarterly/EDUCAUSEQuarterlyMagazineVolum/MobileTeachingVersusMobileLear/225846

Rudd, T., Sutch, D., & Facer, K. (2006). Opening education: Towards new learning networks. Retrieved December 12, 2007, from http://www.futurelab.org.uk/research/opening_education.htm

Rudestam, K. E., & Schoenholtz-Read, J. (Eds.). (2010). *Handbook of online learning* (2nd ed.). Thousand Oaks, CA: Sage.

Salmon, G., Edirisingha, P., Mobbs, M., Mobbs, R., & Dennett, C. (2008). *How to create podcasts for education,* Maidenhead, UK: Open University Press.

Sammons, M., & Ruth, S. (2007). The invisible professor and the future of virtual faculty. *International Journal of Technology and Distance Education, 4*(1). Retrieved December 12, 2007, from http://www.itdl.org/Journal/Jan_07/article01.htm

Schaffert, S., Bischof, D., Buerger, T., Gruber, A., Hilzensauer, W., & Schaffert, S. (2006, June 11–14). *Learning with semantic wikis: Proceedings of the first workshop on semantic wikis—From wiki to semantics* (Sem/Wiki2006, pp. 109–123). Budva, Montenegro. Retrieved December 12, 2007, from http://www.wastl.net/download/paper/Schaffert06_Sem-WikiLearning.pdf

Schwarz, O. (2011). Who moved my conversation? Instant messaging, intertextuality and new regimes of intimacy and truth. *Media Culture Society, 33*(1), 71–187.

Second Life and Education. (n.d.). Retrieved from http://secondlife.onmason.com/second-life-education/

Second Life for Education. (n.d.). Retrieved from http://wiki.secondlife.com/wiki/Second_Life_Education

Second Life Grid Survey—Economics Metrics. (2011, 2012). Linden Lab. http://www.gridsurvey.com/economy.php Tyche Shepherd 2012

Shachar, M., & Neumann, Y. (2010). Twenty years of research on the academic performance differences between traditional and distance learning: Summative meta-analysis and trend examination. *Journal of Online Learning and Teaching, 6*(2), 146–154.

Sharoff, L. (2011, August 17). Integrating YouTube into the nursing curriculum. *OJIN: The Online Journal of Issues in Nursing, 16*(3). Retrieved from http://www.nursingworld.org/MainMenuCategories/ANAMarketplace/ANAPeriodicals/OJIN/TableofContents/Vol-16-2011/No3-Sept-2011/Articles-Previous-Topics/YouTube-and-Nursing-Curriculum.aspx#Trier07Part1

Sharpe, R., Benfield, G., Roberts, G., & Francis, R. (2006). *The undergraduate experience of blended e-learning: A review of UK literature and practice.* A Report to the Higher Education Academy. Retrieved December 12, 2007, from http://www.heacademy.ac.uk/resources/detail/ourwork/research/Undergraduate_Experience

Siemens, G. (2004). Connectivism: A learning theory for the digital age. *elearnspace.* Retrieved December 12, 2007, from http://www.elearnspace.org/Articles/connectivism.htm

Smith, M. A., & Kollock, P. (Eds.). (1999). *Communities in cyberspace.* London: Routledge.

Stephenson, K. (n.d.). *What knowledge tears apart, networks make whole.* Retrieved December 12, 2007, from http://www.netform.com/html/icf.pdf

Stevens, V. (2006). Revisiting multiliteracies in collaborative learning environments: Impact on teacher professional development. *Teaching English as a Second Language, 10*(2). Retrieved December 12, 2007, from http://www-writing.berkeley.edu/TESL-EJ/ej38/int.html

Stiggins, R. (2004). New assessment beliefs for a new school mission. *Phi Delta Kappan, 86*(1), 22–27. Retrieved December 12, 2007, from http://www.assessmentinst.com/documents/NewBeliefs.pdf

Tait, A., & Mills, R. (Eds.). (1999). *The convergence of distance and conventional education: Patterns of flexibility for the individual learner.* New York: Routledge.

Tapscott, D. (1998). *Growing up digital: The rise of the net generation.* New York: McGraw-Hill.

Tarleton State University. (2004). About distributed education, What is distributed education? Retrieved December 12, 2007, from http://www.qualityresearchinternational.com/glossary/distributededucation.htm

TED ED Lessons Worth Sharing. (n.d.). http://ed.ted.com/

Thompson, J. (2007). Is education 1.0 ready for web 2.0 students? *Innovate, 3*(4). Retrieved December 12, 2007, from http://www.innovateonlineinfo/index.php?view=article&id=393

Timmis, S. (2012). Constant companions: Instant messaging conversations as sustainable supportive study structures amongst undergraduate peers. *Computers & Education, 59*(1), 3-18. Retrieved from http://www.sciencedirect.com/science/article/pii/S0360131511002430

Towers, J. M. (1996). An elementary school principal's experience with implementing an outcome-based curriculum. *Catalyst for Change, 25*(Winter), 19–23.

Trier, J. (2007). "Cool" engagements with YouTube. *Journal of Adolescent &Adult Literacy, 50*(5), 408–412.

Veen, W. (2004). A new force for change: Homo zappiens. *Learning Citizen Cluster Newsletter.* Retrieved December 12, 2007, from http://www. learningcitizen.net/articles/AnewforceforchangeHo.shtml

Veen, W., & Vrakking, B. (2006). *Homo zappiens: Growing up in a digital age.* London: Continuum International.

Vovides, Y., Sanchez-Alonso, S., Mitropoulou, V., & Nickmans, G. (2007). The use of e-learning course management systems to support learning strategies and to improve self-regulated learning. *Educational Research Review, 2*(1), 64–74.

Vygotsky, L. (1978). *Mind and society: The development of higher psychological processes.* Cambridge, MA: Harvard University Press.

Waller, V. (2007, January). Are we all learning designers now? *Inside Learning Technologies.* Retrieved December 12, 2007, from http://www.learningtechnologies.co.uk

Weller, M. (2007a). The distance from isolation: Why communities are the logical conclusion in e-learning. *Computers and Education, 49*(2), 148–159.

Weller, M. (2007b, June). Blogging workshop, the ed techie. Retrieved December 12, 2007, from http://nogoodreason.typepad.co.uk/no_good_reason/2007/06/index.html

Weller, M. (2011). *The digital scholar: How technology is transforming scholarly practice.* London, UK: Bloomsbury Academic Press.

Wenger, E. (1998). *Communities-of-practice: Learning, meaning and identity*. Cambridge, UK: Cambridge University Press.

Weyers, J., Adamson, M., & Murie, D. (2004). 2004 student e-learning survey, University of Dundee. Retrieved December 12, 2007, from http://www.dundee.ac.uk/learning/dol/ELS_final_report.pdf

Wheeler, S., Yeomans, P., & Wheeler, D. (2008). The good, the bad and the wiki:E valuating student-generated content for collaborative learning. *British Journal of Educational Technology, 39*(6), 987–995.

Wheeler, S. (2009). Teaching with Twitter. Retrieved June 11, 2012, from http://steve-wheeler.blogspot.com/2009/01/teaching-with-twitter.html

Whitton, N. (2010). *Learning with digital games: A practical guide to engaging students in higher education*. New York: Routledge.

Whitton, N., & Hollins, P. (2008). Collaborative virtual gaming worlds in higher education. *Research in Learning Technology, 16*(3). Retrieved from http://www.researchinlearningtechnology.net/index.php/rlt/article/view/10900

Wilson, C. (2001, November 2). Faculty attitudes about distance learning. *Educause Quarterly*. Retrieved December 12, 2007, from http://www.educause.edu/ir/library/pdf/eqm0128.pdf

Wise, L. Z., Skues, J., & Williams, B. (2011). Facebook in higher education promotes social but not academic engagement. In G. Williams, P. Statham, N. Brown, & B. Cleland (Eds.), *Changing demands, changing directions. Proceedings ascilite Hobart 2011: Concise Paper* (pp. 1332–1342). Retrieved from http://www.ascilite.org.au/conferences/hobart11/procs/Wise-full.pdf

Woods, R., & Ebersole, S. (2003), Social networking in the online classroom: Foundations of effective online learning. *eJournal, 12–13*(1). Retrieved December 12, 2007, from http://www.ucalgary.ca/ejournal/archive/v1213/v12-13n1Woods-browse.html

Woody, W. D., Daniel, D. B., & Baker, C. A. (2010). E-books or textbooks: Students prefer textbooks. *Computers & Education, 55*(3), 945–948.

Yen-Yu Kang, Mao-Jiun J. Wang, & Rungtai Lin. (2009). Usability evaluation of e-books *Displays*, 30(2), 49–52.

Young, J. (2002). "Hybrid" teaching seeks to end the divide between traditional and online instruction. *The Chronicle of Higher Education, 48*(28). Retrieved December 12, 2007, from http://chronicle.com/free/v48/i28/ 28a03301.htm

# INDEX